Indian Theatre

Indian Theatre

Theatre of Origin,
Theatre of Freedom

Ralph Yarrow

CURZON

First Published in 2001
by Curzon Press
Richmond, Surrey
http://www.curzonpress.co.uk

© 2001 Ralph Yarrow

Typeset in Centaur by LaserScript Ltd, Mitcham, Surrey
Printed and bound in Great Britain by
Biddles Ltd, Guildford and King's Lynn

British Library Cataloguing in Publication Data
A catalogue record of this book is available from the British Library

Library of Congress Cataloguing in Publication Data
A catalogue record for this book has been requested

ISBN 0–7007–1412–X

Contents

Acknowledgements	vii
List of Illustrations	ix
Note on Spellings	xi
Map	xiii

Chapter One: Introduction	I
Theatre: a space for the extension of being	I
Some 'Western' questions	4
Some 'Eastern' answers	8
A theatre of origin?	16
Theatre of freedom?	20
India, the current situation and this book	27

Chapter Two: Text	32
Forms of 'text' and approaches	32
Narrative as the basis of performance forms	36
Narrative and myth	39
'Origins' of narrative	42
Narrative authority and the shift towards performance	45
The story of stories	51
Sanskrit drama as text	55
20th century drama as text	57

Chapter Three: Performance   61

    Models of categorisation   61

    Outline of some performance forms   68

    Women in performance   86

Chapter Four: Theory   95

    The changing nature of theory   96

    Aesthetics   96

    Ethics and politics   127

Chapter Five: Indian Theatre in the contemporary world:
        cultural politics in India   142

    Identity, diversity and consciousness   142

    Categories of contemporary theatre activity   146

    Summary   195

Chapter Six: Indian Theatre in the contemporary world:
        East-West traffic   198

    Introduction: what the west has won   198

    Performance training   204

    Understanding of performance forms   207

    Multicultural curry   210

Bibliography   215

Index   221

Acknowledgements

Principally I must thank many friends and colleagues in India for their generosity and expertise: Dr Kapila Vatsyayan, who first indicated to me many of the people I should talk to; Kavalam Narayana Pannikar, for several fruitful meetings; Professor C.D. Narasimhaiah, for the use of his library resource at Dhvanyaloka; the late Professor G. Sankara Pillai; Anjum Katyal and all at Seagull Foundation for the Arts; and many others including Kailash Pandya, Sanjoy Ganguly, Usha Ganguli, Geeta Krishnankutty, Dr Ananda Lal, K.V. Subbana, Professor N.N. Pillai ('Omcheri'), Dr R. Krishna-moorthy, Satish Alekar, Dr B. Chandrika, Professor Mohan Ramanan, Professor R.A. Malagi, Dr S.D. Desai. Above all however I owe an enormous debt of gratitude to those who have consistently encouraged and supported my work in India over many years and repeated visits: Professor K. Ayyappa Paniker, Dr Parasuram Ramamoorthi, Dr Digish Mehta, and Mallika and Mrinalini Sarabhai.

My profound thanks also to my colleagues and friends in the UK who have supported, advised, read and commented on my work: John Martin, Tony Gash, Tony Frost, Michael Robinson and Peter Malekin.

All these people have shared a great deal of their vision and generosity of spirit with me: I hope that this book can reflect a little of it back.

Permission to use the photographs is gratefully acknowledged.

Illustrations

Illustrations: (between pp. 66 and 67).

1. *Patayani* (Keralan ritual form): Madan, Kalan, Marutha. Courtesy Traditional Arts Project, School of Drama, University of Calicut.

2. *Chakyar Koothu* (Keralan mono-narrative). Courtesy Traditional Arts Project, School of Drama, University of Calicut.

3. Sopanam Theatre Institute in *Madhyamavyoyagam*, by Bhasa, directed by Kavalam Narayana Panikkar. Courtesy Anamika Sangam Research and Publications, Calcutta.

4. Theatre Academy, Pune in *Begum Barve*, by Satish Alekar, directed by Alekar, featuring Mohan Agashe (left). Courtesy Anamika Sangam Research and Publications, Calcutta.

5. Aryan Theatre, Manipur in *Antigone*, directed by Nongthombam Premchand. Courtesy Seagull Foundation for the Arts, Calcutta.

6. Mallika Sarabhai in *V for...* Courtesy Darpana Academy of Performing Arts, Ahmedabad.

7. Darpana/UNESCO health education project, Gujarat: *Bhavai* performance. Courtesy Darpana Academy of Performing Arts, Ahmedabad.

8. Jana Sanskriti performing in rural West Bengal. Courtesy Jana Sanskriti, West Bengal.

Note on spellings

Sanskrit diacritical marks are not used. In most cases spelling of terms from Sanskrit or other Indian languages follows the recognised 'English' phonetic pattern, e.g. *moksha, Yakshagana*. The major exception here is *Natya Sastra*, where I have retained this most usual spelling of the title rather than substitute 'Shastra'.

In some cases more than one version of a name exists, and I have opted for one of them! (*Therukuttu* could also be written *T(h)erukoothu*; *Jatra* and *Yatra* both exist.)

I have usually referred to Madras rather than Chennai, and to Bombay rather than Mumbai: apologies if anyone finds this offensive!

Map of India

CHAPTER ONE

Introduction

THEATRE: A SPACE FOR THE EXTENSION OF BEING

I started work on this book to investigate why so many 'Western' theatre workers in the last fifty years have been drawn to Indian (and other Asian) theatre. Jean-Marie Pradier (Pradier 1997) suggests that during this period, western interest has shifted to perceive Indian theatre's status not just as an orientalist curiosity, but as evidence for kinds of physical and mental capacity which art in the west has tried to track down since Modernism, but post-Enlightenment thought has marginalised or written out. (Peter Malekin and I discuss this further in Malekin & Yarrow 1997.) The shorthand terms for these capacities used in this book are 'origin' and 'freedom': they refer to extended understandings of the dynamic of consciousness in operation, of the ways we perceive, conceive, express and interact, as materialised in the mental and physical process which is theatre.

So the book looks at aspects of the history, theory, performance forms and texts of Indian theatre in order to explore how it offers access to these capacities. The evidence that it assembles and the questions it asks are focused around this exploration: they are selective, though the purpose of the selection is to investigate a capacity fundamental to all creative human acts.

It thus attempts a view of Indian theatre in the light of available – but decidedly not mainstream – contemporary philosophical and scientific understandings which imply dimensions to human experience which most western post-Enlightenment thought has ruled out. It also asks how far the world-view underlying much of the history and theory of Indian theatre can be understood in the same light.

I

Books are written by individuals living at a particular moment in space-time, drawing on both a personal and a communal history. To indicate the journey I am making with this book, I need to mention three recent publications.

Black Athena (Bernal, 1987) examines ways in which the relationship between Egyptian and Greek civilisation has been inscribed, and indicates that the last 150 years or so have seen an erasing of the traces of Egyptian presence and a recasting of the notion of the 'Classical' in much a more 'Aryan' light.

India and the Romantic Imagination (Drew, 1987) explores perceptions of India by European 'Orientalists' and creative writers, letting us see how and why they presented and interpreted it in the language of Platonic thought or attempted to establish its linguistic or mythological location within the 'Indo-European' fold.

La Scène et la Fabrique des Corps (Pradier, 1997) proposes that recent western fascination with Asian theatre is underpinned by the intuition that its forms rest upon an understanding of the relationship of mind and body which has not been (officially) available in 'the West' since Descartes at least.

It is not important to defend the arguments of these books here. What they signal is the way in which cultures and cultural artefacts are constantly and inevitably re-evaluated or repositioned by whoever is doing the evaluation. There are historical reasons for this (history understood here as both personal and cultural/racial/national etc.). I write this way because I live here and now and because I have had these experiences.

So I also am subject to this. This book aims in large measure to trace why practitioners in the west have turned to Indian theatre in the last half-century; and that question inevitably has to do with their perception of what 'Indian theatre' might be and what they might get out of it. It also necessarily begs the question: is that what practitioners in India think it is, and do they have similar or completely different goals in wanting to go on practising it?

And my 'take' on all these questions derives from my own image of India and its theatre. That perspective is not total (for all sorts of reasons which I touch on later, I don't believe anyone's is); it may be deficient in many ways, and it certainly is in that I do not read or speak an Indian language fluently. It will, I hope, be apparent from the text that I have spent a lot of time in India and both experienced and participated in many kinds of performance; but my perspective is still limited. Moreover, the desire to write this book, to revisit

India frequently and to explore the issues which I set out to write about, arises from my experience and understanding: firstly, via a practice of meditation derived from India, that there is more to consciousness and the ways it operates through the body than conventional western science gives credence to; and secondly, via a practice of theatre as teacher, director, performer and writer, founded on a sense of the pivotal status of the improvisatory now-moment, that theatre is a place and an activity of discovery which, particularly in the way it is recorded in Indian tradition, makes this extension of being available.

As such my intention coincides with Grotowski's sense that theatre is 'a place of provocation' which urges us to ask:

> Why are we concerned with art? To cross our frontiers, exceed our limitations, fill our emptiness – fulfil ourselves. This is not a condition but a process in which what is dark in us slowly becomes transparent.
>
> (Grotowski 1969, 21)

It may coincide also with the quest of Brook, Mnouchkine, Barba and others, in so far as they too recognise that search for light from a state of darkness, for inspiration from or reconnection with a theatre which seems to reinstate the intelligence of the whole body. Caution may be in order however in respect of the revivalist metaphor, which may conceal neo-colonialist practice of the kind Brook is charged with on his Indian travels (see e.g. Bharucha in Williams 1991). I hope this book doesn't try to appropriate, but to respect what I have encountered and see how it relates to what theatre in the west and/or in the world may be in search of.

So I write not out of but from within *my* skin. It is a white skin in and outside India (in spite of an article in an Indian newspaper which described me as 'a balding, slightly built, deeply tanned man who would not stand out in a crowd' [*The Hindu*, 1998], which I presume may have been a compliment ...). I cannot escape this altogether; although my concern is also, passionately, with what theatre stimulates in us which is not limited by race or gender or nationality or immediate local history; and I write because I am concerned to demonstrate the presence of this in Indian theatre of many times and forms and to claim that, in spite of pressing and complex current Indian concerns about the nature and value of cultural tradition, it still has major significance.

3

SOME 'WESTERN' QUESTIONS

The book sets out from the question: why have so many 'western' theatre workers (actor trainers, directors etc.) come to India and what were they looking for? What is it that seemed to be lacking in western performance and understanding of the nature and function of theatre? So the investigation starts from the western end, with an acknowledgement of the cultural piracy that may be involved. But in order to answer the question I have to look at: a) Indian tradition, i.e. the 'performance manual' *Natya Sastra*, Sanskrit drama, aesthetic and reception theory: what has been thought and written about the functions of performance in India; b) how that has worked in practice — i.e. an overview of the vast variety of performance forms from story-telling to 'classical' styles — and what that indicates about the nature of performance as articulated also by contemporary western theorists like Schechner; c) the nature of 'text' in the Indian spectrum and how that relates to 'performance-text'. So in these sections I give an account, by no means exhaustive but nonetheless fairly comprehensive, of the nature and significance of traditional performance forms and the major ways of theorising them. I interrogate the responses in the light of the perceived needs of western seekers, and see what that tells us about theatre. And then I take a look, both at what the west has got from the east, in terms of additions to the spectrum of performance modes and insights, and also at how contemporary Indian theatre workers are dealing with their own tradition: how, post-Independence and, for example, post IPTA (Indian People's Theatre Association), they are developing new forms and using traditional material, how their understanding of the business of theatre in their own contemporary context is shifting and developing.

Western theatre in the twentieth century, in common with other art forms, can be seen to be working through a series of crises which are based in uncertainty about underlying premises concerning: (a) the nature of 'reality' and its relation to the status of subject, object and the process of perception; (b) identity and the meaning of individual existence; (c) language and the truth-status of the versions of reality it proposes; (d) political and social structures as ways of organising and thus giving meaning to human life. The plurality of aesthetic forms which have attempted to articulate these questions is evidence both of the deep-seated nature of the uncertainties and, more positively, of their ability to generate new responses.

4

Some of those responses in theatre include not merely the embodiment of the questions indicated above (as empty or problematic spaces of being, duplicitous language, questioning of gender and role, framing or fracturing the confidence of public acts) but also, at a more direct level, the institution of alternative status for performance and alternative behaviour for performers and participant-receivers: work to initiate closer encounters with emotion and intelligence, moves to reorientate theatre space and the relations within it.

Theatre of this kind does not 'solve' the Modernist crisis: it *enacts* it precisely because it can produce a physical, psychological and affective equivalent for a situation which continually moves beyond definition. It is

> a provocation, a raging challenge to our orderly pigeon-holing minds ... Artaud's vehement, unrestrained language and Van Gogh's blazing pictures burst all frameworks: 'probably our life too is whole and infinitely richer in extent and possibility than the hemisphere we are familiar with at present' (Van Gogh)
>
> (Stok & Hänssler 1981)

Not just in the scale and range of its perceptions but also in the mode of its grasping and reshaping of the *process* of perception and thought, theatre of this kind fulfils Artaud's requirements to operate surgically upon performers and receivers alike. In so doing it does not merely align an analogy but produces an equivalent of the dynamic and non-linear, non-circumscribable universe revealed by quantum physics:

> Modern physics ... pictures matter not at all as passive and inert, but as being in a continuous dancing and vibrating motion whose rhythmic patterns are determined by the molecular, atomic and nuclear structures. This is also the way in which the Eastern mystics see the material world. They all emphasise that the universe has to be grasped dynamically, as it moves, vibrates and dances; that nature is not in a static, but a dynamic equilibrium.
>
> (Capra, 1976, 205)

That is to say, one major way in which such developments in theatre in the west can be understood is that they move all those engaged with it towards a dynamic rather than a static grasp of living.

To be on a level with, acting at the same rhythm as, a 'dynamic equilibrium' is no mean task. Such a goal might be identified in the aims of virtually all actor-trainers from Copeau (who initiated the use of the *neutral mask* in training in the 1920s) onward. Broadly speaking, there are two stages to this work: stepping *out* of everyday functioning and moving *into* other modes. Copeau, and after him Jacques Lecoq (enormously influential on western performance style since the 1950s), use the neutral mask, which 'edits out' the familiar, for the first stage: it both marks a break with the everyday, the accepted, the habitual (bringing about a psychological and perceptual repositioning) and aims to set up a condition of mental and physical readiness, balanced availability, in which the performer is asked to undertake a rediscovery of him/herself; they, together with Grotowski, Barba and others then work through physical exercises, mime and improvisation to alter the quality of energy and kind of focus of the body in performance (Barba aims for *bios*, scenic energy, and an 'extra-daily' quality to the body; not dissimilar conditions are sought even in the more naturalistic training of Stanislavsky and Michael Chekhov). Keith Johnstone's *Impro* – like Lecoq's work, another vital force in actor-training – encourages 'those who say yes', who are prepared to enter into new conditions and relationships. Much of this work focuses on and through the body, or makes use of the improvisatory tradition of games, play, freewheeling inventiveness and readiness to accept offers, because it is concerned to escape from the domination of the analytical, to encourage 'left-hemisphere' activity (spontaneous, creative, relational) and to move towards holistic performance intelligence. It is thus leaning out, as it were, from the umbrella of western thought (and the concepts of the body, self, identity and so on which this implies) towards models which are both more ambivalent and more generous.

It is therefore not surprising, even if actors have not always apparently been powerful in theatre politics, if the results have gradually rubbed off onto directors and even onto expectations of what it means to be a member of a theatre audience. (I take these issues up further in Chapter 6.)

For Barba, performance initiates an 'extra-daily' mode of behaviour; for Schechner, it 'transports' (temporarily) or 'transforms' (permanently) its participants. Schechner reminds us too of Susanne Langer's understanding of the tragic protagonist as a symbolic condensation concentrated on one way of challenging the 'limit of his possible development' (Langer 1953, 357).

Additionally, performance theory in the last few decades has stretched consideration of theatre and drama beyond the written text towards a 'rich' dynamics of performance, which takes into account a wide range of semiotic transfer and a high degree of flexibility from performers and audience. That is to say that current thinking not only sees the dynamics of performance situations as embracing most of the parameters of our individual and communal life, but also that such situations can be shown to require of their participants a more than ordinary conjunction of functioning, which consistently transcends the boundaries of given categories.

Emerging from the confrontation with time, space, being, language, truth and reality which marks the journey of modernist art, the innovative legacy of the 1950s and 60s has been mainly that of the 'absurd', which involves the explosion of formal, verbal and logical categories and the sceptical exploration of individual and communal meaning and the ways in which it is generated and underpinned (leading into structuralist methodology). Theatre practice of this kind makes bewilderment or unease a central part of the theatrical experience.

What drives this is not only suspicion or dissatisfaction with accepted explanatory models (of science, language, religion), but more fundamentally, the intuition that these 'systems and systematisations', as Ionesco calls them, or forms of Lacan's 'Symbolic Order', function as protection or masking against the unknowable and ungraspable real; Ionesco's theatre, like Genet's, deliberately 'theatricalises' these forms. In a discussion of links between psychoanalysis and the theatrical, Elizabeth Wright says:

> The communal belief in the symbolic, enshrined in language, hides the fact of death and the cessation of desire which it endlessly promises to fulfil. The theatrical cannot help but show this disruption at the heart of drama, so that the effect is not simply an exorcism of anger, fear and resentment, but a recognition of the risk that is at the heart of all play ...
>
> (Wright, 1996, 178)

In other words drama from Shakespeare to Ionesco inherently (by its nature as the play of illusion, as the presentation of what is, but also is not there) makes manifest the fact that the images we give to our experience have only the substance of shadows; what *is* real is our unceasing inability to 'grasp' anything, as well as our constantly renewed desire to do so, to pin down, Faust-like, the passing moment. 'I can't go on, I must go on', says Beckett, Eeyore-like and masochistically resigned; yet his theatre, however ruefully, works again and again precisely with the risk of play (physical and verbal) from the most fragmentary of residual matter, turning us back from the 'enlightened' formulae of our so-called knowledge through loss, emptiness and darkness as the only trajectory to renewal.

These perspectives may suggest why we find in practitioners like Artaud, Grotowski, Lecoq, Copeau, Barba, Brook, Keith Johnstone, Stanislavsky and Meyerhold, explicit demands to draw upon new physical, emotional and spiritual resources, to pass beyond the known and habitual, to create new symbolic forms and 'languages'; in other words, to energise the acts of performance and reception by a constant stretching beyond the familiar. The post-1970s rediscovery of 'physical theatre' is but the latest manifestation of this drive, which many twentieth-century texts from Symbolism to the Absurd similarly require.

SOME 'EASTERN' ANSWERS

What resources then might be found in the Eastern forms to which Artaud, Brecht, Barba, Grotowski and others have turned and in the assumptions and insights underlying them?

Some of the major characteristics and outcomes of Indian forms as perceived by these western seekers (this perception of course is dependent on their situation, their desires and the extent of information available to them, and for the most part is based on assumptions about 'traditional' rather than contemporary practice) could be framed as follows:

(i) liminality
(ii) plurality
(iii) physicality
(iv) transcendence.

I discuss these further below. For now, they indicate the kinds of response which seemed available and attractive in answer to the problematic outlined above. Taken together, they compose a model of theatre as a site of change, as a locus of negotiation on and across the borders of the familiar and the known, as a launching-place for extended configurations of self and world.

The forms of theatre, as of all art, manifest certain basic assumptions about life. In the case of Indian theatre, these are largely Vedic/Hindu, but close parallels exist in e.g. Buddhism and Taoism. The following are of central importance, because they display a conception of form as dynamic and of the continuity between 'reality' and 'illusion':

1. Brahma/Vishnu/Shiva (creation/preservation/destruction): Indian thought envisages the forces found throughout creation, from the micro- (where they are known as *gunas* or tendencies) to the macrocosmic level, in the form of this triad (*trimurti*) of 'gods'; their interaction comprises
2. The universe as the play of form (*lila*).
3. Underlying this play is *Brahman*, the unmoving source of movement, the potential of all form. *Brahman* is the most profound level of reality; from that perspective, the play of form is seen to be *maya* (illusion), i.e. to have only transient status.

The Eastern view, as suggested in the quote from Fritjof Capra above (Capra 1976), sees the material universe as the play of form. Matter constantly regenerates itself, reconstitutes itself. Hence in Hinduism there is not one god but a trinity – *Brahma Vishnu Shiva* – of creative and destructive forces plus the 'glue' which holds them together (preservation, or, more actively, a continual resetting of the balance: Vishnu incarnates in mythology in ten different appropriate forms or *avatars* when things get out of line). Matter puts itself together and then disaggregates itself; all stages are intimately linked, and so you often see statues which are plural, ambivalent or indeed also androgynous: a particular force or quality is not seen as exclusively masculine or feminine. (E.g. *Shakti* is the feminine principle equivalent to Shiva; *Kali* – often simplistically used by Western writers as a demonic female figure – is seen in Indian tradition as more of a Shiva equivalent in the sense of destroying in favour of a new state.) On the microscopic level (and sometimes on the macrocosmic also) these forces, termed *gunas*, represent tendencies inherent in all matter: parallels with quantum physics, which explores energy in states of potentiality from which it may move in apparently contradictory ways, or with the tendency of organisms to seek a condition of homeostasis or internal balance, are not irrelevant.

What can be said then is that everything is in motion and everything is multiple: nothing is ever just what it seems. The world then is the play of form. The Sanskrit word for this is *lila*. Play of form is of course also theatre, as in the title *Ramlila*: the play about Rama, and also incidentally, the largest annual performance in the world, using different areas of the town and many of the inhabitants of Banares/Varanasi.

Parallels with Plato's Cave analogy are not hard to see. Here also the shadows which are taken to be solid are transient, they are not essential. In Hindu thought the essential is *Brahman*: that potential which gives rise to forms and forming, and which is accessible to each individual through the *Atman* (sometimes translated as 'soul', but 'spirit' or 'immortal spark' might be closer; or perhaps better, using a holographic model, the capacity of each part to reflect the whole). *Brahman* is accessible as awareness, by merging the individual consciousness with it: those who have traditionally been thought to be adept at this and to possess the formulae for so doing form the highest (*Brahmin* or priestly) caste. Brahman gives rise to the ceaseless activity of Brahma/Vishnu/Shiva and the *gunas*; activity which we take to be 'real' but is in another sense only illusion, *maya*: partly because it's never still, never the separate entity nineteenth-century physics or materialism aspired to pin down, partly, as Derrida would say because it is always différe/ance, never identical with itself, always changing. But illusion also, literally, means 'in play' (Latin il-ludere).

If we now return to the perspective of twentieth-century western seekers, we can see what might appeal here. Firstly, most Modernist thinkers were dissatisfied with models and structures which failed to take account of the insights referred to by Capra, but which were also evident in the enormous changes occurring in the late nineteenth and early twentieth centuries in psychology, politics, linguistics etc. The certainties (relative or apparent, of course) of the nineteenth-century worldview give way to the famous 'Uncertainty Principle' of Heisenberg. Nothing is quite what it seemed to be before, and yet the 'overarching myths' Lyotard identifies are still those which privilege fixity. So there is a perceived need for a model or models which acknowledge the flux. The notion of *maya*, for instance, is a very close parallel to the perception of Ionesco and others referred to above, i.e. that the Symbolic forms in which we have encapsulated what we take to be knowledge, truth or reality are, in fact, merely forms with no absolute status.

Secondly therefore, here is a whole framework which appears to take precise account of the awareness of the instability of matter but has incorporated this effortlessly into a mythology and a whole range of extremely colourful and lively aesthetic forms. In fact in this view instability is experienced not as insecurity but rather as the natural process of creativity: *Brahman*, though itself a condition of utter stillness, nevertheless generates the movement of those forms which both are and are not *Brahman*. The ambiguous note of Beckett's view of unceasing production is less evident, or, if you like, play is still risk but the death it contains is the merging and re-emerging of life.

Thirdly, although nothing as comforting as final salvation or permanent vindication of individual status might be on offer, there does seem to be a sense in which each individual is seen as having the capacity to function at times in the same way or state as the first cause or condition of generative power from which forms arise. A more extensive sense of 'I' is available as part of the creative project: 'I' have something in common with the forces which organise all matter, and I can consciously and actively participate in that.

The underlying premisses about the nature of life and form look promising, then. How does Indian aesthetic theory map onto this scenario, and what does it see as the function of performance?

All Indian aesthetic theory refers back to the *Natya Sastra*, a comprehensive theory-cum-manual dealing with all aspects of performance from the size and composition of the stage to the detailed hand-gestures (*mudras*); variously dated between 450BC and 1200AD, ascribed to one Bharata, one of the renderings of whose name curiously enough means 'India'. (Not dissimilar manuals were compiled for example by *Noh* performers/teacher(s) singly or collectively under the name of Zeami.) Central to the *Natya Sastra* is the theory of *rasa*: not only is performance transmitted through the presentation of affective 'flavours', a bit like Indian cuisine's use of a subtle blend of spices, but more fundamentally the ultimate aim is to cultivate the receptive faculties of the receivers who should ideally develop the qualities of an adept or *rasika*.

Precisely because performance is so rich, it activates a whole range of channels of response: through movement, colour, text, music, rhythm etc. The aim is a condition of wholeness or harmony (*samhita*). That this is taken seriously is indicated by the fact that the *Natya Sastra* is known as the 'fifth *Veda*'. *Veda* means knowledge, or more accurately the whole process of knowing: the *Vedas* are the basic scriptural texts of Hinduism. Thus performance is understood as an individual and communal act which aims at the transcendence of everyday limits of consciousness by the precise cultivation of holistic functioning of multi-channelled awareness. The relevance of such theory to western mid-twentieth-century concerns and understanding about the aesthetic, social and political function of theatre is clear in what has been said above, and in the range of theatrical practitioners who found something appropriate: the desire to extend the internal and communicative resources of *actors* (Stanislavsky, Meyerhold,

Artaud, Grotowski, Lecoq, Brook, Barba ...); to arouse the *audience* either intellectually and/or imaginatively to greater conscious participation (Brecht, Artaud, Grotowski, Fo, Mnouchkine ...); to intensify the impact of the *performance-text* by all possible – and usually unexpected – means (Grotowski, Kantor, Beckett, Genet, Schechner, Savary ...).

Having seen then how the basic philosophical and aesthetic patterning offers responses to the western quest, we can return to the characteristics of Indian performance outlined earlier.

Liminality identifies the 'betweenness' of the performance event. The term is taken from anthropologists Arnold Van Gennep and Victor Turner, for whom it marks the function of performance in rites of passage. In such events, participants are changing their role within a community and the performance validates the crossing of a threshold (from childhood to maturity, from life to death). By extension the term is useful to indicate the ways in which performance operates in times and spaces which are themselves in some way transitional, and produces shifts across states of being. Much traditional Indian performance is rooted in ritual and temple forms, in folk and community tradition: performance has both communal and individual significance, but tends to lie nearer the 'efficacy' end of Schechner's 'efficacy-entertainment braid' (Schechner 1988, 120–24): it is *part of* the texture of 'daily' life whilst at the same time being quite explicitly 'extra-daily': highly 'theatrical', with no attempt at a realistic 'fourth wall', rich in dense theatrical signs and so on. That is to say, 'extraordinary' faculties are perceived as belonging to the repertoire of individual and community life. Performance often lasts all night, or occurs as part of a festival/celebration; it frequently takes place in the village centre or temple courtyard, rather than in a designated 'theatre'. What Rilke calls the 'other side' of life is not separated off: the 'magic', 'epic' or 'divine' world *co-exists* with the everyday: the audience comes and goes, children play and fall asleep, dreaming and waking alternate and the time of performance stretches across the darkness into the light of dawn. In this setting it is not difficult to concur that 'we are such stuff as dreams are made on': liminality becomes a condition of playing out an understanding of the transience and the transitional quality of individual existence against the background of the community or structure which frames and retains. It looks here as though performance enacts a negotiation or transference across the borders where self and environment (other, community, world) meet.

Sometimes the boundaries are confirmed, sometimes they are bypassed or blurred; but the transaction has to do with the fundamental redefinitions of being, time and space which face western artists from Modernism onwards. (Chapter 3 looks at some examples and other ways of understanding this kind of performance.)

Plurality similarly implies a passing across borders; much oriental performance is 'plural' in the sense that it does not make sharp distinctions between, on the one hand, dance, theatre, music etc., and on the other hand between the sacred and the profane: it does not recognise the same boundaries with which the west is familiar. This does not necessarily mean that 'reality' is *less* compartmentalised, but it is compartmentalised along different lines (e.g. the caste system). Moreover in one sense there is no single entity called 'Indian theatre', just as there is no single Indian language, but fifteen major ones (plus English); five or six major religions; and in that with the greatest number of adherents, Hinduism, a multiplicity of often indistinguishable, overlapping, divine forces, frequently crossing gender or status divides. Performance forms are multiple (e.g. *Bhavai, Kathakali, Therukoothu, Purulia Chhau, Theyyam*) ranging from highly stylised to folk/improvisatory, from delicate mask to elaborate make-up, from ritual exorcism to moral tale (one of the best-known recent works on the subject in India is subtitled *Multiple Streams* (Vatsyayan, 1980). Discussion of a range of forms and their significant features will be found in Chapter 3. What specifically appeals to western scouts here is the flexibility of form and the easy shift across genre, which open up possibilities of rich and inventive combinations of performance meaning more appropriate to render complex perceptions of reality. (In another sense, certain forms of Indian performance display particularly 'plural' versions of the performer/role, e.g. *Kudiyattam*'s mono-acting.) These have of course been present within western tradition at different times, but the 'Asian' or 'oriental' model (however inaccurate or generalised) offers a particularly powerful nexus at a particular historical period. As in the case of liminality, and indeed with what follows below, my argument implies that you tend to find what you have in mind when you start to look. That may not always be exactly what the custodians think they are operating.

Asian, and specifically Indian, performance spaces and the events which take place in them, and the forms and modes of those performances, offer models then which respond in important ways to the perceived needs of western practitioners. So too do methods of training and using the body in performance: *physicality*. Further

13

consideration of the west's booty in this area appears in Chapter 6; for now it's worth recalling briefly the mention above of the tradition of Copeau and Lecoq, and of other actor-trainers like Brook, Mnouchkine, Grotowski, Barba, Schechner and Zarilli who have made explicit study and use of aspects of Indian actor-training and performance methods. On the immediate level, they are looking for ways of freeing up and using physical capacity, of extending the range of the actor's resources; and eastern practice from yoga to breath-control appears to offer many useful techniques to develop a new range of skills and escape from the tyranny of acting from the neck up (part of the western hierarchisation of the written, the Lacanian Symbolic, the Ideal). In many cases however this apparent quick-fix solution founders on the realisation that such training forms part, firstly of a very lengthy apprenticeship often starting in childhood, and secondly of a whole cultural tradition. It cannot, as many theatre workers have since acknowledged, be simply packaged and bolted on. Indeed Copeau and Lecoq worked instead with physical and mask-routines drawn from European culture (*commedia*, sports education) to great effect.

But beyond this seeming blind alley, an important door in fact lies in wait: an alternative approach to the relationship of mind and body. It would be grossly unfair to Brook, Barba, Grotowski and others to suggest that they have not been aware of this dimension and consciously seeking to explore it. Indeed the various 'secrets' coveted by what has been regarded as a new form of 'orientalism' or cultural piracy all exemplify this further, crucial, border-crossing: actor-training methods offering control, flexibility and versatility beyond the range of most western-trained actors; possible access to 'alternative' states of consciousness (shamanic trance, ecstasy, etc.) which fascinated both Artaud and Schechner, though in rather different ways; and/or to the possibility of a 'pre-expressive' condition which seems to underlie and to generate what to some western eyes appears to be a special quality of dynamic availability or 'presence' manifested by *Kathakali* dancers or *Noh* performers (see especially Barba & Savarese 1991). Discussion of the nature, status and function of these performative conditions occurs in several different contexts below. It is also irrelevant for the present argument whether and how Indian performers (or indeed performers from other traditions) evaluate or recognise them. What is important here is their place in the western quest, which thereby identifies as one of its principal goals alternative understandings and practices in which mind and body, consciousness and matter, are experienced as a continuum, and where work at subtle strata cannot clearly be allocated to an exclusive category, but is seen as breathing vitality into performance.

This analysis indicates that, just as the previous headings of liminality and plurality point beyond narrow categorisation, so too physicality in this understanding moves beyond itself and becomes a form of *transcendence*. It is not just restrictive criteria which are left behind, but the mind-set upon which they are based. Indian performance provides the conditions for theatre which is 'holy' (Brook, Grotowski), 'cruel' (Artaud), 'sacred' (Genet), 'anthropo-cosmic' (Nuñez), or in other formulae 'physical', 'rich', 'theatre of imagination', and so on. Its nature is intentionally transformative and its process transcendental because it is rooted in and articulates experience of self and world, sensation and intelligence, energy and attention which can only adequately be explained by moving beyond the restrictions of conventional western thought. Vatsyayan declares: 'how and when the Indian considered the body as an essential prerequisite for transcending the body constitutes a total history of Indian thought' (1980, 8). In other words the 'extra-daily' activity generated by theatre in performers and receivers is not just a handy performance technique; it is a precisely-composed journey across levels of psychophysical functioning which effects an extension beyond the egoic self.

There is however another important perspective on the foregrounding of the physical which has occurred in western theatre after Brecht and Artaud: it marks a recognition, already referred to above, of 'the gap between the body as a discursive construct and its felt embodiment in experience, between the representational and the real' (Wright, 1996, 189). On the face of it, this appears to contradict and indeed to reject on ideological grounds any possibility of transcendence, by insisting on the irreducible physicality/ mortality/transience of performer and performance. Nevertheless, although psychoanalysis itself has some trouble acknowledging this, a 'fall' into the real in this sense, entailing as it does a shift 'out' of the Symbolic, creates precisely that space for a rescripting of self which neutral and other mask work seeks. It is perhaps significant that, whereas in much western usage, 'masking' tends to refer to covering up or hiding what one does not want to be seen (i.e. one's vulnerability, physical or moral frailty etc.), in this kind of work the understanding is much closer to Asian practice in which to put on a mask means to enter into an 'otherness' which is both liberating and vitalising. The loss of the Symbolic is also the chance of gaining the real, which is a condition of becoming, of flux, of moving into and through a succession of forms.

Indian theatre, it should be said, can itself also adopt a whole range of forms from the material to the spiritual: it can be 'epic' – in Brecht's sense as well as generically, carnivalesque, 'third', political, 'for the oppressed', and also 'westernised' proscenium-arch, naturalistic. The contemporary spectrum is discussed in Chapter 5. Totality, whether in the sense of the *Gesamtkunstwerk*, of a receptive state of *samhita*, or of formal diversity, also functions as a mode of transcendence. Schechner's concept of a 'fan' covering a whole range of performance events (e.g. ritual, art-making, play, sports, ceremonies: 1988, 6) can be applied here, in an extended sense.

A THEATRE OF ORIGIN?

Western practitioners have turned to India to look for something they felt was missing. To some extent they perhaps constitute thereby a further wave of orientalism, a fascination for the 'exotic'; but the fact that this is fuelled by a sense of lack is significant. Whether that lack is understood as psychospiritual, technical, aesthetic, or a combination of them all, it suggests that Indian theatre is perceived as possessing something fundamental at the very least to the business of theatre and probably, by extension, to its relationship to individual and social life.

Indian practice and traditional scholarship has, through the *Natya Sastra* and the critical debate it has consistently inspired, accorded to performance a similarly significant role within the philosophical, religious and aesthetic spectrum.

It therefore looks as though the assumption of the existence of something powerful is common to both eastern and western approaches. Although I am aware that Schechner, for one, views theories of origin as on the whole misleading and unhelpful (Schechner 1988, 6) – I concur with him in many respects and will take this up in Chapter 4 – it is worth asking whether we are not actually here encountering something like a claim for a theatre of origin (rather than an origin for theatre). Let's look briefly at the case for this, which will be developed subsequently.

I. The *Natya Sastra* postulates a 'divine' origin for theatrical performance via a myth or story, according to which Brahma responds to the request of the gods for an object of diversion by entrusting the sage Bharata with its development.

I think there are three main ways of understanding terms like 'gods' and 'divine': (i) as natural forces (wind, fire, spring, etc.); (ii) as a ruling order (either abstract, i.e. the function of governing or ordering – reified as a creator God – or imaged upon those who govern or hold power); (iii) as events, processes or modes of operation in consciousness ('unusual' qualities or powers of perception and action). The three may overlap or interweave in mythological account: e.g. those who fall into category (i) or (ii) may in certain circumstances be credited with (iii), or those who possess (iii) may be designated as belonging to (ii). This model is best thought of as one level of operation manifesting in three different ways.

Definitions in category (i) may generally be thought of as anthropological; those in (ii) as political and religious; and those in (iii) as psychological (in the sense of psychospiritual, rather than in the more limited western sense).

The opening myth in *Natya Sastra* seems accessible to interpretations using categories (ii) and (iii). Those in category (ii) propose that the (individual or collective) author 'Bharata' claims divine origin in an attempt to acquire more credibility, or perhaps (debatably) to validate non-Aryan features of performance (see Ghosh and Shekhar, quoted in Byrski 1974, 6–7). In other words, this is a political and/or historical ploy to confer upon the *Natya Sastra* the status of a *Veda* and achieve an easier passage for the arts it promotes. This is not implausible; but theories of this kind require historical grounding as proof (which is particularly difficult in the Indian context) and parallel the 'origin of theatre' model which Schechner is sceptical about.

Moreover, the reduction of the territory delineated by 'divine' etc. to that of power play, however cynically accurate in terms of the frequent invocation of 'scriptural authority' for otherwise unacceptable practices, leaves out of account the equally widespread tendency to perceive the aesthetic as having something to do with 'more than ordinary' modes of being. That sort of intuition seems to underlie the western quest I have outlined above. Theatre as a practice is commonly (and certainly in Shakespeare) conceived of as a production of multiple versions of the self and multiple forms of being; there seems no reason why Bharata should not make the same claim, particularly in a text which goes on to elaborate both an extremely wide range of forms and a high degree of precision about their production. If 'divine' can refer to the ability to generate or move into alternative modes of being, and 'gods' to the kinds of archetypal forms or characters which might be put in play and thus stimulate more-than-everyday degrees of understanding in receivers, we come closer to an account of the process which is theatre in operation, rather than to speculation about when it might have 'started'.

Viewed in this light, the 'source-book' of Indian theatre enters a claim that performance (the originating of active and signifying forms) has its beginnings in the conjunction of 'human' and 'universal' (or individual and para-individual) modes of perception and action. One of the principal functions of myth is to trace and analogise ways in which consciousness operates in such modes: the beings and events described there can be read as 'agents' and 'operators' in a psychological as well as a physical and/or political sense. The *Natya Sastra* myth about the creation of drama involves, for instance, a debate between 'gods' and 'demons' (agents and operators on the divine level, as it were). One way of looking at these terms is as attempts to describe tendencies or desires. The desire to create a harmonious or idealised version (a pleasant 'diversion' or a positive model) is represented by the 'gods', whereas 'demons' raise objections, point out that things aren't quite like that, seek to destabilise the given order, and ultimately function as the grit in the oyster which provokes a new construction. Gods and demons are therefore both formal and psychological drives. Their interaction is the process of constructing form, in this case dramatic form or the story of life, carried out by 'human' operators ('Bharata' and his 'hundred sons'). The 'divine' level here could be a way of presenting the genesis and process of action. Although the reading proposed above could be analogous in some degree to Nietzsche's Apollo/Dionysos or Freud's superego/ego/id models, I suspect we are also talking about subtle aspects of the functioning of motivation which need a rather more extensive model of consciousness than Freud's to account for them fully. I will take up these issues further in Chapter 4; in Chapter 3 I analyse some Indian performance forms in terms of inner and outer process. I would also argue that all creative activity may be understood in this light; but the point here is that the *Natya Sastra* consciously recognises and foregrounds this, and bases its claim for the importance of performance upon it.

2. The texts from which much Indian performance derives are themselves viewed as of 'divine' origin or inspiration and seen as fundamental to an understanding of the culture, social organisation, moral and religious precepts and 'history' (in the Indian rather than the western sense; closer both to scriptural connotations of 'revealed truth' and to the poststructuralist reading 'his story') of the country. I will look at some of the debates this gives rise to later; but it's worth noting that here again the claim is made and in some measure at least supported: firstly by the fact that the epics and scriptural texts generate so many versions, narratives, adaptations, discussions, etc. that they certainly have given and continue to give rise to an apparently endless stream of material suitable for performance in a whole variety of forms and contexts, a richness further underpinned by their 'mythical' status in the sense I outline above; and secondly that the language they are framed in (Sanskrit) is itself perceived in Indian tradition as a seed language, not just of the Indo-European linguistic family but also in the sense that it is considered to possess an exact or vibratory equivalence with fundamental levels of material existence. Sceptical as most western linguists are of such claims, there are arguments worth making, particularly in the context of performance, where features such as rhythm and breath can be seen to affect meaning profoundly. Sanskrit also has the property of generating innumerable forms from root syllables.

3. Indian performers in many traditions are rigorously trained, often from an age and to a level which invites comparisons with monastic discipline. This training is certainly at least on a par with what western academies provide, and is particularly adept at producing precise and thorough physical control and application (muscular, vocal, gymnastic etc.). Performers generally receive this training within the *guru* tradition, in which the teacher is accorded the highest respect. They often view their training and the performance in which it issues as a kind of devotional offering. That is to say, the act of performance itself is seen as a raising of human capacity to a divine level, in order, as the *Natya Sastra* expounds, to assist the receivers to tread the same path and perceive further dimensions to existence. Performance is a heightening and refinement of sense and sensibility both for performers and audience; Grotowski's pursuit of the sacrificial is similar but, in most cases, significantly different: Polish history and Catholic tradition provide a rather more masochistic flavour than the joy which Indian performers often convey. (Again of

19

course there are those, particularly contemporary, practitioners in India who would take issue with some aspects of this – and equally, many who would defend it; further discussion of this occurs in Chapter 5, but I want here to point to what remains a widespread perception.) In addition, what is of particular significance is the capacity of Indian performers to achieve physical and mental balance or stillness – in part deriving from particular physical training and mastery of a centred, low-gravity stance – from which dynamic activity emerges.

So in the areas of aesthetic theory, text and performance, Indian theatre does seem to be quite conscious of itself as offering to extend the range of human capacity and experience, to operate on the borderline between 'human' and 'divine'. And in each case this can be understood in terms of conducting operations *at the point of origin* of form, language, meaning and physical action. Performance is both understood and practised as a coming-in-tune with a mental and physical condition 'outside', 'beyond', 'beneath' or 'prior to' conventionally recognised expressive structures and moving into creative activity from there.

If this is so, we are indeed talking about the origins of many of the activities which make up theatre. Not origins which are buried in the past, however, but those which, provided appropriate means of access are available, can be regularly revisited. Part of the work of this book will be to explore, in the chapters dealing with text, performance and theory, the extent to which these suggestions can be verified. If they can be, the importance of Indian theatre for theatre practice throughout the world will be demonstrated.

THEATRE OF FREEDOM?

It is worth recapping two shorthand lists from earlier sections, which look like this:

'western problematics'	'eastern characteristics'
reality	liminality
identity/meaning	plurality
language/truth	physicality
political/social structures	transcendence

They were not intended to parallel each other exactly, but juxtaposing them is useful because it reveals that whereas the problems seem to be related to the relative inflexibility of the categories employed (and hence of the mind-set which gives rise to them), the 'answers' found in eastern practice all move away from boundaries towards increasing flexibility or freedom. Much of my argument in the preceding section also suggests that it is not just conventional or deferential to view the aims and outcomes of Indian performance as opening up extended kinds of meaning and functioning.

But it would be grossly oversimplistic to leave it at that and to imply that Indian practice and western needs form a neat match. For a start, it is up to western artists to find their own answers with reference to their own cultural modes and historical situations: they have been doing it for a long time, and plenty of evidence exists to suggest that they have been pretty successful (from Shakespeare to Beckett, from *Commedia dell'arte* to Théâtre de Complicité). In this process there is massive interference between the concepts and practices listed, which could be applied perfectly appropriately to much Modernist art. Secondly, Indian artists are both questioning their own traditions and practice and trying to accommodate these to precise political and historical circumstances, as well as engaging in their own interrogation of categories. They would not all accept transcendence as an unquestioned aim, though many would see themselves as in the business of active intervention within and pushing beyond the aesthetic and/or political status quo, at least. Nor am I hereby sanctioning a monopoly view of Indian theatre as 'tradition', as a 'given', as a defensive cultural asset: as Bharucha points out, this would be for Indians to '"orientalize" [their own] past by refusing to confront the mutations of [...] history' (Bharucha 1993, 206). Indian theatre, I think, needs to be recognised both for its contemporary refocusing in the light of current circumstances and for the subtlety and power of its grasp of the nature and operation of individual and communal effects as embedded in its performance traditions and in the *Natya Sastra*.

There are, it seems to me, senses in which theatre can be both a means of liberation from confining systems and structures and a positive engagement with them. The spectrum in play here involves differing dimensions of confrontation with self and other, as well as different categories of performance and their effects on audiences. It has to do with the role of 'self' in the environment of human possibility, and the role of theatre in the environment of social organisation; with kinds of awareness engendered by theatre and performance and with ways in which they translate into action.

21

There is a tendency for much performance to work towards what might be called border confrontation; the border can be thought of as that of self/other, both in terms of a challenge to how individual performers and receivers experience themselves and also in terms of how performance defines itself within its social and cultural context. Both these dimensions are found in theatre and performance East and West.

In Indian practice there are many forms which this mobility and transferability can take. As already indicated, the understanding of performance articulated in *Natya Sastra* and the intended outcome of much theatrical semiosis in 'traditional' forms is that it should stimulate significant psychospiritual modifications in receivers, both individually and collectively (the latter in more ritualistic forms). Sanskrit drama too rests on this premiss, but also aims to produce aesthetic refinement in its receivers through a poetic and symbolic use of language in a more extended way; Tagore's early twentieth-century stage writing in English and Bengali draws on this tradition. Towards the more overt and public end of the spectrum, political theatre and street theatre are particularly evident during the last fifty years, but go back to 'folk' practice: Badal Sircar's 'third theatre' and much IPTA-inspired work (for example that of Safdar Hashmi and, in his early years, Habib Tanvir) uses innovative forms which mix presentation, entertainment and debate, for specific social, political and/or psychological intervention. Within both traditional and contemporary work there is extensive use of mask, for purposes which include the shamanistic, the aesthetic and the comic, targeting both individuals and communities. There is also theatre which quite legitimately adopts 'conventional' Indian or western performance modes but does so in order to question accepted thought or behaviour for its – usually but not exclusively urban – target audience; and an understanding of theatre in many forms as a practice which empowers because it gives its participants the experience of using their own capacities more fully (which, together with other aspects of the contemporary scene, is discussed further in Chapter 5). Much of this work constructs the performance event (space, time, form, audience etc.) differently according to its intentions.

The shift across self and role has a number of important dimensions. Performance of a certain kind frees up its participants, but within relatively 'conventional' limits: taking on recognisable but distinct roles (social, political, psychological), exploring a range of 'types'. For both performers and audience, the emphasis tends here to be largely conscious and deconstructive, a recognition of the relativity of these configurations. This is indeed a form of liberation: I can experience myself as not having to be only what is being revealed about each particular role. (I think this is similar to what Schechner means by his 'not me/not not me' formula, which he applies to Olivier as Hamlet [Schechner 1985, 110].) I gain thereby both a sense of increased potential and a precision of discrimination: I am enabled to experience the nature and limitations of boundaries (habitual role-behaviour) more clearly and to discover that some part of me is able to operate outside these boundaries. The self/other work taking place here is largely within the sphere of Lacan's Symbolic, but it also offers, through a sharper sense of how roles in this domain or Order are constructed, the chance of what I earlier refer to as 'stepping outside', or in more Indian terms, of observing the play of *maya*. Categories are becoming less watertight, different spaces are being opened up for play.

Performance can also take its participants towards less familiar forms of otherness which lie further away from the definable world of language or habit, through more radical forms of the extra-daily; shifts of this kind are more usually approached through trans- formations or substitutions initiated in the *body*, its attitudes, rhythms and style of operation; in other words, through an act of direct *incorporation* of 'otherness' *within* the territory experienced as 'self', rather than as (intellectual) standing apart or appreciating a distinction *between* the two (though there is a sense in which the two routes converge).

Whereas in the first model above the actor takes on a secondary, but recognisable, persona, in work of this kind I am likely to be much less confident about who or what 'I' may turn into. Improvisation, mask-work, trance or rhythmic activity may initiate a shift into something more 'unknown' and less accessible to rational under- standing. What is met with here may be monstrous or outrageous, emerging from or as desires, fears, psychic drives, anarchic forces, things of darkness which lament or celebrate modes of being my everyday 'I' scarcely admits.

In one dimension, then, the intellectual or consciously perceived borders of self are being renegotiated; in another, the sense and space of 'I' is subject to pressures of a more visceral, felt kind. I begin to think and feel 'myself' to *be* in some way 'other'.

Both performer and receiver can be affected; in both dimensions (as, for example, in the experience of political satire and exorcistic

23

ritual) a reconfiguration of the interface between the individual and the extra-individual (me as part of the *polis*, me as part of *communitas*) could well be taking place.

In practice these dimensions can and frequently do overlap and co-exist; so that work of a Brechtian kind does not rule out access to encounters with the psychic unknown, or moments in a ritual event can be suddenly transformed by down-to-earth humour. Part of Stanislavsky's exploration is to investigate the ground between these modes, whereby for instance 'memory' extends beyond the merely personal or where recollection begins to establish what Susanne Langer calls 'the form of feeling'. Clowns, shape-shifters, tricksters in Indian and western tradition cross all kinds of linguistic, political, social and psychological borders. As John Emigh puts it, 'masks and puppets lend themselves particularly well to this sort of ontological acrobatics' (Emigh 1996, 29), but his delightful final phrase is appropriate to most of the kinds of transformation I have outlined above. Again, for both performers and receivers, or receiver/ participants, in practice these conditions are likely to alternate. Both 'character' and 'mask' performers may experience periods of complete immersion in the 'other' ('flow episodes', in Emigh's citation of psychologist Mihaly Csikszentmihalyi: 1996, 26); receivers likewise will have periods of completely focused involve-ment in which, like performers in many fields including both art and sport, everything seems to be working effortlessly and with great precision. And both parties will at other times experience a degree of detachment. In both periods it could be said that they are experiencing 'not me/not not me'. As Coleridge puts it, they could be 'in their right mind'; but it would be more accurate to say that they can be in their right *minds*.

Or alternatively, mind functions here in such a way as to make available awareness of what was previously 'beyond' self, unseen or unknown. The 'daily' range of action and understanding is, during this phase of alternation, supplemented by an extension of or even beyond knowing, which occurs both organically and conceptually. I 'know' I am not my everyday self; I also 'know' that whatever role I adopt draws on that everyday self but is not limited to it. And this 'knowing' is therefore of a different order to what I previously 'knew' as myself. Usually it stops there; but it is also possible that this 'not knowing' becomes heightened to such a degree that I experience myself as *only* that, without trace of any role. From the complete suspension of this beyondness (what Indian thought calls *moksha*, or absolute freedom), knowing itself emerges transformed. In any case, the process of juxtaposition leads in this direction.

If I am not 'me' and not not me, who or what am I? Something like an ambassador, conducting frequent sorties on either side of the border? In that situation I am beginning to stake some claim on a 'no-man's land', a cross-border territory in which I become more comfortable the more I go on shuttling back and forth. I (my mind) is more extensively conscious; what I add to 'me' is a potentiality to be other. That 'other' is more; it is a gain, not a loss; 'I' am enriched by it.

Within the space of the shuttling, I am 'not me/not not me': what I am is potential. A sort of 'gap' has opened up. The self as previously known is left behind. Or better, it is suspended. It is not lost, but it is lost to awareness for a brief time or space. The self as other is likewise in suspension, not quite inhabited as yet. This in-betweenness (recalling a term used earlier about liminality) is crucial because it marks the moment when freedom from the known becomes a possibility. This is in fact what is marked by Schechner's diagonal (/). As an experience it can engender fear or delight, or anything in between; though properly speaking this does not occur at the moment of loss, because at that moment there is no I to experience. What there is, however, is awareness.

Chapter 4 will take up this discussion again. Here it leads me to say something more about the gain. When I live this quality of awareness (and I hope the above discussion has indicated that I think it can occur in many forms of theatre at many times to many people), I am at my most available: I am not determined solely by what I was (and by the beliefs and habits attaching to this), nor by what I will become. I am open.

I am not the known and defined I, but rather, I as potential: the potential to move into form, the potential to be 'me', 'not me' and 'not not me'. That I-ness can enable I to extend to other. The otherness can be aspects of myself which I 'normally' prefer to leave unilluminated, or potentialities of sensibility activated by something outside me. It can also, in certain circumstances, be something more. It is interesting that the sequence above indicates progressive degrees of 'me' moving to 'other' through increasing factors of negation (not > not not). Perhaps the supreme proponent of the double (and sometimes the triple) negative in the west is Samuel Beckett, whose protagonists are intensely motivated to rid themselves of the everyday egoic self.

In marked similarity, the *Upanishads* define Brahman, towards which the Self (i.e. the more-than-everyday) gravitates, by degrees of 'notness': it is not this, not that, it cannot be seized this way or that. But by negotiating the 'gap' I give myself the chance of becoming, or becoming one with, this other, whatever it may be, rather than of shrinking from it or pushing it away. To register all the possibilities and to slightly extend Schechner's formula, here 'I' is/am the potential to be me; the potential to be other; not me; not not me; and pure not (recalling Beckett again via Mr Knott in *Watt*).

Within the play of theatre, this loss – or perhaps better, this sacrifice of what Alan Watts calls 'the skin-encapsulated ego' – which is a necessary condition of facing the real otherness of the other, is negotiated. Emigh offers a parallel between Turner's 'liminality' and child psychoanalyst D.W. Winnicot's 'potential space' for play, which are both 'events called into being by the experience of gaps in continuity' (Emigh 1996, 3); this condition allows the (masked) performer to '[work] within the plane of similitude to create the amalgam of self and other' (1996, 278).

And this 'otherness' may then be discovered as the *real*, in several senses. By incorporating and activating in myself what I most fear in myself, or designate as alien to me, I rehabilitate it. It may be strange or disturbing. It may be what lies beyond the limits of what I usually know (myself to be). I may in other ('everyday') situations therefore be very scared of it. But it is also what subtends all the 'known' forms of my being: it is *me as not me*, it is *both* the death *and* the life of 'me'. It is both the utter viscosity of my transience and the simple potential for my multiple being. It is the real of my limits and my power to move beyond them. So it is also the best resource for negotiators. Acquiring it is the most direct and most fundamental way in which the skill of border-crossing can be cultivated. That has pragmatic consequences in a multicultural and transpersonal world.

Given these views, it perhaps comes as no surprise that I believe all politicians should receive theatre training! Not of course in order to allow them to perform their familiar roles with more conviction; rather, to offer them the evidence of the limitations of these roles and the chance of improving on them. All the same, this exploration of the potential for freedom in theatre needs to take account too of theatre's role in the political spectrum.

The argument above suggests that although theatre may not, as Bharucha says, have changed the world so far, 'it is possible to change our own lives through theatre' (Bharucha 1993, 10). Among the motivations to change which its activity on the fringes offers are: redrawing of the boundaries of understanding and possible action; focus in many forms on issues which would otherwise be overlooked; expression by voices which would otherwise be silent. In India, theatre activity has not infrequently been at the centre of radical political and social movements, for instance in the case of Hashmi's Janam; it constitutes at present an important part of the political and cultural debate about identity, tradition and values (Chapter 5 addresses this further). More fundamentally it provides a means of individual realignment which then underpins changes in perception, understanding, articulation and action.

All this can be in part encouraged or stifled by the availability of finance: funding is important for training, production, status and visibility; and its lack, and the consequent lack of adequate facilities in many areas, is serious. Nevertheless, the activity of theatre and performance is widespread throughout India even where adequate funding does not exist. This suggests that people find it stimulating, rewarding and useful, and that they want to go on experiencing directly those ways in which it can open up life for them and lead them in new directions both personal and public.

INDIA, THE CURRENT SITUATION AND THIS BOOK

Indian theatre, its history, theory and practice, has become increasingly important in the West in the past half-century, both for the reasons outlined above and in the context of debates about 'postcolonialism'. Lal claims that 'no analysis of contemporary Indian theatre can afford to ignore the profound Indian influence on world theatre' (1995, I). Concurrently in India, in this post-independence era, theatre has passed from relative neglect to the status of a national cultural icon with all the problems that brings with it. Theatre practitioners in India are now having to deal with the problem of its relevance and ability to respond to contemporary socio-political realities whilst at the same time rethinking its rationale in the context of new models and theories of performance which have dominated recent critical approaches to theatre and drama. Additionally, major transformations of Indian life and 'invasions' by westernised cultural forms and economic practice mean that indigenous culture is itself in a kind of 'modern' crisis: though it is true to say that India is so large and complex that there is always at least one crisis going on somewhere, and it still continues to survive.

27

Indian theatre has thus become, both in India and in the world of performance, a major site of reappraisal and renewal. The West has looked to it as a multi-dimensional performance model, not without the twin dangers of a new 'orientalist' appropriation and a tendency to view it as a convenient form of postmodernist pluralism: acquisitive and reductive approaches which overlook cultural embedding, reflected not least in the tendency to think of Indian theatre as a single phenomenon. Chapters 3 and 5 in particular of this book will attempt to recognise that the multiplicity of 'traditional' and 'contemporary' manifestations cannot be neatly subsumed; indeed they impinge constantly on and across each other, and much of the current debate within India centres on major questions underpinning performance theory as it has existed for centuries in India, namely the functions of theatre and the ways it affects its audience. On the other hand, recent writers have also pointed out that to overlook the specific historical situation of Indian theatre in India and in the world today is a form of marginalisation. If theatre anywhere is relevant to the context it inhabits, it needs to be able to dialogue with it, not retire from it.

Over the last half-century there have been a number of very significant applications of oriental theatre forms by western practitioners, directors and actor-trainers from Brecht and Artaud to Grotowski and Brook. That practice has been further developed in workshop and study contexts by UK organisations like *Pan Project* and the *Centre for Performance Research*; feeding into European performance work either via direct 'importation' as in the case of Mnouchkine, Barba, etc. or through exposure to training methods; and in Britain and the USA emerging quite extensively in the work of practitioners of Indian origin (Jatinder Verma's directing at the National and with Tara Arts, numerous well-known dancers and groups, for example Shobana Jeyasingh) and of theatre workers/academics like Schechner and Philip Zarilli. Barba has used Orissi dancer Sanjukhta Panigrahi extensively in his theoretical and practical investigations of 'theatre anthropology'.

There have also been studies of article length of Indian and related forms, by Barba, Schechner and others, and books largely or entirely focused on Indian forms by Schechner and Zarilli. In addition there exists much traditional Indian scholarship on textual forms and aesthetic theory, and a few books (not widely known or available in the West) on the current or recent state of such forms and related practice (e.g. *Traditional Indian Theatre: Multiple Streams* by Kapila Vatsyayan [1980]; *Yaksagana* by K.S. Karanth [1973, new edition 1997]; *History of Indian Theatre* by M.L. Varadpande [1992]). Important recent studies dealing largely or partly with Indian theatre include Rustom Bharucha's *Theatre and the World* (1993) and Eugène van Erven's *The Playful Revolution* (1992). Both offer challenging critiques of 'orientalising' perspectives (as does the collection of essays on Brook's *Mahabharata* edited by David Williams: 1991) and ways of asserting the liberating socio-political potential of mobilising indigenous tradition. At the same time, neither provides a subtle and specific enough account of this tradition to fully relate past to present practice.

Richmond et al indicate in *Indian Theatre: Traditions of Performance* (1990) that they are attempting an 'introduction to Indian theatre [...] written by Western scholars from their own perspective' (xi) and propose that this is 'part of a larger rewriting of the history of theatre/performance that is currently underway' (3). As such it is potentially – and in terms of its use in American academic circles – a significant volume, containing material organised along historical and descriptive lines according to the categories *classical, folk/popular, ritual, devotional and modern*. It doesn't however attempt to analyse the implications of the nature, basis and development of Indian forms; and Lal (1995) points out that it contains a considerable number of errors and misrepresentations. It is also particularly vague in its definition of 'modern' theatre, for which it relies heavily on material from 1950–60s urban theatre.

Lal also indicates that the errors are reproduced in the *Cambridge Guide to Theatre* (1992), where all the 53 entries on India are by Richmond, and further recycled into the *Cambridge Guide to Asian Theatre*. His detailed critique (Lal 1995, 24–27) is appropriately framed as a demand for increased vigilance from both Indian and foreign theatre scholars.

In *Rasa: The Indian Performing Arts in the Last Twenty-five Years (Vol. II – Theatre and Cinema)* (1995), Lal introduces thirty-three essays on theatre, all but two by Indian writers: sixteen 'overviews' of theatre in different languages, and essays on training, design, arts policy, economics, interculturalism, the 'folk' question, and others. The range of topics is significant, though even here the editor points out geographical and thematic lacunae. What is important for both Indian and western critics is to take into account as much of the spectrum represented by this collection as possible.

Given these salutary indications, plus the range and variety indicated by Vatsyayan's subtitle, it is probably foolish for a non-Indian to offer another inevitably partial account. I do so however because there isn't a book which attempts to analyse the basic structures of Indian theatre in both philosophical and performance terms, and to relate them to recent theatre history, theory and practice in the West. This book aims to fill this gap, and to appeal to those in both East and West who have an interest in the practice of performance and the nature of the meanings it conveys. Its intention is to explore the underlying causes of the profound impact Indian theatre has had and can have on the understanding of the active exchange between performers and audience which major western practitioners locate as the core of the theatrical process.

This book therefore does *not* set out to be a scholarly exegesis of texts, nor a full historical description of all the extremely numerous Indian forms. I am not qualified to do that, and the Indian works mentioned above, plus others indicated in the Bibliography, together come close to fulfilling these tasks. Rather it involves a discussion of styles of performance, of the criteria underlying them and the kinds of meaning they invite, their relevance to the contexts of theatre in India and the world at the present time. In the course of this discussion, I use conventional categories like 'text', 'performance' and 'theory', but I suggest that the evidence from Indian theatre requires them to be thought of as interrelated and to some extent transferable, rather than as watertight.

The book tries to do two main things therefore which I don't think anyone else does: 1) give an account of how and why Indian theatre contributes significantly to our understanding of everything that 'theatre' is about in the light of contemporary perceptions both eastern and western; and 2) look at how it is going about its business now. This penultimate and longest chapter draws on accounts by Indian writers which have appeared in the last decade and on my own investigations in India.

The sources and resources on which I have drawn come principally from my involvement with the practice of theatre as a director, a performer and a teacher; my work with Indian performers and institutions, in Britain and in India; activities with students in both countries; long familiarity with Indian thought and with its practical expression in a practice of meditation. These have fed into much of my work which has been made public both as performance and as writing.

During the fifteen or so years that I have been travelling frequently to India I have no doubt gone through many phases, from bewilderment to cultural tourism to varieties of postcolonialist guilt. They will probably be reflected in what follows. But essentially I've been in India to *do* things: to teach, to direct, to work with people, to initiate projects. For me doing theatre is about making things work. Although everyone brings along their own personal baggage, the process may persuade them to leave much of it aside and get on with the meeting and the creating. So I have not spent a lot of time agonising about the political correctness of what I have been doing, nor indeed about the political correctness of writing this book. If either activity has been some use to some people, so much the better. If it stimulates them to think and/or to behave in different ways, I don't mind if those ways are in conflict with some of mine.

CHAPTER TWO

Text

FORMS OF 'TEXT' AND APPROACHES

Where are the 'origins' of Indian theatre: in performance or in 'text'; and if, in part at least, in the latter, what kind(s) of text are we talking about? Common-sense suggests that performing and recording of performance in some form, for example as cave-paintings of ritual relationships to the world around, develop together. But most theatre criticism has tended to start from the primacy of text, and this has until fairly recently been true of India as much as of the West, though in a slightly different sense: where in western approaches the written *play*-text was seen as the starting point, in India critical work more commonly took the form of revaluations or reinterpretations of aspects of the 'classical' *theoretical* text on *how* to perform, the *Natya Sastra*. The written text however is on one hand a stimulus to performance, and on the other, what is crystallised out of performance; in other words it rarely presents, even as 'stage directions' or performance indications, anything approaching the range of effects and procedures which occur in the performance itself. Indian and other 'plural' performance forms make this particularly clear.

Such forms can't easily be pinned down to any simple version of text or genre of performance, as we have already seen to some extent in terms of cross-border activity between categories such as 'folk' and 'classical', 'ritual' and 'theatre'; the same situation holds for the opposition or more accurately the continuum 'text'/'performance'. This book is not especially concerned with the problems of whether the texts of the epics, or of earlier narratives which were later incorporated into them, existed wholly or partly in written form at any particular point in the outgrowth of performance forms. There is evidence on both sides, some of which will be referred to below and in the next chapter.

For my purpose it is more appropriate to use a model of dialogue between text and performance, because what I am mainly concerned with is the state which that dialogue has reached today, its repercussions on theatre in both hemispheres, and the ways in which it fuels creative activity.

If I thus bracket out the issue of a sharp distinction between text and performance, the question remains: why put a chapter on 'text' first? Whilst there is in my view no complete justification for doing so (maybe it should come last, or not at all), the pragmatic reason in this case is that I want to talk about *narrative*. Narrative as the basis of dramatic performance in many Indian forms; narrative as generative process; the development and the undercutting or relativisation of narrative as dramatic practices; narrative as the myth of creation, the story of stories; narrative as the incitement to imaginative activation, to the plurality of forms in theatre. About narrative in its relationship to drama and performance then, both as content and as structuring mechanism.

It is however also worth briefly positioning other western approaches to 'text' in Indian theatre, because it helps to elucidate what people were looking for. Early work deals almost exclusively with Sanskrit drama, which could in fact be accessed as *written text* (albeit in translation, necessarily incorporating the perspective on India of the translator at the time, such as Sir William Jones, who first translated *Shakuntala* in 1789). Arthur Ryder's early twentieth-century translation (undated, but post 1910), refers to Kalidasa as 'the greatest of Sanskrit poets' (vii): there is little reference to the play in or as performance. In contrast, most approaches during the period I am discussing (i.e. 1930 and after) tend to focus on *performance* features of the so-called 'folk' or 'traditional' forms; in this perspective script, written text and even spoken dialogue is what receives virtually no reference; in part because much of it is not written down, but also because it is in languages inaccessible to the investigators (i.e. Prakrit, contemporary Indian languages and dialect forms). In other words, early seekers found 'classical' and 'canonical' text, which could be offered, for instance, as comprehensible to early Romantic writers in Europe who were intensely concerned with inner states of being and with the revelatory quality of language. Twentieth-century travellers however 'discovered' socio-anthropological event-structures, rich theatre semiotics and powerful performance techniques which answered their needs outlined in Chapter 1. For the former, there may be a sense of relief that the otherness of 'oriental' *practice* can be avoided by a reading which welcomes Kalidasa into both Classical and Romantic folds; for the latter, the relief is generated by the realisation that the otherness of Indian *languages* can be 'safely' overlooked by designating the performative events as significant in themselves. From Artaud onwards, western practitioners have claimed to 'read' the performance-text without reference to the written or spoken languages it includes. Like Artaud, many of them have understood some important things; they have also not infrequently misunderstood, even if not quite as spectacularly as he did. Peter Brook's and Jean-Claude Carrière's truncating of the *Mahabharata* is one example of what can happen. Emigh highlights the 'preposterous' claim that their version was the first time anyone had staged the whole epic, which, he indicates, is both inaccurate and insulting (Emigh 1996, 282).

We can only deal with so much otherness, it seems; so we ignore what we find particularly uncomfortable and recuperate other aspects into more familiar paradigms. It so happens that these paradigms are themselves gambits for or moves towards the 'unknown' or the unconventional (Romantic and Modernist quests for heightened sensibility, escape from excesses of ratiocentricity). Attitudes to 'text' and performance highlight the way envoys on this territory have behaved, and suggest that there are further dimensions of otherness which need to be met; I will take up this question and related issues in Chapter 6.

This analysis indicates another reason for treating text and performance together, in order to avoid the editing out of one or other of these crucial elements. So my discussion of typical performance forms (in Chapter 3) is preceded here by some examination of the epic texts from which they mainly derive. And in post-Independence Indian theatre (and in earlier work particularly in Bengal and Maharashtra) there is also a strong textual element: eclecticism, in the sense of drawing upon all appropriate resources and contexts including the scripted text, is important in current considerations of what theatre can be. Lal (1995) underlines the importance of the publication of translated play-scripts, both into English and between Indian languages: part of Indian theatre's current task is to negotiate the space between canon and folklore.

So this chapter will give some thought to both Sanskrit drama and contemporary Indian theatre as text in the relatively conventional sense of the term. It will also explore some features of the epics (*Mahabharata* and *Ramayana*), source-texts for much traditional and a certain amount of contemporary performance; in part because one basic question that an audience asks is 'what is it about?'. The desire or need to know is one aspect which motivates its presence as audience. It may be that interrogating an epic and interrogating a performance produce something of the same result: a recognition that acquisition of 'objects' of knowledge, or experiencing completion, is not quite what it's about, and that the act and process of knowing may be more crucial, and in a curious way more substantial, than any finite 'product'. In order to explore more fully some ways in which that awareness is mediated, I need to look, as well as at features of performance, which I will take up in the next chapter, at what in a way underlies 'text': the nature and modalities of *narrative*.

There are good reasons for starting with narrative, since it is where many other things start. Even an abstract performance requires (for directors and performers at least) a narrative of some sort. All theatre tells a story, even where it is the story of how we tell stories and even — or especially — when it is only completed or fully articulated by the receivers. Narrative demonstrates by its inevitable drive towards teleology our perpetual desire to make sense, and we 'read' everything that happens on stage with a similar intention. Additionally in the Indian context, sound (*vac*) is understood as the first expression of the impetus to form. Speech emerges from sound, and, in contrast to Derrida and his followers, is perceived as the primary form of language rather than what is written down. Major 'texts' like the epics (in common, of course, with other epic literature from e.g. Greece and Scandinavia) and the *Vedas* have been primarily preserved through *oral* transmission, which has ensured that they are always essentially *performed*, and that they always not only produce but consciously (as in chanting of the *Vedas*) aim to make use of the physical effects of sound and rhythm upon receivers. The interaction between narrative (even the prospect of narrative) and receiver stimulates our sense-making capabilities; oral performance functions as a deliberate part of the process by causing specific changes in the receptor mechanism and thus affecting the quality of what is received: the listeners listen better and hear more, and this is a model for the effects of performance as understood in Vedic thought, in which, clearly (as in the best renderings of Shakespeare) the sound and rhythm of the words is not in the least arbitrary.

NARRATIVE AS THE BASIS OF PERFORMANCE FORMS

Most Indian performances still derive from the major Hindu epics *Mahabharata* and *Ramayana*, two of the largest and most famous narrative compilations in the world. This applies to dance as well as drama, and is true of performance both at the more 'classical' end of the spectrum and of 'folk'-oriented forms. There are many forms currently in existence which illustrate this in different ways. Some employ a 'narrator', often a mix of director and stage-manager on stage, who may introduce characters, narrate events, fill in background detail, prompt performers, dialogue with them etc. (known as the *Sutradhara* – from *sutra*, thread or core statement – or as *Bhagawata* in *Yakshagana*). Others make use of the comic character (*Vidushaka* in *Kudiyattam*, *Katiyakkaran* in *Therukoothu*) for aspects of the same functions. Others use singers to narrate the story, as in *Kathakali*. *Kuttu*, the basis of *Kudiyattam*, is a one-man dramatised narrative form. There are many forms which cover the spectrum between narrative and performance, in which the basis or principal motivation is narration and some aspects are dramatised or physicalised using puppets, musicians and/or a certain amount of dialogue, gesture etc. There also still exist picture showmen, who use a kind of sing-song to narrate incidents depicted on a scroll or painting which is displayed or unfurled (*Chithra Katha, Pabuji Ki Phad* from Rajasthan, other forms for example in Maharashtra; see Chapter 3 for further discussion).

K.N. Panikkar writes, challengingly if perhaps somewhat over-programmatically: 'The traditional concepts of Indian theatre can really be explained only in terms of the process of evolution of the actor from an official shaman to storyteller to performer and subsequently to character, and from the village bard to the *sutradhara*' (Panikkar 1995, 110).

Much of what goes on in Indian theatre has its impetus then in narrative energy, in the desire to narrate and the act and process of narrating. So we need to look at the 'sources' of this narrative drive. Who narrates? Why? What is being narrated?

To engage with these questions we have to say something about the *Mahabharata* and the *Ramayana*; and we also have to say something about the world-view which they articulate and/or on the basis of which they arise. (I am not going to talk about the history of the epics in any detail, but they do need to be placed in the context of Vedic thought.)

According to W.J.Wilkins (*Hindu Mythology,* first published 1882, reprinted 1986) the Vedas 'are amongst the oldest literary productions of the world' (7); but since they derive from oral transmission no precise date is possible. They have been dated from before 1,400BC (Colebrooke) to 1,200–200BC (Max Müller). *Mahabharata* and *Ramayana* are dated roughly between 1,000 and 100BC, though *Mahabharata* does not appear in written form until c.400AD; *Natya Sastra* between 200BC and 200AD; the major playwrights of Sanskrit theatre between 150BC and 700AD (after Greek and Roman theatre, before other major Asian forms and European medieval theatre).

As far as the dating of various gods and attributed legends goes, it bears out Schechner's view that origin theories are not terribly helpful. Nomenclature was and still is highly volatile and interchangeable (e.g. Krishna is an avatar or incarnation of Vishnu but sometimes a god in his own right, Rama likewise, Shiva and Vishnu, Krishna and Vishnu are in certain circumstances joined, Brahma Shiva and Vishnu are aspects of each other and/or of creative energies, Durga has many names and forms of which Kali is one, and so on); they are more credibly and helpfully envisaged as tendencies, kinds of energy, principles, ideal or archetypal forms; and they recur over and over again in different times and places. Trying to construct a linear history (e.g. worship of Agni gave way at some point to worship of Shiva who incorporates some or all aspects of Agni ...) is highly speculative, although the *Vedas* offer some clues.

The *Rg Veda* gives an account from several different points of view of the origin and process of creation. One aspect of this account is analysed through a consideration of the opening phrases (see below, p. 85); others are found in Muir's transposition, quoted by Wilkins:

There was neither aught nor naught ...
[. .]
The One breathed calmly, self-sustained ...
[. .]
That One, a void in chaos wrapt, by inward fervour grew.
Within it first arose desire, the primal germ of mind,
Which nothing with existence links ...

Although to guess from its poetic language and form, this owes a good deal to nineteenth-century Imperialist assumptions (Wilkins in the Preface to the Second Edition [1900] says condescendingly 'the sages of India were not in complete darkness' [xi]), it nevertheless offers a reasonable insight not inconsistent with a variety of interpretative perspectives, as follows:

- linguistic (sound arises from silence, thought from intention);
- psychoanalytic (desire is the impetus to action);
- philosophical (the many emerging from the One, mind as the outgrowth of the Self-sufficient becoming conscious of itself);
- aesthetic (form emerging from the potential or absence of form).

Relating these interpretations back to the discussion of basic premisses in Chapter I is not too difficult. Nor is it difficult to see the likelihood that understandings of this kind should be transferred into all Indian performance forms including, but not exclusively, Sanskrit theatre. What they underline is that the process of 'creation', 'manifestation' or 'incarnation' – the way things take shape, idea becomes form – moves through different psychophysiological stages and across different vehicles or media. (Vedic 'gods' operate as forces which appear as different forms and are presented riding on animate 'vehicles' – Ganesh, for instance, on a rat – and thus enter into the play and interplay of the world-as-transformation.)

So the *Vedas* offer a consistent view of the performative structure of creative acts, and it is not surprising that this perception underpins epic literature and is transferred into theatre. The transfer can be located in textual form in the *Vedas*: as instructions for rituals and/or 'sacrifice', which operate the merging of individual and para-individual; in the dialogue of Yama and Yami in *Rg Veda*, which embodies a resolute and active questioning of gender, sexuality, relationship and procreation; in the epics and other texts, as myth and story, as exemplary action; or via performance instructions in the *Natya Sastra*. All these have firmly to do with setting creative acts in motion and exploring their dynamics, with beginning therefore to articulate a *dramatology*.

The figures and events of *Mahabharata* and *Ramayana*, usually thought of as archetypal, are drawn from the following sources, which explains their range of action and their scale:

(a) *the religious tradition*: figures are larger-than-life/superhuman in order to function as moral and spiritual models; they also tend to imply an exclusive role for certain castes who have privileged access to such mysteries and powers, e.g. the tradition of *sidhis*, 'abnormal' powers and attributes acquired through prolonged spiritual practice.

(b) *temporal rulers and historical events*: for example, the postulated Aryan invasion and colonisation (images of battles and weapons; the battle of Kurukshetra, 900–800BC, for which archaeological evidence exists, understood as a dynastic dispute between Kurus and Panchalas (who become the *Mahabharata's* Kauravas and Pandavas); the story of Rama's conquest of Ravana in Sri Lanka as a retelling of the invasion of the Dravidian south by Aryan forces from the north; examples of social and military structures from major empires like the Mauryas in the north (321–104BC, including the reign of Ashoka) and the Cholas, Pallavas and Pandyas in the south (500–1,250AD).

These figures and events therefore represent actions in the personal, social and political, and cosmic domains in order to illustrate and explicate *dharma*: right action in both the cosmic and the contemporary context, analysis of how the individual can act in accord with communal, even 'universal', modalities for good. They thus offer models and examples of action on all psychospiritual and sociohistorical levels.

So the who/what/why questions above cannot be answered simply; principally because the epic and the mythological are open to interpretation on many levels. *Mahabharata* and *Ramayana* can be viewed from one angle as repositories of spiritual teaching, from another as social and moral instruction, from another as a version of the history of ancient India, or as a kind of cultural blueprint. They can and do give rise to interpretation from theological, psychological, historicist and anthropological standpoints among others. They tend to move across disciplines and genres; they are networks of significance which invite networks of performative development.

NARRATIVE AND MYTH

Myth is by its very nature capable of many kinds of interpretation, and thus subject also to many ways of classification. It can be thought of as a kind of historical narrative (in Indian tradition the epics are classed as *itihasas*, which implies just this). It then imparts in fictional form all kinds of guidelines and belief structures about, for instance, ideal characteristics and forms of behaviour. In another perspective myth is a kind or level of utterance: Greek apparently classifies four such levels, namely *logos* (divine), *mythos* (poetic), *epos* (historical) and *rhema* (lyrical) (Kanellakos 1972), which are identified according to the subtlety and complexity of significance which they articulate. So *mythos* refers to a highly compacted, potent, resonant level in which utterance is charged with possibility (in the case of *Mahabharata* and *Ramayana*, the contention is strengthened by the generative structure of Sanskrit referred to above). It is a quality of language resonant with meaning, that is to say it is implicitly fabricative, enactive or performative. Another approach would see it as a kind of narrative structure, a means of accessing and exploiting the kinds of linguistic resonance just mentioned; and yet another would read from it anthropological evidence of stages in social development. At one extreme it is close to religion, in the sense that it describes the relationship between human beings and the cosmos, often by means of images of superhuman beings. At another extreme it is a form of political or moral persuasion.

All these possibilities are relevant to *Ramayana* and *Mahabharata*, and indicate again their potential as sources of entertainment, instruction, speculative thought and dramatic action. There could be many other ways of approaching these and other myths: each discipline (theology, philosophy, history, linguistics, anthropology, psychology, literature ...) can draw up its own criteria for classification. There is however another way of looking at myth which is important from my perspective (the attempt to understand forms of performance) and which does not negate any of the others.

Myth (as the above paragraphs imply) crosses borderlines: it is itself a *liminal* situation. That is to say, it operates at the junction of different ways of understanding and classifying. It is evidence of a vision which shifts across the borders, which is capable of holding many possibilities of significance in play simultaneously. To do this such vision must be capable of a quality of very precise attention, in which discreet but potentially contradictory phenomena are perceived and held in balance. In physics this might be the kind of perception which is required to comprehend the existence of different dimensions at the quantum level but the impossibility of measuring them in the same instant. Beckett has an image for it in *Murphy*: in what is described as his 'third zone' of perceptual activity, characterised by a kind of detached floating along with intensely acute awareness, Murphy feels himself to be a part of a continual 'generation and passing away of line' (Beckett, 1977, 65). Awareness in this condition displays an important paradoxical quality (which I will return to in the chapter on theory). It retains its ability to record with great precision, but is able to free itself from attachment to conventional categories and to suspend the normal febrile desire to close off the indeterminate by allocating it to a single system.

If myth and what the Greeks called *poesis* (making) emanates from this condition, it is not surprising if its essence is performative. Whatever other ways of understanding myth we employ – and all may have their uses in particular contexts – it is necessary also to understand it as deriving from this condition of generative openness in consciousness. Such a condition must of course have its psychobiological parameters and be in some sense measurable. Since the Indian theory of *rasa* quite specifically aims to instil a particular 'ideal' state or condition in its receivers, it will be necessary to return to this aspect too in the discussion of theory. As I will be arguing there, however, aesthetics is a practical as well as a theoretical affair. It invites participation, it opens up 'gaps' which incite the activity of the receiver. There are moreover close parallels here with psychophysiological conditions which western practitioners believe they see in Indian performance and which they have sought, by a variety of methods, to cultivate in their performers: these will be discussed in the chapters on performance and theory (Chapters 3 and 4) and further evaluated in Chapter 6.

Hindus moreover do not consider the epics, which still form part of the fabric of daily life in cartoon and cinema, in allusions in political speeches, in figures of speech and styles of behaviour, as well as in millions of icons in temples, on advertisement hoardings, in buses and rickshaws, to be 'myths' in the conventional (negative) western sense of the term, since the forces they incarnate are experienced as part of the web of life. Krishna and Rama are not just regarded as abstract principles or folk heroes, they are felt to be tendencies within the field of experience, or they function as role-models – which can of course have both positive and negative effects.

Myth is a highly complex study, but the attitude to it in these cases suggests that it presents equivalents of states and situations, both 'daily' and 'extra-daily', which its audience may experience: such states and situations are subject to change, they are not fixed once and for all. Myth is liminal, suggestive, interactive; although its content may often appear conservative, its mode of operation is closer to being transgressive. Or perhaps it could be accorded the dual status of preservation and transformation.

'ORIGINS' OF NARRATIVE

So if there is much room for ambiguity about the status of what is narrated, it is equally difficult to say where the narrating has its origin. The epics themselves are ascribed to figures whose historical existence or sole authorial input is in any case not certain, and the mythological account of the origin of the *Mahabharata* is that it was dictated by Vyasa to Ganesh, elephant-headed son of Shiva and Parvati: Ganesh agrees to take dictation so long as Vyasa doesn't pause; Vyasa counters by saying: 'Agreed, I won't, so long as you understand what I've said instantly on all levels and in totality'. So production here is ceaseless emerging of form as narrative, and reception requires total understanding; that is, consciousness functioning in harmony with the potentiality of generative possibility so as to grasp all order at the point at which it moves from the 'implicate' to the 'explicate' stage. Vyasa is thus credited with being not only the narrator but also the progenitor of the lines from which both sides of the warring family – Pandavas and Kauravas – spring. He doesn't just tell of them, he creates them in and through the telling, and in so doing he embodies understanding of all the levels on which they engage in their epic and *dharmic* journey and of all the conflicting positions they adopt.

The *Ramayana* is attributed to Valmiki, supposedly inspired by the manifestation of Brahma, who compliments him on a *sloka* he has just composed and invites him to produce some more: so in this case Valmiki's awareness is in tune with the Brahma-aspect (Brahma is usually represented facing three ways at once), in other words with all phases of manifestation incorporated into the act of telling.

Both epics thus include in the story of their own narration the requirement for totality, which in terms of consciousness must mean operating beyond ordinary space-time and linear modes. If they require the consciousness of the teller to access this most powerful state of symbolic organisation, they also require in their receivers the ability to operate at a similar level.

This is the realm of archetypal narrative, of narrative and narrating as the story of stories, the articulation of how we make sense and of the ways in which we produce variants of sense. Performance can in fact come closer to this in some respects than linear (written) form, because it can more immediately generate co-existence and coherence of levels, modes, dynamics: stillness along with movement, sound balanced against silence, speaking or acting whilst at the same time experiencing a sense of detachment or witnessing. What it doesn't so obviously provide is the opportunity to return to understandings or experiences which the receiver might have 'missed'. In reading it is possible to pick up this intuition of loss and recoup the pay-off. Performance does however have means of allowing this: the extraordinarily elongated rhythm of *Noh* is an obvious one, but other more 'busy' forms provide instances of repetition, reincorporation, recognition and restitution, so that we do ultimately get the chance to explore the full range of possibilities generated by text-in-performance.

This process factor confirms moreover that the origin of narration is less in the writing of a single verifiable author than in the ability to tell stories, to weave meaning from the memories and legends of the past and from the evidence of the present and the aspirations of individuals and societies. Especially since the opening section of the *Mahabharata* frequently has to switch to a new narrative antecedent to the previous one, in order to explain how the 'current' narrator knows what has occurred. 'Knowledge' is not a fixed entity which can be packaged and purveyed, but a dynamic process of transference whose perspectives, forms and participants are constantly being revised. Such, in the days before the contemporary myth of consumerism, was (ideally at least …) the nature of education.

Mahabharata also has 'origin' status in that it is reputed to contain 'everything': if it has happened, it's there, they say. It certainly contains accounts of the beginnings and presumably the end of civilisation, and many of the typical moral and political dilemmas which occur in between (some of Ratan Thiyam's recent staging of episodes has attempted to highlight this sense of the apocalyptic whilst retaining traditional performance-modes). It has been described as less an epic than 'an entire literature' (Maurice Winternitz, quoted in Varadpande 1990, 9).

There is however a difficulty which, it seems to me, quite properly arises when encountering a work of this kind. For an outsider it's remarkably difficult at first to 'make sense' of much of it: there are so many narratives within narratives that it is not clear what the structure or hierarchical relationship of them to each other might be ('whose story are we in now?'); and many of them appear to offer either very similar lessons or no discernible lesson at all. In other words it is quite difficult to keep your (logistic or moral) feet. The epic form seems here to require a similar revision of reading process to that sought by certain kinds of formal experiment in the West, which encourage the reader to gravitate away from exclusively sequential or cumulative reading towards degrees of simultaneity, repetition or paradox.

It seems to me that Indian audiences by and large do not look for 'coherent' meaning in the sense of considering the whole epic at once. Epics don't work that way; especially in cultures where visual or oral transmission is still more accessible than written (in a way much of India is currently involved in the switch from one audio-visual medium – performance, dramatised narratives – to another – tv and film; the problems created are less to do with the switch than with the active/passive nature of the reception in each case). Consumption is piecemeal, in selected incidents and extracts, and their relationship to each other is acquired over time and through repetition. If meaning is cumulative it is probably less as a series of intelligible propositions arranged in order than as a kind of substratum or deposit of assumptions and expectations, picked up at different times across different media, reworked, assimilated through a kind of osmosis.

But surely there are some (relative) certainties? It is true that the 'master narratives', to use Lyotard's term, do appear to be fairly transparent in their transmission of cultural values. There are definitely goodies and baddies in the Pandava/Kaurava conflict, even if here and elsewhere the categories are not as simplistic as I've just made it sound (Hindi movies tend to render them that way in their contemporary versions however); Rama is clearly a nicer chap than Ravana, and heroes are usually expected to display valour, chivalry and obedience to their father and their guru. On the other hand, especially in performance, more complexity is evident: a *Kudiyattam* Ravana, for instance, may have half an hour or more to express all kinds of ambivalence about his intended seduction of Sita and thus reveal himself as incorporating degrees of light and shade which put him more in the Macbeth than the Rambo category.

Some dissident voices have begun to point out recently that women rarely get anything to say and are expected to perform in stereotyped roles, even if they are required to marry five brothers at once; they become 'true example[s] of Indian womanhood ... ideals which defy intelligence and rational explanation, which involve sacrifice and dedication ... and have been kept alive in the popular Indian psyche through the ages, beginning with Sati-Savitri-Sita right down to Nirupa Roy and Chand Usmani in our times ...', as

Mahasweta Devi puts it in 'The Wet Nurse' (1987, 12); and the desired virtues do appear more easily achievable by male brahmins or warrior-rulers than by other less fortunate groups. The function of inculturation in 'national' epic is often to sideline those who don't fit the mould, and anthropological readings to some extent agree with this view by relating the development and spread of the epics to the increasing domination of Aryan as opposed to Dravidian culture.

So in this situation it may be difficult to say 'who' is narrating, because the source of the narrative is deliberately concealed many times over and hence it can only be ascribed to some supernatural or collective entity, which endows it with an authority transcending that of a single individual. It also makes arguing with it more difficult in one sense. On the other hand, the plethora of narratives and narrators-in-the-text may also lead to the view that if everything is in it, every way of reading it is permissible. That view, whatever problems it poses for fundamentalist or morally rigid standpoints, is an advantage for theatre and performance.

NARRATIVE AUTHORITY AND THE SHIFT TOWARDS PERFORMANCE

From one point of view *Mahabharata* is a heavy-weight text: its sheer size and ubiquitousness in Indian life can be overpowering. Within the 'traditional' forms of performance virtually nothing exists outside it, and while it may be tenable to argue that the epic contains the potentiality for all forms of interaction, narration, event etc., there is nevertheless a sense in which this has come to mean a certain amalgam of attitudes and beliefs and to exclude others. Maybe even those British-Indian middle-class coteries which at the end of the nineteenth and the beginning of the twentieth century aped Western naturalistic theatre style were not only enslaving themselves to a 'foreign' cultural matrix but also exploring with some relief a degree of freedom from their own; and this is more so in the case of post-war 'experimental' activity in theatre, dance, visual art etc. produced by Indian artists who have had considerable contact with the rest of the world and have incorporated other attitudes and approaches into their work without necessarily losing touch with their own heritage. There are some things which in general the epics appear not to encourage people to think or talk about – mainly for example forms of behaviour, assumptions about hierarchy, status and role etc. – because to a large extent they form the 'givens' of a so-called traditional view of 'Indianness'. However inaccurate, historically suspect, and indeed unfairly attributed to *Mahabharata* this model may be, it exists as a kind of Panglossian philosophy defending an idealised status quo.

The severe limitations of this view, and of the assumptions it encodes, are obvious enough to anyone who has tried to reconcile the experience of daily life in India with the pronouncements of politicians and pundits (for example, the ongoing sagas of corruption and political infighting in recent years, or revelations about the treatment of women in custody, the continuing existence of 'dowry deaths' and so on).

There is both a history and a strong presence of dissident writing which unpicks or satirises the pomposity, ineptitude, venality and hypocrisy of those in power; for many Indians perhaps the most familiar example is the cartoons of Lakshmann, though a similar, if more gentle version can be discerned in, for instance, R.K. Narayan. Both of these much-loved commentators indicate that any 'official' version of perfect harmony in a perfect society is less than ingenuously accepted by many of its citizens.

If the existence of such a public fiction (which to some extent underpins attempts to 'restore' traditions of performance after Independence – see Chapter 5) can in any way be laid at the door of *Mahabharata* and *Ramayana*, it is perhaps due to the assumption of a dominant narrative position which has tended to be accepted as an orthodoxy. Although it is possible to argue that some aspects of the epics, particularly in performance, do open themselves to the possibility of irreverence and challenge, by and large these are less obvious or marginalised, and it has often required considerable intellectual and moral courage to locate and foreground them. The task of as it were suspending the edifice of traditional assumptions about the epics is rather like the god-like feat reputed to have been performed by Shiva of raising Mount Kailash to serve as an umbrella.

However, performance inherently has the means to question any limitation of viewpoint: across the whole range of traditional forms, comic characters like the *Vidushaka* enjoy a freedom not only to offer different perspectives on the 'noble' characters and the situations they engage in, but also to communicate in a different register and a different language (usually the vernacular, as opposed to the 'higher' forms of Prakrit or Sanskrit employed by more dignified characters). They stand aside from the action both physically and linguistically; they frequently use the codes of the contemporary world in order to relocate and question the issues derived from the epics. So although derived from the epic texts, performance in many periods can recontextualise them; as it does so, it operates its own version of shape-or-category shifting, its own liminal journey which moves narrative across into narrat*ing*. Some contemporary writers, directors and performers have quite deliberately seized on this feature in Indian performance (Brecht would have recognised it too) and used it to take further the deconstruction of the assumptions underlying the stories as they are 'traditionally' depicted. What kinds of narratives about power structures do they provide? What assumptions about gender and role do they 'immortalise'? What attitudes to class, caste or creed do they enshrine? Narrative can be a powerful opiate for the masses, and many an Indian movie appears to cash in on this; the dramatisation of narrative however offers the chance to raise rather than dull awareness. I will look at the practice of some of these theatre workers in the fifth chapter.

The *Mahabharata*'s claim to include everything implies that there is a story for every situation. But stories are always narrated from a particular standpoint; where narrative strategies often tend to conceal this behind authoritarian or 'objective' discourse, the dialogic form of drama nearly always involves an opening up and pluralising of points of view; in any case the story is mediated through performers – and often, especially in Indian theatre, through a multiplicity of performance codes as well – who either implicitly or explicitly act as a framework to the story and offer other perspectives or comments on it. Here too recent western critical perspectives are closer to what happens in Indian practice, in the sense that they have focused on the plurality of 'voices' and the interweaving of discourses in any text.

If the 'what' of narrative consists on one level of the now familiar stories of gods and heroes, battles and marriages, good and bad causes, punishment and reward, noble or scurrilous actions on a grand scale played out against a vast canvas, on another level it is history, poetry, ethics, entertainment, inspiration and indoctrination. It perhaps tells how one racial or cultural group resisted or dominated another; how human beings articulated their relationship with the animals they fought, killed, domesticated, feared or loved; how they made sense of natural forces; how they explained the sweep of time and history; how they tried to understand death. In other words it is the texturing of a world-view, with all the contradictions that implies. Perhaps that view did not so much 'exist' prior to the telling and retelling of the stories, but was born of and in the telling and is reborn as they are told again and again.

Performances in both 'folk' and 'classical' modes, even when they last as they traditionally do in some forms all night or for several successive nights, usually take a short incident or series of incidents from these enormous narrative and philosophical collages. The performance illustrates the episode(s), but it may also explain, recontextualise or elaborate. Thus neither the performance nor the 'script' work in practice as fixed systems, but rather, in a manner compatible with postmodern critical theory and practice, as generative networks, archetypal narrative in the sense that they continually give rise to new formulations; 'text' is not fixed entity but perpetual transformation, intertext reworked in different contexts, textual play, cognate with the notion of *lila*.

Narrative in performance then emerges as impetus and recurrent generative force, rooted in a model which views life as continuous reformulation out of latent energy. This statement is however pre-emptive and in need of considerable qualification in terms of philosophical precision and specification of its relationship to consciousness: the chapter on theory will develop this further.

Mahabharata and *Ramayana* have been discussed as weighty sources and as residues of generative narrative. From the point of view of drama the latter aspect to a large extent balances out any disadvantages of the potential authoritarian impact of the former. Additionally, the interaction of different characters and status roles, and the dialogic structure of much dramatic interchange, offer possibilities of relativisation. I suggest below (Chapter 3) that some of the splendid exhibitionism of *Yakshagana*, for instance, offers room for a sense of irony about the grand figures indulging in it. There is a parallel here with some aspects of European medieval drama (the enactment of Biblical narratives, the taking of carnivalesque liberties), where the doctrinal begins to offer scope for play.

Play, in terms of shifting between different levels of interpreta-tion and across the borders of conventional assumptions (e.g. about 'reality' and fantasy), is even more a feature of myth; and *Mahabharata* and *Ramayana* work in this way too. In spite of their great length and complexity of interweaving narratives, it is possible to see fairly simple basic structures. *Ramayana* in particular presents a model of the quest myth as archetypal narrative structure (see Malekin & Yarrow 1997 for more detail). The hero, Rama, is involved in a picaresque journey to regain his kingdom and his wife, Sita, having been unjustly deprived of both (by the trickery of Manthara and Kaikeyi, by the villainy of Ravana). He accepts his fate in both cases (the need to spend fourteen years in the forest and the need to win Sita back from Ravana by force) and reveals his stature in the performance of the tasks. He finally kills Ravana, is reunited with Sita and returns to claim his kingdom in triumph. (This cursory, though traditional enough account leaves out for the moment any questions we may have about for instance male/female stereotyping, or the way Rama treats his wife after their reunion.)

Mahabharata, though even more involved in terms of sub-plots and digressions, is centred on the feud between the Pandavas and the Kauravas and the questions of moral responsibility highlighted in the *Bhagavad Gita*. The 'quest' and the narrative here centrally involve the unravelling of the issues and forms of action which shape the moral and political structures of a community or a nation. Many embedded narratives deal with incidents in individual characters' development, all of which reflect back on the focal problem: by what means may an individual be enabled to make clear choices of action which will be valid and supportive not just for oneself, but also for the community? And each individual, like Yudhisthira and Dhritirashtra, or like Prospero or Lear, is 'king' in the perceptual structures by which he or she creates his/her own world.

Both epics then are about challenges to and ways of working out 'heroic' qualities which issue into 'kingship'. In both there are severe challenges or crises to overcome (exile, loss, financial ruin, war). If *Ramayana* ends with all restored (except to Sita, perhaps), *Mahabharata*'s vision is much less assured, and modern interpretations at least have dwelt on the apocalyptic vision. Perhaps in neither world is the outcome either certain or altogether comfortable: if so, the model of self-generating narrative is upheld, in that the story must necessarily go on. (As it does, of course, in contemporary reworkings both in drama and in Shashi Taroor's *The Great Indian Novel*, which ironically relocates much of the *Mahabharata* story in terms of post-Independence political infighting.)

There is a goal: fullness of vision and of life, a society in harmony, a coherence of knowledge and action. There is a passage through loss, absence, death. There is a sense of a new order, even if it is as yet unclear how successful its operation will be. The journey through exile, doubt, difficulty, and the essaying of many routes across it, forms the major part of both epics. The issues are existential (personal, political) and the process is enactive: values are created in and through choice and resultant action. Substance and structure here for drama, then: Chapter 4 looks further at implications of structure in Sanskrit drama, compared to western forms.

A play organises the quest of its protagonist(s) (and that of its audience to understand, to empathise, to judge) through the interaction of *sjuzet* (what is narrated) and *fabula* (the way in which it is presented). The linear form of surface communication is interrupted, questioned, enriched. What is known and the way it is known only emerge during the performance, a journey which in traditional Indian contexts passes through the dark, and which in performance everywhere occurs in time-and-space in some way marked off from the everyday. Different modes of knowing are set in motion; often they are initiated by a 'switching off' or 'bl(a)(o)cking out' of more recognisable features. The chapter on performance (Chapter 3) will look at this in more detail. But on all levels the *text* structures of *Ramayana* and *Mahabharata* and the plays which derive from them incorporate this (mythological) form of knowing in different dimensions.

As outlined above, the structure of the epics is that of the continuous generation of narratives. Not only does this suggest an awareness of the importance of the ability to tell stories and to materialise and analyse those stories in many ways and on many levels, but both the form of telling and many of the most frequent themes also open up the possibility of continuous reinterpretation.

I have mentioned above some of the forms still found today in India. That is only a fraction. In a country with around fifteen major languages and hundreds of dialects, it is no surprise that the rhythms of performance are varied, let alone the artistic traditions accompanying and/or determining them (glove or shadow or string puppets, different forms of painting, differences in musical structure between north and south), the huge variety in climate and the influence of several distinct major religions. Precisely because performance in most cases encompasses many or all of these features, the number of permutations increases exponentially. Chapter 3 looks further at a selection of forms.

Narrative as seed form can incite imaginative activity to emerge in many ways: it can offer the symbolic or poetic, it can suggest focus on different aspects. Reading *Mahabharata* or *Ramayana*, I am struck by the sparseness of the discourse, in spite of the sheer volume of stories they contain. Each episode is etched out almost in shorthand, as a series of motifs, many of which recur in many of the stories like cornerstones or departure points at different places: sages or gods performing austerities known as *tapas*, single combats between larger-than-life characters, nugatory moral discourses, symbolic journeys (the geography is closer to the realm of Superman than to flight paths, even those of Indian Airlines).

This may only be another way of making the point about overarching narratives or underlying structures, but in this context it helps to explain why so many different performance-pictures can emerge. Each is rooted both in the Pan-Indianness of the epics and in the historical and cultural specifics of time, place, language and community. In each case there is a reason for the stories being selected in the first place and secondly being told/dramatised in the way they are. A kind of 'efficacy' is always in view, and to a large extent that determines the shaping of the narrative as well as the conditions of its activation. In this sense text always interacts with context as performance event: *Raslila* for instance is a very different event in Vrindavan and in Delhi (simplistically, one is more like communion, the other more like carnival) because it takes place in a different space for a different kind of audience. The former location, with its mytho-historical echoes of Krishna, engenders a more devotional atmosphere, whereas an urban audience is more immediately appreciative of external play and display, as well as concerned about getting back home in a city where transport is difficult to find after 10pm.

THE STORY OF STORIES

Theatre in a way is itself the story of stories, because as Goethe said: 'Am Anfang war die Tat' (in the beginning was action). To return, then, to beginnings: in Vedic phonetics the sound *a* is not only the initiation of the alphabet but the setting in motion, the activation of all phenomenal manifestation; and it is the first sound of the *Rg Veda*, considered to be the first *Veda*.

Rg Veda begins with the words: 'Agnimile purohitam ...': literally, 'I behave in a priest-like fashion to Agni'. Very possibly then, 'I prepare to make a sacrifice to Agni'. Agni is the 'god' of fire, that is the principle or element which transforms, the Shiva element which burns up one state in order for it to be transmuted into another.

Where, in Indian performance, is Agni? Centre stage, from the beginning: the flame lit before a performance which remains present throughout (see photo of *Chakyar Kuttu*). Dance recitals frequently start with an invocation, often to Agni. Ritual events frequently centre around a fire. More prosaically, even in proscenium-arch auditoria, the lights go up to signal the start of the event.

So theatre begins with Agni, takes place in the presence of or by the grace of Agni. Metaphor for illumination and transformation, yes; but what about the *action* signalled in *Rg Veda*? A careful exploration might yield the following possibilities:

(i) I bring my awareness in tune with the state or condition represented by Agni; I come to that level of my being.

(ii) I suspend, put on one side, 'sacrifice' my everyday self and habitual behaviour: I leave the egoic self behind.

(iii) I become that which transmutes and transforms matter.

Now, since 'the state represented by Agni' is the phoenix-flame of transformability, what this means is that I access, physically and mentally, within myself, the point at which forms arise, mutate and reform. In a sense, then, this equates to the putting into form of the potential of Brahman; as Eliot has it:

> At the still point of the turning world [...]
> there the dance is [...]
> Except for the point, the still point,
> There would be no dance, and there is only the dance.

And in this condition, he is:

> surrounded
> By a grace of sense, a white light still and moving,
> (Burnt Norton).

Understood in terms of performance dynamics and practical behaviour, this means to access the waiting-but-tensile state of alert consciousness which precedes performance at its most lively level, where the performer is fully open to his/her faculties, mental, physical and affective, but not yet deploying them in a specific direction: in the 'potential space' for play (see also Chapter I, pp. 22–27). Here one is right on the threshold of action but not quite active.

Or we could say, open to the active process of reception/transformation which takes place when one goes to a performance or is involved in performing, provided that the conditions described above (getting in touch with the inner Agni) have been met or are set in operation by the event.

Rg Veda, then, opens by locating in its initial phrase the condition in which performance most propitiously arises. Indian theatre has the means to refer back to that condition by placing performance within the field of Agni as visible icon and indexical reminder.

In its initial sound (*a*), *Rg Veda* locates the openness from which utterance arises, both as metaphor for the multiplicity of linguistic forms and as physical act. Production of the fullest vowel-sound entails opening the mouth and expelling breath (lots of performers do it as a warm-up before going on). Like the experience of suddenly seeing light in darkness, it is directly tactile and affective; both phenomena also reproduce the first acts most babies perform (they open their eyes, see the light and shout). We are on 'origin' territory again here.

The basis of light and sound is vibration. At the start of the 'big vibrations' (to pinch an ironic aside from Russell Hoban) which make up the infinite Babel of language is an open mouth, another potential space for play (and you don't have to be a dentist to enjoy it).

The g which follows the a of Agni is the initial act of limitation (i.e. giving specific form), whereby the definiteness of *g* intervenes in the infinity of *a*, and the unlimited vowel of the power to create is stopped and shaped by a (consonant) act. But in order for there to be forms there must be boundaries, and in order for sounds to be identifiable there must be teeth and tongue. Beckett's *Not I* opens with, or as, a mouth on its own going through the extraordinary contortions which the production of language requires; managing also to look like a painful act of giving birth, accurately enough since the restriction of pure sound to specific syllables (and hence eventually to crystallised and ultimately stagnant text) is a kind of loss. But, as I said before, you can also think of it as a gain.

This activation of language – as phonetics but also as speech-acts – is not an origin-theory in any 'historical' sense. What it articulates is the way that forms – linguistic or whatever – emerge from a psychophysiological condition of relaxed but not specifically-focused alertness at any point in time when such a condition is accessed. The important thing is the identification of the process of activation and the nature of the impetus.

This condition precedes performance, as identified in *Rg Veda* and as practised by performers in and beyond India. The flame is placed *before* the performance; the Agni-state allows the maximum range to play, both physical and linguistic. It determines the way in which text will emerge as performance-text.

So to get to the start of the act of utterance (performance of language) is to bring the awareness back to the launching-pad of intention, to that physical and mental state in which the whole of the organism is focused towards the next move/sound/impulse. Stanislavsky indicates that all performance-behaviour needs to identify the underlying intention, to wind action back to, and perhaps beyond, memory-trace and desire. What kinds of nascent moves underlie the texturing of word and deed?

Text in performance is also the playing of 'sub-text'. What language may imply or suggest on levels other than the everyday, as well as what it may cover up, needs to be given expression in the codes of dramatic performance. In this sense a performed text is always fuller, or 'richer' than the blueprint of the written version. Sub-text is often the revelation of intention or desire, of the psychological motivation of the action. But it can also be the physicalisation of what might normally be considered unknowable or unpresentable: in Indian and other eastern performance this can be made available, not as verbalisation, but as music, rhythm, mood and movement. The sub-text is in many ways much more 'visible' than the text: in *Noh* and *Kathakali*, for instance, the text is sung by musicians (on stage but either at the side or the back or seated): the whole task of the actor is to perform the physical expression of that text, not to 'say' it. Text in this model is therefore clearly a *dialogue*, not between two performers on the same (expressed verbal) level, but between different levels or ways of signifying; the half-understood, that which is only partly-present or intuited, is materialised in its journey into the consciousness of the protagonist.

Noh theatre (and to some extent *Kabuki* as well) is often structured around the appearance of a ghost, signalling an absence, something unfulfilled or not understood which has to be brought to awareness and in some way completed. Indian folk/ritual forms like *Bhuta* and *Theyyam* tend to physicalise their ghosts and/or ancestors even more immanently and powerfully in order more directly to stimulate the process of 'remembering', 'identifying', or in some way entering into understanding or communion with them.

In a sense, then, text of this kind includes what it 'leaves out' or doesn't directly say, setting up a 'gap' which is partly filled by visual and aural cues which act as a stimulus to the audience: text is completed through performance and in the process of reception. What is 'remembered' here are the sources of my being, acting and speaking in the here and now, whether these are seen as ancestors or events, dreams or desires, buried fragments or dim memories. The business of theatre is understood to include 'texturing' this material.

This examination of the narrative – performance spectrum has enabled me to indicate why 'text' in Indian theatre needs to be viewed flexibly. I will now take a brief look at a few 'texts' in the more traditional sense of the term, in order to check to what extent this judgement holds good. So I will explore some aspects of both ancient (Sanskrit) and modern playscripts: other notes on contemporary writers will be found in Chapter 5, and further discussion of the mechanics of Sanskrit drama in Chapter 4.

SANSKRIT DRAMA AS TEXT

Reading a Sanskrit play text makes it clear that the script offers scope for expansion: it is both highly poetic and condensed and evidently requires filling out by the director and performers. It looks to some extent like a 'pre-text', calling for the wealth of symbolic gestural detail, musical accompaniment etc. which characterises forms like *Kathakali*. At first sight, the narrative sequence of events may seem very rapid, but those words which are there need to be mined for their layers of sub-textual suggestion. Psychological and political motivation has generally to be sought and supplied in performance. The text itself tends to move from the depiction of one major emotional tone (*bhava* or *rasa*) to another. Moreover, as already noted, Sanskrit is a highly compacted language in which almost every syllable encodes a range of different implications in its structure. But placing alongside this the instructions in the *Natya Sastra* on empathetic and mimetic investment of emotional states, it is clear that performers have to trace out for themselves something like a Stanislavskian sub-textual itinerary in order to fill out the performance with the necessary dimensions of felt meaning.

The major Sanskrit playwrights are:

- Bhasa, c. 400AD. 13 of his plays survive and were published in 1912.
- Sudraka, author of *Mrcchakatika* (*The Little Clay Cart*), possibly plagiarised from Bhasa (350–500AD).
- Kalidasa: 3 plays survive, including *Shakuntala*, the best known Sanskrit play outside India (150BC–500AD).
- Bhavabhuti (700AD): three plays.
- Harsa (8th century): two plays.

(Translations of Sanskrit classical plays into English, as also of the second century Tamil epics *Shilappadikaram* and *Manimekhalai*, are published by Penguin.)

Ujjain (Madhya Pradesh) still regularly mounts festivals of Sanskrit drama. These include both 'preservative' versions and modern renderings, for example several productions of Bhasa by K.N. Panikkar and others plays directed by Habib Tanvir, M.K. Raina and others. It is the textual sparseness referred to above which attracts Panikkar: 'The most significant aspect of a Bhasa play is that it has 'minimal script'. This gives the contemporary director total manoeuvrability, whereby he can unravel new meaning, interpretations and create a totally new dramatic sub-text within the main framework of the play' (newspaper article on Panikkar reproduced in Sopanam brochure 1997). Just as contemporary versions of *Shakuntala* can explore a range of different possibilities in the interpretation of gender roles, Panikkar's production of Bhasa's *Swapna Vasavadattam* focuses on an exploration of dream and reality and the status of the two women in Vasavadatta's life.

This expandable facility of text in large measure derives from the nature of the epics from which most plays are taken. As described above, *Mahabharata* and *Ramayana* function as generative narrative energies inviting development and completion (though as in many narratives, the latter is a necessary lure rather than a likely attainment). One brief example is a sentence from the *Ramayana*: 'Viswaamitra was a king who had attained sainthood ... he exhibited his spiritual powers by starting to create another Brahma and a rival universe' (Rajagopalachari 1951, 19). This virtual reality scenario offers room for just about anything, but also invites speculation and imaginative work on what the relation between 'king' and 'saint' might be, for instance, and how they might manifest themselves. Additionally, the ability to 'create another universe' itself signals the potential of theatre.

What I have not dealt with in this section is the history of (literary) text in relation to Sanskrit drama. It is true that my focus is on how 'text' is construed and why it should issue into performance, rather than on specific detail of the written forms it takes. However, it is important to note that here too the plural is more appropriate than the singular, and that at every stage of theatre in India, close links with many written texts can be identified. Vatsyayan provides a useful overview of these complex interrelationships (Vatsyayan 1980,

181–184), and also notes that 'a continuous history of Sanskrit theatre of nearly eight hundred years can be reconstructed' from material found in both north and south India (1980, 16). This history, as well as affording evidence of sophisticated cultural development, provides a glimpse of the range of transfer between different versions and between languages (Sanskrit, Prakrit and regional languages, plus, in the south, special literary forms combining Sanskrit with Malayalam and Tamil, both of which were given the name of Manipravala). I may also have inadvertently given the impression that there is one *Mahabharata* and one *Ramayana*: there isn't, of course, there are many, written in different languages and at different times (Vatsyayan selects seven *Ramayana* versions in different south Indian languages composed between the eighth and the fourteenth century, followed by four eastern and northern language versions between the sixteenth and eighteenth century). There are also other major Sanskrit works, like for example the *Gita-Govinda*, which also fed into performance traditions. Although Sanskrit continued to be widespread until the fifteenth and sixteenth centuries, not only are other major northern Indian languages (Hindi, Marathi, Bengali etc.) developing from the eleventh century, but there is also a flourishing literary tradition in the south in Tamil, Malayalam and Kannada or mixtures with Sanskrit; the celebrated Tamil work *Shilappadikaram*, attributed to the second century, includes a metatheatrical focus on performance – one of its protagonists is a dancer – implying the existence of a strong performance tradition whilst emphasising the text > performance link. Any single text thus forms a tiny part of a historical, cultural and linguistic mosaic; this pattern of change and interrelation is however constant in providing, in all periods and many languages, lines of communication between great literary works and forms of performance which draw on them.

20TH CENTURY DRAMA AS TEXT

It is perhaps curious that text and performance have been subject to a sort of status dance in recent times. Whereas early western approaches to Indian theatre perceived it (erroneously) as almost entirely a literary form and thus, to the extent that they were linguistically competent, foregrounded the status of text as outlined above, much twentieth-century work, by focusing on performance values, underplayed the importance of the written.

Initial post-Independence cultural policy in India also tended to privilege 'traditional' and 'folk' material (in ways which I will discuss further in Chapter 5) rather than to support new writing. So the status of text is part of the cultural debate both within and outside India. There is now an increasing amount of scripted material available; though publication is still somewhat haphazard, it is important as a marker of recognition and of cultural/linguistic identity. In spite of major gaps in publication in regional languages and in translation between them, there are scripts of many kinds which form the basis of productions, and the current theatre scene is one which is highly conscious of the many stages of transference between page and stage. I will briefly look at plays of three different types to illustrate some of the ways in which this exchange is operating.

Certain kinds of twentieth-century Indian theatre use apparently conventional western-style playscripts. But here too things are not so simple; firstly because the mere acceptance of 'colonial' forms is subject to extreme suspicion, secondly because the contemporary focus is on mining all the riches of indigenous performance traditions without necessarily abandoning the virtues of a degree of scripted, coherent material. Contemporary texts by e.g. Habib Tanvir and Girish Karnad, as well as reworkings of *Mahabharata* by directors like Ratan Thiyam (all discussed further in Chapter 5), draw explicitly upon traditional regional forms, as well as on mythological, historical or local material, in order to create an appropriate semiotic richness. On the other hand they display a thoroughly contemporary attitude, as well as making explicit the crossover between the enacted events and the present situation. Here too then, the scripted text is 'porous', in that it requires completion in the form of music, dance or acting styles. Karnad's plays moreover not infrequently offer two or more alternative endings in the published version, and he has sanctioned further alternatives in performance.

Kavalam Panikkar's *Theyya Theyyam* (1991) takes both its narrative and its form from ritual practice, but aligns that practice with contemporary reality. Two narratives work in parallel, in that the protagonists of the first (an agricultural worker who avenges the attempted rape of his girl friend) are also performers within the second, the annual *theyyam* ritual. The second narrative portrays a version of Ravana's abduction of Sita in a local setting, thereby presenting in fact the background to narrative I. Just as the attempted rapist landlord is killed by the hero, so the villainous

Ravana-figure is eliminated by a Hanuman character. But the agricultural worker in narrative I plays the Ravana character in narrative 2: returning to the village to perform in the *theyyam*, he is beaten to death. The juxtaposition of the two stories highlights some questionable features of *theyyam* whereby the aggressor is deified (that is the purpose of the ritual) and the hero is killed. The plots are interwoven and performers take roles in both narratives and in the chorus, signalling shifts of role by simple and emblematic costume changes; the play operates both on the 'realistic' level of the contemporary narrative and the social issues it raises, and as an entry into the world of the *theyyam*, with aspects of dance, rhythmic percussion, trance and so on. It is clear that in many senses the text here becomes pluralised, inviting both performers and audience to discover ways of operating on many different levels of involvement and judgement at once.

A third group of post-1950s writing – again some examples are discussed in Chapter 5 – uses mainly 'western' models of dialogue and action. Into this category falls much of Vijay Tendulkar's work, as well as that of Mahesh Elkunchwar, G.P. Deshpande, Omcheri and Mahasweta Devi. The problems addressed, whether seen from an 'urban' or 'rural' perspective, are either recognisably 'Indian', or they take up 'universal' issues observed from an Indian perspective. Devi's plays, adapted from her fiction, focus mainly on marginalised groups and the historical causes of marginalisation; Deshpande's theatre of ideas is concerned with the politics of class and state, Elkunchwar's examines generational and family problems in an Indian context; Omcheri's *The Flood* looks ironically at the nuclear holocaust scenario. The themes are varied, but what these plays share in common is a greater commitment to scripted dialogue: it takes up most of the page, whereas in the categories examined above, dialogue is on the pithy and minimal side and instructions or suggestions about stage business are correspondingly more important. Tendulkar, Devi *et al* do also make use of appropriate business or stage machinery (rural music and dance in Devi, multi-purpose screens providing different size perspectives in Omcheri), but the thrust of the plays is towards (linguistic) dialectic or exposition. 'Text' here functions in a more 'traditional' (western) manner; but the playwrights in question write like this because they see it as the best way to address the Indian issues they feel to be of most importance. So this model has parallels with the Indian assimilation of English; it becomes a part of the resources available, a 'text' which is itself an intertext.

Where, as in many of the above cases, the work is also available in English translation (or, as in the case of Karnad, self-translation), English as intertext becomes English as intermediary. Theatre written directly in English also exists, although it has tended to suffer from somewhat belated anti-colonialist bigotry, and Indian work in drama in English is much less visible than in fiction and poetry.

It is however the case that much of the debate about theatre forms, and particularly about the relationship between theatre and politics, has been carried on in English. Not because it is the language of the former colonialists, but because it is a language in which Indians of a certain degree of education can speak to each other. The same may be true of the way text functions here in the third category discussed above; it is a coded model for a particular kind of investigation, one which is driven principally – though not exclusively – by intellectual discrimination. Its approach, by and large, is more obviously 'deconstructive' than that of the models previously discussed – though here again there are qualifications, for example in the case of the Panikkar play, which aims to raise questions, although going about it by the use of parallel processing and imaginative suggestion. What this implies is that here too there is a 'spectrum', 'fan' or 'web', stretching perhaps from 'text' as an activation of intellectual analysis (à la Brecht) to 'text' as an amalgam of sensory and imaginative stimuli (Artaud). The aim of both is to 'perform', to achieve an outcome which passes through text into texturing and emerges in what is received by the audience. The next chapter develops this perspective further.

♦ CHAPTER THREE ♦

Performance

Chapter 2 has suggested dimensions in which text and performance overlap. This chapter will outline some of the many forms within the spectrum of Indian performance and will take a look at the contexts in which they arise and at their functions within those contexts. It will also look at their effects on performers and spectators/ participants, and try to assess what kinds of influence they have. It will however confine itself (if that is the right word) to 'traditional' forms as discussed by e.g. Vatsyayan (1980), Varadpande (1992) and Richmond *et al* (1990); the contemporary situation is profiled and discussed in Chapter 5. Some questions which are considered in this chapter are: What perspectives on performance does Indian theatre invite? Are these in any way compatible with aspects of contemporary western 'performance theory'? Does performance instigate or make available new or extended ways of being and acting? If so, can we understand its processes as fundamental to mental, physical and emotional activity? The final section looks at the image and role of women in performance. The whole chapter, both by discussing different categories under which performance may be approached and by exploring some aspects of the kinds of processes it represents, points forward also to the question of how performance is theorised, which is the topic of Chapter 4.

MODELS OF CATEGORISATION

The very tendency for forms to proliferate can be seen as evidence of the variety of creative origination. Where does this variety come from? It seems likely that humans attempt by as many channels as possible to explore and express — and perhaps to influence — our status as individuals, our position in the scheme of things cosmic, comic or constitutional.

It is worth saying that this chapter is (i) central, in that I am claiming that Indian theatre is essentially performance – as performance-text, performance-theory and multiple performance-forms, and (ii) the most problematic to organise, because performance crosses so many boundaries, manifests itself in so many different ways, is a mobile and flexible phenomenon. It is in fact precisely this problem of pinning it down which is a mark of its essential vitality, its status as life rather than idealisation. This poses problems for 'scholars' of the traditional kind, but also for the element of scholar, or the desire to operate with relatively fixed categories, in me and all of us. Theatre (and Indian theatre is a magnificent example) has a tendency to sweep aside this pigeon-holing anality. On the other hand, what I am writing and you are reading is a book, not (quite) a performance; it has to operate with the categories and limits of sequential language. So we do need some kind of pattern.

What frequently has been taken to be synonymous with Indian theatre in the past is Sanskrit drama, and perhaps precisely because it does provide such a pattern. It also looks as though it might be the historical origin of much Indian performance. Sanskrit drama is also discussed in the context of theory in the next chapter; I am more concerned here with its status within the event-spectrum of performance. What kinds of event does it represent, and for whom?

Schechner says: 'origin theories are irrelevant to understanding theater' (1988, 6). Nevertheless, most books on Indian theatre start with (and many do not get beyond) a discussion of Sanskrit drama, which thereby comes to be thought of as the original form. Apart from Schechner's valid objections, which I will come to later, this myth of origin needs to be reconsidered on its own terms. Where it is partially valid is in the sense that Sanskrit theatre provides a defining model for what can be thought of as 'classical Indian theatre'. This term reveals its own limits on examination: 'classical' seems essentially to mean a historically-circumscribed textually extant form recognisable to and classifiable by scholars; the slipperiness of 'Indian', 'theatre' and 'history' have already been referred to in Chapter I. However, the main identifiable elements of this model are:

– a consistent formal pattern or structure;
– an underlying aesthetic based on an identifiable source (*Natya Sastra*);

- repeatable performance criteria;
- thematic material derived from identifiable sources (*Mahabharata*, *Ramayana*, the *Puranas* etc.);
- named (if not precisely identifiable) authors;
- some elements of relatively precise dating;
- some fragments of performance history.

In other words, the kinds of things that make scholars happy and give them material for theories of various kinds. Some of these theories (notably those relating to aesthetic experience and to the existence or otherwise of the tragic) will be discussed in Chapter 4. But the elements listed are in themselves stable enough to provide a shape, to indicate a style. For a long time it was a style only intermittently acknowledged in the west, though Goethe was enthusiastic about Kalidasa, for instance, and textual material relevant to theatre was significant to investigations of language and culture carried out by 'orientalising' Sanskritists and others at either end of the nineteenth century.

The elements do make it fairly clear that a generic model for performance of this kind existed; its main theatrical features are the mythopoetic textual base, the use of non-realistic settings, largely presentational (as opposed to dialogic/interactive) acting require-ments, the important role of music, and fidelity to criteria laid down in the *Natya Sastra*. *Kathakali* offers a degree of similarity to this model, which seems to afford the imaginative richness and linguistic subtlety Goethe valued; *Yakshagana* also comes close in some respects; *Kudiyattam*, though now very much a specialist activity, is 'easily the most prominent survivor among the forms containing some essential elements of content and structural features of the Sanskrit theatre' (Vatsyayan 1980, 15); and there have been deliberate 'revivals' of Sanskrit drama at the Ujjain festival. *Kudiyattam* is particularly notable for its elaborate gestural coding and 'slow-paced' nature, in that a short incident from *Ramayana* may be the impetus for performance of several hours' duration; it signals also the requirement on the part of the spectators for a high degree of attentiveness and sophistication in recognising, interpreting and evaluating the details of any particular interpretation. Performance aesthetics, as entered into by the receivers, are highly valued as a mark of cultural, spiritual and probably also social distinction.

However, although such an audience may appear to be exclusive or privileged, during the past century it has become clear, both in India and to interested parties elsewhere, that Sanskrit theatre must have existed within a wide diversity of forms. What has survived may possibly be regarded as a refinement or crystallisation of some of them, though that view is open to challenge.

That diversity is now seen as the primary scenario; historically, the position of Sanskrit theatre has thus shifted and been relativised by later 'discoveries', particularly since in many cases the other forms thus highlighted have a continuous performance history and/or still flourish. Sanskrit drama, on the other hand, only exists in performance as and when it is consciously preserved (as in the Academy and festivals at Bhopal and Ujjain) or revived. So the current situation is that the 'classical' or written form which for a long time was thought to be the principal manifestation of Indian theatre needs to be seen as an important element, but only one element, in a rich canvas. So, useful as the Sanskrit drama model is, it needs to be supplemented.

Theatre, even in this sense, is not quite the same as performance; or rather, as the drift of my argument so far implies, performance includes theatre rather than the reverse. It is tempting to assume that this relatively precise model 'comes first'; and it is true that many kinds of Indian performance draw on similar aesthetic intentions and make use of material from the same sources. In other words the elements singled out above can indeed be useful, because they are to be found in Sanskrit drama, which is important because it is historically the first written form of which we have evidence, and because it was clearly a highly developed model with clearly-defined performance features. But Schechner can be helpful here in that he offers a different and extended compass of what 'performance' may be, which enables us to see Sanskrit drama as one set of formal moves within a whole range of possibilities, as a significant option rather than as the only blueprint.

Schechner replaces the idea of 'origin' with the 'fan' and the 'web' (Schechner 1988, xii–xv). The *fan* stretches across the following:

ritualization/rites + ceremonies/shamanism
art-making process
play/performance in daily life/sports etc.
eruption and resolution of crisis.

The *web* links origins (European and non-European) to rites and to play, and crisis behaviour to 'environmental theatre' (see below, Chapter 4) as forms of dynamic activity. Theatre is part of a spectrum of events; these events interact as history interacts with private and public consciousness in art. 'Performance' has an extended time-span which includes the build-up, the framing of the event, and the 'cooling-off', for performers and receivers and thus relates to 'ongoing systems of social and aesthetic life' (1988, xiv), both in its structure and in its mode of operation. The *fan* thus stretches to an overview of kinds of public activity, whilst the *web* links them together as modes of behaviour which respond to critical situations and/or instigate change.

This approach does not rule out the kinds of event represented by Sanskrit drama, which may in some respects offer archetypal features by which to understand much else; but it locates them as part of a mobile canvas: both diachronically, as part of the transfer, poaching, interaction, mimicry, of performance behaviour in any period and through time, and synchronically, as part of the processes which make up the dynamic of 'transportation' or 'transformation' initiated by performative events at any one moment (Schechner 1985, 117–151). This kind of model widens the optic within which Indian performance can be understood, even though it too has its limitations of focus, as suggested in Chapter 1.

This also feels much more like the experience of performance in India. Whether one is caught up in a procession or demonstration, of which street theatre may be one end of a spectrum, or watching a Bollywood movie, or attending a classical concert or a performance of *Bharatanatyam* or *Kathakali*, or seeing women dancing in traditional costume with no audience at all at 11pm in a country village, the actions and the event are, at least immediately, much less insulated from the community and its daily concerns than is the case with proscenium arch theatre. This in spite of the fact that the performance forms are only minimally 'realistic': the presence of the 'extra-daily', to use Barba's term, is not regarded as strange in Indian life. Performance occurs as part of the social and communal situation rather than something separated off from it, as is the case with 'art' in the western post-medieval sense.

This view of performance construes it as in a variety of senses purposeful: for Schechner, it lies at the efficacy end of his 'efficacy/ entertainment braid' (1988, 120–124). Given the wide range of performance forms in India, it is reasonable to suppose that they fulfilled different shades of purpose, speaking different languages (performative as well as linguistic) to different constituents; and that Sanskrit drama, directed largely at court or upper levels of the caste hierarchy, falls within this range. However, Schechner's approach, which highlights performative circumstances within the framework of community, and Barba's, which focuses on performance technique and behaviour, both also contribute to a wider vision. It is noticeable that Indian scholars too have found it necessary to construct flexible or plural models.

Varadpande (1992) identifies multiple forms related to different cultural, political and historical purposes: entertainment, instruction, inculturation (preservation of heritage via myths, tradition), ritual, exorcism (community and cultural, religious and anthropological values), appeasement of perceived or believed powers, political and or social comment, sometimes subversive.

The forms and their purposes therefore overlap; Sanskrit drama served some of the above purposes, operating within a particular social nexus in order to validate and maintain rights and forms of behaviour. Both it and many 'folk' (not forgetting Vatsyayan's caution about this term) forms were rooted in similar belief-structures, and frequently used metaphorical narrative and exemplary detail from common myth/epic sources. These stories were no doubt conveyed by upper-caste, frequently Brahmin, authority-figures. Sanskrit theatre does not necessarily represent 'higher' values or aspirations, social, religious and/or aesthetic, than do other forms, though it does consciously strive to articulate these values, which necessarily take different modes of expression depending on the participants and receivers.

The attributes ascribed to theatre in the myth of its origin proposed in *Natya Sastra* (as a compilation from the poetry/recitation of *Rg Veda*, the song of *Sama Veda*, the performance process of *Yajur Veda* and the aesthetics of *Atharva Veda*) do include 'special knowledge' and 'sacred material' in order to perform 'sacrifice in honor of the gods' (Richmond et al 1990, 27); but this does not serve to differentiate either Sanskrit drama or the more 'classical' performance forms from others, all of which in some measure accommodate many of the purposes and processes sketched out by Schechner and Varadpande (see also the discussion of Sanskrit Drama in Chapter 4).

Indeed one of the specific aims of the devotional/folk form *Raslila* is to produce a state of *anand* (bliss), cognate with the aesthetic pleasure of *rasa*; and the early *Nata* community of artists believed they had a 'sacred duty to make people laugh' (Varadpande 1992, 9). Laughter, of course, is a form of release, both physical and psychological; it arises as and encourages 'space for play'; it is, as Hermann Hesse (another traveller to the East) makes clear, a means to freedom from imprisonment in single role and egoic self. Some of

Plate 1. *Patayani* (Keralan ritual form): Madan, Kalan, Marutha. Courtesy Traditional Arts Project, School of Drama, University of Calicut.

Plate 2. *Chakyar Koothu* (Keralan mono-narrative). Courtesy Traditional Arts Project, School of Drama, University of Calicut.

Plate 3. Sopanam Theatre Institute in *Madhyamavyoyagam*, by Bhasa, directed by Kavalam Narayana Panikkar. Courtesy Anamika Sangam Research and Publications, Calcutta.

Plate 4. Theatre Academy, Pune in *Begum Barve*, by Satish Alekar, directed by Alekar, featuring Mohan Agashe (left). Courtesy Anamika Sangam Research and Publications, Calcutta.

Plate 5. Aryan Theatre, Manipur in *Antigone*, directed by Nongthombam Premchand. Courtesy Seagull Foundation for the Arts, Calcutta.

Plate 6. Mallika Sarabhai in *V for ...* Courtesy Darpana Academy of Performing Arts, Ahmedabad.

Plate 7. Darpana/UNESCO health education project, Gujarat: *Bhavai* performance. Courtesy Darpana Academy of Performing Arts, Ahmedabad.

Plate 8. Jana Sanskriti performing in rural West Bengal. Courtesy Jana Sanskriti, West Bengal.

its more important functions may survive better outside more formal modes: Varadpande proposes that the *Vidushaka* figure (clown, but also director, stage manager, narrator, commentator etc.) 'died of suffocation in Sanskrit theatre' (10) but lives on in the *Kattiyakaran* of *Therukoothu*, the *Bhagavata* of *Yakshagana*, and in many other forms.

Performance in India evolves through both ritual and temple forms, from narrative traditions and from communal celebrations. 'Folk' and 'classical' form a continuum, as do efficacy and entertainment. Narrative issues into and crosses with epic and dramatic criteria. Nowhere is there the exclusive 'realism' of the European nineteenth-century tradition. Indian performance can be epic; historical; didactic; documentary; dialectic; socially cohesive; controversial; entertainment/diversion; sentimental; demanding/ empowering; elevating. Because the mytho-poetic base remains dominant, all forms retain the possibility of many levels of meaning and consequently of interpretative engagement (and thus escape being merely a reinforcement of authority-structures which would otherwise be likely given their derivation from a 'sacred' cachet).

Richmond, Swann and Zarilli (Richmond et al 1990) categorise forms as *classical, folk/popular, ritual, devotional* and *modern*. This scheme allows them to differentiate usefully in some respects. The *classical* is more historically reliant on patronage, involves control by the *guru* tradition, is closer to the aesthetic principles of the *Natya Sastra*; *folk* suggests more exuberance and accessibility, closer regional affiliations, more profane material and a professional or semi-professional structure; Schechner's categories of *efficacy* (for *ritual*), *transportation* (for *devotional*) and *entertainment* (for *modern*) are invoked, though not acknowledged. But this schematisation, like most others, is, as the authors concede, inadequate in so far as all categories overlap continually. However, it does allow them to indicate for example factors such as reliance on patronage as opposed to a more professional or semi-professional structure and the incorporation of more westernised models in the nineteenth and twentieth centuries. Economics are important in theatre anywhere and especially so in terms of the possible developments open to performers, directors and promoters: these issues will be looked at particularly with reference to the contemporary situation in Chapter 5.

Vatsyayan's categories include 'ballad' form (she places *Pabuji ki pada* and *Burra Katha* here); cycle plays like *Ramlila* and *Raslila* (somewhat similar to European 'mysteries'); forms which draw on the epics but with a strong emphasis on local culture (*Bhavai, Tamasa,*

Therukoothu, Nautanki, Yatra etc.); those which can be located somewhere between the formal sophistication of e.g. *Kudiyattam* and the improvisational 'street-theatre' quality of the preceding group, e.g. *Yakshagana, Bhagavatamela*; those where elaborate formal sophistication is paramount (*Kathakali* is the obvious example); and those, like the *Chhau* group, in which dance is the most important element (Vatsyayan 1980, 10).

What we therefore have in these different models is a mosaic of overlapping criteria and features indicative of enormous richness and dynamism. In most cases examples of these forms are still extant, sometimes, as for instance in the case of *Kathakali*, following a 'revival' (which itself followed an eighteenth-and-nineteenth-century upper-class orientation towards forms imported by the British and a consequent marginalising of some traditional forms); and they all, or nearly all, have the resources to respond to the contemporary situation. This we shall return to in Chapter 5.

OUTLINE OF SOME PERFORMANCE FORMS

What follows is a *brief* account of some of the many forms to be found in India. For more detail the reader is referred to the descriptions of specific forms to be found in the works cited by Varadpande, Vatsyayan and, with the caveat mentioned in Chapter 1, Richmond *et al.* Das (1992) lists 84 forms with brief descriptions, but this is by no means all-inclusive (for instance, neither *Kathakali* nor *Yakshagana* appear in her list). The subsequent discussion again considers only some forms in order to bring out significant features.

Although I think that the classifications attempted by the above writers are in many cases very useful in revealing key features, the discussion so far has indicated that what I see underlying them is a tendency towards flexibility and interrelation. I will come back to the implications of this and examine them in the light of other approaches. However, the categories which I set up below are deliberately simpler and, in one case at least, much more inclusive than those referred to in the books mentioned. It is in a way no accident that they become progressively looser.

Narrative forms

I have discussed the status and function of some of these in Chapter 2 in terms of the emergence of performance from narrative. There are many *mainly narrative forms* using musicians, main narrator, some dialogue and gesture, etc., filling the gap between narrative and full dramatic performance; for example:

Pandavani (Madhya Pradesh)
Oja-Pali (Assam)
Tal-maddale (Karnataka)
Burra Katha (Andhra Pradesh)
Gondhal, Keertan, Powada (Maharashtra)

In addition there exist also several forms in which the central performer is a picture-showman, sometimes assisted, for instance by his wife:

Chitrakatha (Pushkar, Rajasthan)
Bhopa (Bhopal)
other forms in Maharashtra
Pabuji Ki Phad, Rajasthani picture-ceremonies/narratives.

These employ variants on the use of picture-scrolls (*Phad*) – sometimes unfurled slowly, sometimes displayed all at once, with the narrator using a pointer to guide the spectators through the characters and incidents displayed. Stories are mainly drawn from epic material, frequently adapted to local circumstances and thus functioning both as moral framework and repository of local history (NB some of these are somewhat differently classified by Vatsyayan). *Puppets* also illustrate narrative (glove puppets mainly in Kerala and Orissa, also sometimes shadow-puppets).

Further story-telling traditions include those practised by the Kathaka and Suta castes: the *Chakyars* of Kerala are descended from the latter. *Kuttu* is a narrative Chakyar form (performed by the Nambiar caste), in which, in a virtuoso display of monoacting extending the story-teller's art into more developed role-play, the Chakyar acts all parts as the *Vidushaka*: it develops further into *Kudiyattam*, which uses several actors (on the lines of the evolution in Greek theatre from one chorus figure, to dialogue of two actors, to protagonist + antagonist + chorus). The secrets of *Chakyar Kuttu* performance are traditionally transmitted from uncle to nephew; narration takes twenty-one days or more, and during the first twelve the performer is at liberty to improvise, weave in contemporary references, use and interact with the audience, make mocking comments on people of nominally high status, and so on. This functions both as a performance methodology (assuring the audience's interest and repeated presence before progressing to the last section) and as a claim for another kind of totality or extension: the performer becomes the source of both contemporary and traditional wisdom, he exemplifies a kind of all-knowingness which parallels the organic or cosmic dimensions of ritual performance.

Narrative issues into and crosses with epic and dramatic modes in for instance the presence of the *Sutradhara/Bhagavata* figure in e.g. *Yakshagana* and the singer/narrator in *Kathakali*. There are many gradations in between; similarly there is a spectrum or continuum of forms and effects and an interchangeability of many elements between 'folk' and 'classical': in most cases they draw on the epics, on Brahminic tradition and/or Dravidian ritual practices, often in equal measure. Different forms however emphasise different performance aspects, e.g. *Kathakali* mixes *abhinaya* (expressive gesture) and the martial art form *Kalari*, *Manipuri* makes extensive use of dance, *Ras-lila* is structured around poetry and music. All these forms 'dramatise' or theatricalise narrative in one way or another (sometimes in several at once).

Ritual-related forms

These are directly at the 'efficacy' end of Schechner's braid (though there is little in Indian theatre, as opposed to Indian cinema, which is not in some sense or other). They are frequently preceded by rites lasting up to forty-one days, sometimes including the preparation of a *kalam* (drawing) which is then wholly or partly erased and, as it were, transformed into the action. Examples include:

Mudiyettu: Kali kills Darika, usually in a spectacular chase and fight sequence.

Theyyam: three-part event including Thottam – recitation and drumming – and Theyyam – possession by 'god' or entity. Some writers suggest that *Kathakali* represents an upper-class aestheticisation.

Bhuta: possession by devils/ancestors as 'ghosts', who act as judges, reminders of 'proper' behaviour.

Ras-lila: the play of Krishna = ras = joyous essence: aim is to achieve *ananda*; dance is the external form used as an aide-mémoire to more central meditation-function; performed at Vrindavan and Mathura; dance origins in rural circle forms, developed to include sophisticated movement similar to *Kathak*.

Krishna-attam: only in Kerala temples: the purpose is to beget a male child, or to get a good husband: male-oriented rites in a matriarchy?

In order to explore important features in more depth, I am going to look at one form: *Theyyam*.

Theyyam is a Keralan form which has been widely written about (articles in *The Drama Review*, Sankara Pillai's book mentioned below). The *Theyyam* performer is called the *Kolakarran*: 'the man who takes the form of a god' (the formulation is interesting: see my remarks in Chapters 1 and 4). There are many different *Theyyams* in different districts.

Common features, similar in other forms, include strong rhythmic and visual elements, e.g. drumming throughout; in the case of *Theyyam* the early section, *Thottam*, consists of several hours of drumming as ritual invocation. Other parts are to some extent open-ended, allowing for new elements and/or repetition, but the sequence is (i) invocation; (ii) recitation of deity's story (*Thottam*); (iii) possession dance (*Theyyam*); (iv) further stories in the first person, marking a shift from narrative to performative mode; (v) blessings from deity; (vi) removal of headgear. As in Sanskrit drama there is therefore a distinct relationship between sequence and intended effect (see Chapter 4): as Schechner indicates, there is both a substantial building-up and cooling-off period.

Massive headgear, brilliant colour, repetitive dance/display, chanting, burning torches and/or coloured powders help to create a sense of the powerful and 'other-worldly' presence which the performer who incarnates the *Theyyam* takes on. Contact with the earth is strengthened by dancing, drumming and the heart-beat rhythms; costumes and headgear are made from natural materials; fire, water, earth and air frame and punctuate the event. It is attended by the whole community; the performers come from around twelve 'scheduled' castes and during most of the year are farmers, tailors, witch doctors etc. The event starts as the sun sets and continues until dawn. The level of intensity fluctuates; everyone from babies to elders is there, but their attention is relaxed or focused alternately: captured by the initial call of the drums, fascinated by the first appearance of the performer-*Theyyam*, make-up and headgear in an intermediate stage; in between these the rhythm may relax, with other focal points – *puja*, rises and falls in the pitch and tempo of the drumming – until the second emergence of the *Theyyam* in full regalia;

thereafter too there are processional or more measured phases, punctuated by dramatic display or aggressively playful sorties towards the spectator/participants and culminating in crucial moments of ecstatic action. At these points the mood builds rapidly from 'cool' to 'hot': walking on hot coals, eating raw eggs or a live chicken, in which the otherness of the god is performed in the body of the actor, and hence his/her visitation is confirmed and the propitiousness of the outcome assured.

But not without passing through 'dangerous' stages, both for performer and for spectators, who are often closer to Boal's 'spectactors' in that they both inhabit the immediacy of the event to their own cultural situation and look to it to provide tangible results. The effort and kinds of behaviour required of the performer – whether or not he is 'really' in some form of trance – pushes at the borders of the 'normally' possible; the *Theyyam* may charge the crowd for real and is sometimes – particularly since this happens at night and to the accompaniment of hypnotic drumming – disturbing, menacing or incomprehensible. The visceral effect of such performance depends upon the achievement by the performer of a liminal status, paralleled by the liminal performance space and time, both familiar and unfamiliar in that they are within the communal locality but yet outside it both by virtue of being made 'sacred' for the duration of performance and by virtue of occurring outside quotidian time-scales. He is in between actor and shaman, in between his well-known everyday self and the functioning of extra-personal forces, in between the time of everyday life and the round of seasonal occurrences or the whole life-span of the community: he becomes a 'moving icon' (Varadpande 1992, 145), similar to the Trickster/Fool figure in European theatrical tradition and iconography in, for instance, Shakespeare and Dada. Like Fools and Tricksters, he can be both frightening and comic: if he is performing 'out of his skin', he can also shake receivers out of theirs into another dimension where they both experience their vulnerability and can begin to feel comfortable with it (or able to accept being uncomfortable). He shifts his function as he shifts his status: performance too operates this shift since it is action, yet not ordinary action, and its effects on the receivers are also more than ordinary and may produce transformations in their awareness and their subsequent functioning. Kavalam Panikkar recounts that an actress in his company, asked to take a receptive role at a *Theyyam*, was, much to her distress, overcome in spite of her determination to remain unaffected; she felt her rational, recognisable self to have been 'defeated', yet her later development as an actress was 'remarkable' (Panikkar, 1995, 112).

G. Sankara Pillai's *The Theatre of the Earth is Never Dead* (1986) lists some 55 ritual forms in Kerala alone, documented by the School of Drama at Trissur (Trichur) (the aim of the project was to record forms related to (a) the 'mother' cult and (b) fertility cults); a parallel operation at Udupi in Karnataka has recorded South Kanara forms (both with financial backing from the Ford Foundation). What emerges is a flexible spectrum or 'braid' encompassing the following:

   (i) performance/spectacle/ritual/theatre
  (ii) 'believing'/'acting'
 (iii) vitality/moribundity of form
 (iv) minimal/full-time training of performers
  (v) simple/ornate make-up, costume, headgear
 (vi) single performer/communal celebration
 (vii) special event/regular occurrence
(viii) no text/improvisation/sections of text/mainly textual narrative
 (ix) clapping/drumming/several instruments/mainly musical

So there is enormous variety even within this category, which already contains many features of others, just as there is considerable overlap with 'folk' forms in other states. There is a sense in which all forms draw on similar roots and preoccupations, although they articulate these differently and place the emphasis on different aspects: for instance, stories derived from the *Mahabharata* used in the more 'classical' *Kathakali* may emphasise the importance of *dharma* (morality, ethics, social and political structures), whereas *Therukuttu* and similar 'folk' forms tend to focus more on 'carnivalesque' physical links with the organic world, on exorcising physical ills or perceived threats to the community, on the recollection and celebration of communal and familial structures and on the celebration of natural and seasonal patterns.

But in all cases – whether, as in ritual-related forms, through participation, mediumistic 'possession', or sympathetic involvement; or, as in more 'sophisticated' forms, through a heightened state of aesthetic receptivity – the performance event can be seen as an effective means of extending individual and communal being (linking with extra-individual forces, getting in harmony with the 'divine', rarefying sense-perception towards synaesthesia and perhaps some form of transcendence of the senses). Sankara Pillai notes that 'in the case of rituals the aim has been and is a process of consummated sublimation' (1986, iii); in her introduction to his book, Kapila Vatsyayan suggests that these forms 'represent the turning of man to paradoxically internalise archetypes and ... cosmoscise himself.'

This double movement seems to parallel Meyer-Dinkgräfe's model of paradox (discussed further in the next chapter), whose presence he identifies in various forms in all aspects of the performer-character-spectator-event transactions of theatre, and which signals that the occurrence of something new/different/as-yet-unexplained is crucial. Although Sankara Pillai warns that in order to qualify as 'ritualistic theatre', theatre would need to have similar aims to ritual, my sense is that theatre which shares the underlying understandings of its function with those encoded in many Indian forms can indeed be said to do so. Where ritual forms do differ, as Pillai notes, is in the degree of their cultural embedding: many rituals are specific to locale, belief structure and social organisation. However, the nature and function of ritual, as outlined above, is more universal.

What Vatsyayan refers to as a kind of cosmic outreach of the individual and Sankara Pillai calls 'sublimation', K. Ayyappa Paniker, in an essay in the same book, discusses in terms of 'sacrifice'. I want to pick this whole issue up in Chapter 4, because it is of central importance in terms of theories of how Indian (and other) theatre may be working; but I will touch on it here.

Paniker is writing about *Patayani*, a form which overlaps ritual, mask and narrative (in Sankara Pillai, 1986, 1–7). The single performer in the Mask-Dance of the God of Death has to 'play' three characters whilst the narrative is chanted in the background. He thus, says Paniker, presents 'the entire dialectic of death' (4). The performer as death god is the killer (he is trying to kill the boy Markandeya according to his fate). But he is also the killed (the death god is killed by Shiva because the boy embraces a Shivalingam and the death god tries to drag this away with him, thus arousing Shiva's fury). And he is the killing: he enacts the process of dying, of being killed, whilst trying to kill someone else.

Thus this apparently 'primitive' form is in fact a piece of metatheatre (the performer has to play three different roles with differing degrees of involvement, i.e. to embody/enter into/be possessed by and to indicate/present) which both marks out and transcends its own limits. In it, 'death is revealed as the death of death', which 'takes us beyond the frontiers of drama in the perspective of the theatre as illusion' (4). It also goes way beyond any narrowly focused ritual outcome, situating the performative function as opening up capacities of insight across apparently contradictory modes of being. Paniker comments:

> In all art there is a constant striving to go beyond the forbidden. You don't need an artist to do what anyone else can do as well' (5).

> Drama probably holds out the possibility of human survival through the surrender of the personal, through ... self-transcendence. The village artist who performs his role in these ritual dances knowingly or unknowingly seems to hold the key to the secret of all art in this sense: by taking on other roles one sees life from angles other than one's own ... The joy that only tragedy can give arises from this aesthetic process of sacrificing the self (7).

There are many resonances here. Paniker not only neatly side-steps the apparently fascinating but probably diversionary issue of whether or not performers in rituals are 'really' possessed, he also enters a claim for an Indian (but by no means exclusive) understanding of tragedy; and he pin-points the nature and meaning of 'sacrifice' in ritual practice as the fading out of the everyday egoic self in favour of a dynamic, pluralist and performative capacity. All these are vital to the understanding of the purposes of Indian theatre throughout history and in the present day. I will be returning to them. In the context of the present chapter it is also important to highlight firstly that these insights derive from one of the forms which would not be accorded 'classical' status; and secondly that this form is itself a hybrid containing theatrical, ritual and metatheatrical elements. As a demonstration of the fluidity and profundity of performance forms operating as fan and web it could hardly be bettered.

Highly pluralised forms

This rather loose category comprises everything else (including in fact much contemporary work, though that is discussed in Chapter 5). In addition to the virtual impossibility of finding any watertight classification, as I have indicated, I use this holdall appellation to signal that whatever else has occurred, elements of ritual content and form remain ubiquitous.

However, it is wise perhaps to start this section by dealing with the forms which fit least well under this heading, namely those which in spite of considerable narrative sophistication nevertheless display

75

strong ritual elements and a great deal of formal precision. *Kathakali* is the principal case, but it is useful to consider it alongside *Yakshagana*, which in some ways resembles it.

Yakshagana and *Kathakali*

Yakshagana can appear to be a slightly brasher form of *Kathakali*, using a similar style and telling similar episodes from e.g. *Mahabharata*. The moustaches are flamboyant, the colours even brighter (much red and gold); the actors leap and dance more than in *Kathakali*, they speak some of their own lines. (See Vatsyayan 1980, 42–5 for useful comparisons of costume and make-up in *Yakshagana* and *Kathakali*.) The dialogue and interaction is a bit more down-market, as it were; there's more than a hint of bravado, conveying a sense that this depiction of (male) heroic behaviour is at least on the verge of irony. Sometimes this occurs in *Kathakali* too, but often things are a touch more solemn. There is an exuberance about *Yakshagana*; and in contrast to the singer-narrators in *Kathakali*, the *Bhagavata* not only narrates but also appears to foreground his own narrating as part of an ironic stance. His adoption of the *Sutradhara* role, pulling the strings, is in keeping with what is always embryonically present in Sanskrit drama, if conventionally truncated to a brief introductory scene; but it picks up on the liberty of the director/performer to adapt traditional material for contemporary contexts. If in *Kathakali*, narrative is splendidly presented by the statuesque body enhanced by elaborate costume, delivered by subtle and precise gradations of gesture, expression and signing, and counterpointed by drumming and the chanted text, in *Yakshagana*, narrative is enthusiastically and somewhat less reverently enlivened; both offer rich models of performance at work with its components.

In addition however to the gaudy facade, which has led in recent years to a proliferation of *Yakshagana* troupes at the popular entertainment end of the spectrum, its repertoire of around sixty plays draws on rich and distinguished literary and musical sources (Kannada literature, which enjoyed five grand phases from before 850AD to post 1850, and a blend of Hindustani and Carnatic musical systems). It also contains passages of pure dance, as well as spectacular jumps and distinctive gaits including a kind of virtuoso pirouetting on the knees. Its magnificent make-up and costuming divides characters into eight to ten categories (more than *Kathakali*). Red is used, as in *Kathakali*, for evil and heroism, but heroic characters use a base of pinkish-yellow as opposed to *Kathakali*'s green;

moustaches are used instead of the cardboard and rice-paper 'collar' or *chutti*. All these features indicate an intricate and elaborate form which balances acting, recitative, dance movement, stylised gaits, music and rhythm and brilliant costuming. (For more detailed descriptions see Vatsyayan 1980 and Karanth 1973; *Dodatta* and *Bhagawata Mela* are among other forms of the *Yakshagana* type, found mainly in Karnataka and some parts of Kerala and Tamil Nadu.)

Kathakali has experienced a twentieth-century revival established by Vallatol Narayana Menon's founding of the Kerala Kalamandalam at Cheruthuruthi, near Trissur (Trichur) in the 1930s – permanently from 1937. The Kalamandalam, which features a school and a *Kuttambalam* (performance space reproducing the dimensions laid down in the *Natya Sastra*) is criticised for its 'Western' academy model by Chitra Panikkar (in Nair & Paniker 1993, 43–4); but Elappamanna Subrahmanian Nambudirippad sees it more positively as having 'popularized *Kathakali* even abroad, and established a systematic training' (Nair & Paniker, 48). Margi (in Trivandrum, founded 1974), functions as a kind of postgraduate institute taking artists on further than the Kalamandalam in the *Kaliyogam* style (*yogams* were troupes supported by patronage); it currently has the largest *Kathakali* repertoire and goes in for more lengthy (i.e. traditional) performances of both *Kathakali* and *Kudiyattam*. Other companies in places like Kochi (Cochin) provide 'packaged' versions for the tourist market. All of this indicates that *Kathakali* is in some ways in a relatively healthy state, though it certainly forms part of the debate about current practice which will be taken up in Chapter 5.

The many forms of classification of criteria for performance and of specific performance techniques (*mudras*, facial expressions etc.) set out in *Natya Sastra* and followed quite closely in *Kathakali* have an extraordinary thoroughness. This ranges from specifics of movement (four head actions, thirty-six kinds of glance, nine movements of eyelids and eyeballs, twenty-four single hand *mudras* etc.) to details about stage space and measurements, and to the classification of characters and the appropriate stylisation of make-up: these, for instance, are (in *Kathakali*):

sattvik or *pacha* (virtuous): green face
rajsic (heroic): green and gold
tamsik or *rakshasic* (destructive/demonic): red, white, black
(plus female characters and *rishis*/saints, who have less elaborate make-up)

Iyer notes that the make-up patterns 'reveal that the colours used are selected for their sensitiveness to communicate ideas and their transforming qualities' (Iyer 1983, 44). Considerable variation and subtlety in the patterning permits a whole range of refinements, for example villainous characters may exhibit some green, or the red of anger may appear in a variety of locations.

The above divisions mirror the three *gunas* or tendencies in nature (*sattva, rajas, tamas*), themselves clearly paralleling the creation/maintenance/destruction spectrum of the *trimurti* Brahma/Vishnu/Shiva.

The modes of representation are similarly comprehensively classified in e.g. *Bharatanatyam*, across:

vachika (voice),	linked principally to	**Rg Veda**
sattvika (mind),	"	**Atharva Veda**
angika (body),	"	**Yajur Veda**
aharya (décor, deportment),	"	**Sama Veda**

The above details are taken from Gopal (1951) but can also be found in Kale (1974) and elsewhere. To this can be added the 'nine *rasas*' or facial expressions (illustrated in Gopal) and the emotional states they convey, plus other areas (gaits, kinds of laughter) similarly classified. Other forms have their own coding of make-up, costume, movement etc. and, like *Kathakali*, are animated by particular musical rhythms.

What can be seen from this is a ubiquitous tendency to thoroughness, all-inclusiveness. It is a tendency which is evident in all Indian forms of systematisation: the so-called Six Systems of Philosophy are better comprehended as different vantage points which offer complementary ways of understanding and categorising 'reality'. Even Ayurvedic medicine classifies body-types as overlapping: any individual can be *Pitta*, *Vata* or *Kapha* or any combination of the three. On the one hand there is a kind of obsession with classification; on the other hand, the classifying principle operates more like Schechner's fan than as rigid compartmentalisation. What is at work here is a kind of generous and essentially performative or process-oriented intelligence: just as Ayurveda prescribes treatment in terms of the tendency dominant at the time but in the awareness that others also operate in some measure, so the classification of performance modes implies the awareness that any or all of them may be suitable within a mobile context, but that each needs to be classified, because the goal of the performance is to produce 'treatment' or cause an effect which can be monitored. What these overlapping systems of classification reveal is that Indian theatre is perceived as a special case of what is always a dynamic view of life as forms in continuously generative motion.

Although *Kudiyattam*, with its extremely elaborate *abhinaya* (expressive coding) is closest to Sanskrit drama, *Kathakali*, according to Nair & Paniker (1993), can be understood fully in terms of the aesthetics of the *Natya Sastra*, although it sometimes departs from its precepts or adds facets of its own. It is defined as *pakarnattom*, or 'multiple transformational acting' (1993, 8). Not only does each actor present 'multiple appearances and behaviour' (88) (e.g. the actor playing Hanuman also 'plays' both Sita and Ravana when recounting her abduction to Rama), but the performers undergo a 'radical transformation of the human face and figure' (88); the performance is intended 'to change the *laukika* (worldly) nature of things to the *alaukika* (non-worldly)' (86) and the ultimate aim is to arrive at a non-dualistic state in which performer, performance and reception are one (4).

The means to do this include: (i) non-mimetic stylisation etc., preventing 'identification'; (ii) the gap-structure of narrative and action (reinforced by the disjunction of text and action as in a film by Godard or Robbe-Grillet or in a Brecht play); (iii) the co-existence of opposing demands upon spectators, who have to perform very abstract decoding operations (re. the *mudras*) and are also subject to 'strident vitality' (Chaitanya, 1986, 25) recalling the visceral effects of parts of ritual performance. In other words they have to operate across several kinds of border and in several different receptive and cognitive modes simultaneously: they are required to extend themselves considerably.

These features suggest a suspension of everyday modes of behaviour and perception whose purpose is to assist the transfer across into an 'otherness' of functioning. The performers 'become' highly imposing heroic or divine entities resplendent in elaborate costume and make-up; they stamp heavily onto the playing area and adopt a position balanced on the outside of the feet. On their first entry they playfully signal their arrival in character by the alternating conceal/reveal use of the hand-held curtain. As audience we know they are there from the beginning, because they wear bells on their ankles and don't try to walk quietly; their progressive revelation shows us how *much* they are there, how 'different' they are: it celebrates their otherness. It also relies on the enticement of concealment, the desire to see what is hidden. Often performed in an up-front, jokey fashion like a children's game, this sequence has quite complex significance. It is like the 'peek-a-boo' discussed by Emigh via Winnacott (Emigh 1996, 2) (or what Freud calls 'Fort/Da'), which stimulates the child to imagine what 'isn't there'; it is also a parallel to the rapid concealment and revelation of divine images in Hindu worship, as well as in the devotional performance form *Krishnattam* (Bharucha 1993, 174). The audience's potential to enter the 'divine' is thus stimulated through *play*.

I will come back to aspects of this discussion in the context of theory (Chapter 4), but in terms of performance it's important to note both the practice of using multiple techniques to produce specific effects and the direction of those effects: they work to set up that condition which Chapter 1 discussed in terms of self and other, of 'not me/not not me' and of extension beyond this into a dynamic but unfettered availability which is the ground of radical change in perception, self-evaluation and action. Since the analysis of ritual forms has pointed up similar features, it looks as though consistency of practice and intention is to be found, though it is a consistency which aims to produce not stasis but total availability, the possibility of inhabiting any form. To inhabit this availability means to pass 'beyond' form, out of given frameworks, and to discover the impetus to form in the ability to play (the conjunction of Schiller's *Formtrieb* and *Spieltrieb*).

Paniker comments about *Kathakali*: 'The text should be seen only as the skeletal base for evocative improvisation which diligently seeks to fill in the gaps in it by rendering passages taken from other texts' (Nair & Paniker 1993, 20: this recalls Kavalam Panikkar's comment about why he works with Sanskrit drama quoted on *p. 93* in Chapter 2). Firstly then the 'text' becomes an 'intertext', it intervenes in and is intervened in by other texts, it is part of a continuum (see what I say in Chapter 2 about 'text'). Secondly it becomes an impulse to improvisation (cf. the interaction between musicians and dancer in many forms of Indian – and other – dance): it generates other dimensions and pluralises itself as performative dialogue. Thirdly it requires the active participation of its receivers, rather as Wolfgang Iser's reception theory of reading emphasises the 'gaps' which any narrative offers as invitations to its readers to insert their own response, evaluation, additions etc. (another angle on the imaginative play/ passing-beyond-form process referred to above). The hierarchy Paniker establishes here is: written text > performed text > received text.

We have here a full model of the text > performance > reception process to which I will return in Chapter 4. It designates performance as fluid transformation for text, performer and receiver.

It is thus not quite the case that, as C.N. Ramachandran puts it, 'sophisticated classical theatre in India is characterised by its amazing formal rigidity ... [which] reflects the acceptance and endorsement of a rigidly structured society' (Ramachandran 1993, 21). There is a level on which this analysis works, but Paniker and others also point to ways in which forms like *Kathakali* escape rigidity. Although the distinction between 'classical' and 'folk' is marked by a lessening of formal rigidity which *may* be 'historical' evidence of 'dissatisfaction with formally structured society' (Ramachandran), this proposition also is rather oversimplistic, both as an aesthetic and a political comment.

Other forms

Moving towards varying degrees of more 'informal' or 'folk' performance, we find:

Therukuttu (Theru = street; kuttu = play) dates back two or three centuries, but is based on a Tamil version of the *Mahabharata*, and on the early works *Shilappadikaram* and *Manimekhalai* (c. 200AD). Like the *Ramlila*, *Therukuttu* ends with the burning or destruction of huge effigies with audience-participation, here as a version of the Bhima-Durodhyana fight; it also includes songs and interspersed (*ad lib*) prose elaboration, comic/satirical interruptions by the jester-figure *Kattiyakaran*, fights, physical action, grand stylisation and very colourful costume; stories are taken from *Mahabharata* and many feature the Draupadi cult, which is celebrated in a twenty-one-day festival in rural Draupadi-temples in Tamil Nadu. The ritual functions include *moksha* (rite whereby the soul is liberated) for recently departed relatives.

Bhavai: this 'folk' Gujarati form (also found in Rajasthan) has undergone a deliberate revival by, among others, Janak Dave, Jaswant Thaker and Kailash Pandya (the latter with the assistance of Darpana Academy in Ahmedabad), though here as often there is considerable debate about whether, and if so how much, it in fact 'died out': whether it is perceived to have done so depends very much on the position (location, social status etc.) of the perceiver. Much Indian performance which from a 'westernised' or a 'scholarly' viewpoint appears to have been moribund or non-existent nevertheless continued in e.g. rural areas, where it has subsequently been 'rediscovered'. There is considerable irony here. Kapila Vatsyayan, for instance, believed *Bhavai* to be defunct, but having been shown evidence to the contrary includes an elegant apology in the introduction to her book (Vatsyayan, 1980, ix). I have met many people who assure me that it has been going strong, and others who suggest that it is in various kinds of crisis. As with other forms there are several reasons for this. Either investigators do not have access to what is going on in, for instance, remote rural areas; or new experiments, revivals, activities at local academies etc. are in their early stages and the results are not yet evident; or economic and other factors give rise to relatively sudden changes. Even more recently, traditional *Bhavai* performers who were beginning to lose out to television have again been 'rescued' by Darpana and utilised in a health education project in Mehsana district north of Ahmedabad from 1998; it is a story which is echoed elsewhere.

Bhavai consists of a number of sequences or *veshas* (in *Yakshagana* and other forms the term means impersonation of a particular character-type), under the direction of a *Nayaka* (cf. *Sutradhara*), performed in the open; sometimes on a platform, sometimes not. Women did not perform until the twentieth century. Some material is mythological but much is socio-historical in focus, co-ordinated by the *Ranglo* or *Rangalo* (cf. *Vidushaka*). Costume is based on the naturalistic but with stylised motifs; music and dance is interspersed with dialogue, and draws on folk forms: it offers considerable scope for improvisation. Like many other forms, *Bhavai* displays in its particular regional and linguistic garb the interweaving of the traditional and the contemporary, the stately and the comic, the stylised and the improvised.

Chhau has three forms: *Purulia* and *Seraikella* (*Seraikala*) (masked); and *Mayurbhanj* (unmasked). *Seraikella* has beautiful, 'moon-face' masks reminiscent of Japan; in *Purulia* the masks are more 'earthy' (made in fact from earth and paper, where *Seraikella* masks are traditionally of wood and now of clay); the emphasis in all three of these eastern Indian forms (found in Orissa and Bihar) is more on mime and movement than on narrative. *Purulia* is the only Indian form to use full-body animal masks. Instead of a sacred flame, these open-air performances occur at salient points in the agricultural year in front of a pole representing (Shiva as) the world-tree.

Ankia-nata and *Bhaona* are Assamese forms (*Bhaona* is properly the dramatic presentation element). They contain a strong Sanskrit strand, particularly developed under Sankaradeva in the sixteenth-century; they are performed in a specially-designed prayer-hall with stage and auditorium (*namaghara*); the forms includes sung text, local music and dance. Themes are drawn mainly from the *Puranas*; some characters are masked; only males act; the *Sutradhara* introduces all characters and provides the links.

Ramlila: The Rama legend is pervasive throughout large parts of Asia; Vatsyayan indicates its extent and influence 'in the value system which it represents and the ideals it places before individuals for norms of human conduct'; so performance drawing on it 'must be seen as integral parts of the reality of life and not leisure time entertainment' (1980, 111). Performance draws on any of the innumerable versions of the *Ramayana* in different local languages; the best-known example (Varanasi) is based on that of Tulsidas. Forms range from *Kathakara* (mono-actor, singer), shadow- and rod-puppets (Orissa, Karnataka, Andhra, Kerala, Tamil Nadu) to the *Ramlila*s of North India. Although Vatsyayan classifies the form as in some ways cognate with European mystery or procession plays, she also emphasises that there are very considerable differences. The central point derives from the term *lila* itself: the play of form functions as manifestation and celebration of the unmanifest source (see Chapter 1). The mood and purpose is thus essentially different from most European 'passion plays'.

The Varanasi *Ramlila* is still directed by the Maharaja of Ramnagar/Varanasi and dates from the sixteenth century. It is an urban spectacle involving the whole town for ten to fifteen days by playing different episodes in different locations: one major effect is social cohesion achieved by communal input. Performers come from any caste but the heroes and heroines are played exclusively by young boys of less than fourteen. The text is recited by the narrator (*Vyasa*); music and dance contribution is basic, but major episodes (fights etc.) are grandly presented. There are some masks – mostly of cloth, for e.g. Ravana; Hanuman's mask is, uniquely, made of metal.

Like many other forms, though with different emphases, the *Ramlila* turns mythological narrative into performance spectacle: it is a theatre in which *communitas* (Turner) has clear socio-cultural aims. These could of course be regarded with suspicion, particularly as the director is a Maharaja, and in a sense the *Yatra*, particularly of Bengal, could be said to provide an alternative version.

Yatra: some 300 companies in Bengal employ 20,000 people (more than in film or urban theatre): *Yatra/Jatra* is a processional play, originating in devotional forms (cf. *Raslila, Gita-Govinda*). During the nineteenth century *Yatra* began to make use of social themes, for example in opposition to colonialist educational and artistic models; this continued in the twentieth century with more specifically Marxist-oriented material like episodes from Lenin's life; the form, always highly adaptable, now accommodates prose, contemporary language, political and social references etc.(see Chapter 5). It is very much travelling theatre, with simple and transportable props, sets and costumes.

Nautanki: an 'operatic' form from Uttar Pradesh exhibiting a similar development to *Yatra*, i.e. from the devotional towards an emphasis on contemporary social and political issues. Its origins derive from singing bards called *Chranas*. Few traces of ritual remain; *Nautanki* is characterised by sharp dialogue, melodrama, declamation, singing and dancing, much of it involving the *Vidushaka*/clown figure (*Munshiji*). The actors are professional, though not as highly paid as in *Yakshagana*, and receive training in institutions called Akharas, some of which accept women. There is a strong influence from Hindi movies in contemporary practice; in contrast, Habib Tanvir (see Chapter 5) has adapted *Mrccha-Katika* for *Nautanki*.

Tamasa: (Maharashtra): unlike most other forms, its origins date from as late as the eighteenth century. It is an 'earthy dance-drama [with] occasional obscenities and vulgarity'; but displays the 'potential of high drama' (Vatsyayan 1980, 171). In 1980 there were some eighty companies and 3,000 professional performers, rural and urban; *Tamasa* plays to large audiences in e.g. Pune and Bombay, acted inside or out. Previously, companies were co-operatives. The leading performer is female; the performance is characterised by interchange, both comic and serious, and banter between actors, musicians and the *sardar* (*Sutradhara*), with considerable room for improvisation. P.L. Despande, Vijaya Mehta and others have used the form extensively in contemporary Marathi theatre.

Varadpande notes the continued centrality in very many forms of the *Vidushaka* figure (director, stage manager, narrator, commentator etc. – cf. *Sutradhara*). He parallels in many ways the licensed transgression of the carnival tradition in Europe, and symbolises a subversive quality. His hallmarks are freedom to improvise and variety in the modes of doing so, in a mix of registers, styles and indeed languages. The jester figure can take liberties with any established order – he was frequently dressed for example in mock British gear under the Raj.

Whereas, as mentioned earlier, the *Vidushaka* has a truncated role as a kind of embryonic *Sutradhara* in the Sanskrit drama of Bhasa, much subsequent Indian theatre has taken care to include contemporary and/or alternative perspectives in his person, (whether as *Sutradhara, Bhagavata, Katiyakkaran, Vidushaka, Ranglo* or *Munshiji*) whilst retaining ritual and/or religious structures.

Vatsyayan indicates (i) that the *Sutradhara* links phases in the narrative and serves as a 'chorus' figure, whereas the *Vidushaka* connects past and present, gods and men (1980, 13); and (ii) that these functions persist under different names in many forms (she lists some fourteen: 1980, 186). These figures thus in many ways exemplify the metatheatrical freedom which draws on the narrative and the dramatic, opening their convergence through the spirit of play.

It is not therefore surprising that much theatre invokes Ganesh as its presiding deity. Ganesh is often represented dancing, recalling Shiva as Nataraj and as the energising of creative forces, fertility and flow; Ganesh is also the elephant remover of obstacles, which perhaps are envisaged as inherent in such a potentially disrespectful form or in the attempt it presents at totality. There is more than a hint here of a Dionysos or *lila* quality, with the ability to break open the solemnity of apparently fixed categories and to do the impossible. Remember too Ganesh as totally alert scribe of the *Mahabharata*, able to assimilate, understand and write simultaneously. Like the flexibility and plurality of these forms, the role of clowns and elephant-headed gods seems to stand for requirements and capacities of all human performance. Whether they emerge from narrative, ritual or tradition, they are able both to construct frames and to break out of them.

This section has looked only at a selection from the multiplicity and range of performance forms, but has attempted to indicate the spectrum across which they operate and the extent to which they overlap. They range across categories like formal/informal, sophisticated/spontaneous; interior/exterior; they employ a vast spectrum of performance codes and styles, operating through different combinations and gradations of narrative, song, dance, music, mask, make-up, gesture, movement, costume and so on. Several different theoretical strategies and paradigms are employed to attempt to organise this material from various perspectives. In the next chapter I consider further what they each contribute.

The repertoire of practice sketched out above clearly indicates that Indian theatre as performance articulates the full range of expression and action, in many cases by seeking to return its participants to their 'origins' or, more precisely, originating modes of behaviour. This in itself suggests why its forms may also be appropriate to engage with contemporary concerns, be they socio-political or psychological; Chapter 5 looks at what is happening to and in traditional and regional forms in the current context. The discussion has also focused on ways in which Indian performance aims not just to activate a 'horizontal' richness across forms of behaviour, but also to identify and invite the extension of capacities of understanding and being through a 'vertical' dimension, opening up the full range of perceptual and conceptual potential and offering ways in which 'self' may begin to integrate kinds of 'otherness'. In *STQ* 17, Katyal writes of performance forms from Punjab, Bihar and Orissa, that they represent 'traditions which comfortably transgress what we are being taught are barbed-wire barriers between different systems of religious belief' and which in so doing 'affirm our centuries-old history of sophisticated acceptance of difference, of the other' (Katyal 1998, 2). As such, she claims, they need to be 'cherished'. This debate is pursued in the next chapter.

There is however an aspect of this negotiation which seems to have been glossed over both within the logistics of performance in India and in critical accounts of it. Although a combination of traditional and contemporary Indian and western approaches does cover many senses in which performance produces and transforms the body, some questions remain.

WOMEN IN PERFORMANCE

Many traditional forms, in particular where they are closest to ritual and the classical/courtly, use male performers in female roles: there are established terms, forms of training, groups or castes of performers etc. who in many cases still exist, ranging from the categorisation of 'feminine' acting-style in *Kathakali* as *lasya* (in distinction to *tandava*; similar to the Balinese *kris/manis* distinction), to terms for males who specialise in female roles (*strivesas* in *Yakshagana*), to accepted groups of transvestite eunuch performers (*hijaras*). Men represent all kinds and conditions of women, taking the role of the goddess Kali in ritual forms like *Mudiyettu*, of Rama's wife Sita in *Kathakali*, of mothers, wives and daughters. The only forms where women have traditionally performed are the 'classical dance' *Bharatanatyam* (but this was revived – by a woman, Rukmini Devi – after being suppressed largely by the colonialist powers on moral grounds), *Mohiniattam*, *Kudiyattam*, and forms which tend either towards pure dance (e.g. pot-carrying dances in rural Gujarat) or towards the 'entertainment' end of the spectrum (e.g. *Nautanki* in Uttar Pradesh).

Important changes have occurred particularly during the twentieth century in women's situation as regards status, range of roles, position within the performance economy and its artistic, political and social organisation; the issues are varied, crucial and ongoing, and some of them will be taken up in Chapter 5.

But the changes occurred because a need for change was perceived. It is therefore important to ask why, in a theatre whose performance aesthetic is centrally about extension of possibility (becoming more or other, acquiring new kinds of perceptiveness, 'cosmoscising'), women as performers have been mostly limited to the spheres of entertainment or decoration. In order to address this we shall need to look at women characters as well, where they figure for example in episodes from *Ramayana* and *Mahabharata*; and the issue is of course cultural and historical and in its scope way beyond a few paragraphs. I am not therefore claiming to write the history of women and performance in India, but I do think it's important to state some of the problems. Most accounts of Indian theatre have not engaged with them to any extent.

As far as I can judge there were no governing or *organisational* roles for women in the development of most classical or ritual forms, though they did *perform* in Sanskrit drama; these forms were closely allied to (or in some cases taken over by) Aryan (Brahminic) religious hierarchies and/or the ruling classes with which they were allied, where power resided mainly with male elders. The texts themselves (epics, *Puranas*) from which episodes were derived also reputedly originate from male hands, and the framing of the narratives certainly seems to confirm a male perspective. Although in South India many ritual forms link back to Dravidian culture, which is in considerable measure matriarchal (e.g. pre-eminence of Kali and Draupadi cults), here too in many cases the men played female roles, whether these were of the strong and violent type (e.g. Kali, female demons etc.) or the soft and submissive. Possibly this was a result of Aryanisation of the social structure.

Power to decide the content and form of the performance resides then with men; women, where they appear in their own right, do so in closely-circumscribed behavioural zones as dancers, light entertainers or behind a mask; they remain as it were veiled or cloaked in aspects of the functions prescribed upon them; they do not, for the most part, speak. (It's true that in some forms neither do men – the text is sung or spoken by others, but traditionally those others have nearly always been men too. The *Bhagavata* can speak for female characters, but it has, until recently, been rare for the *Bhagavata* role to be taken by a woman who speaks either for her own sex or for both.) Where women are represented by men, this is transmitted through a stylisation of movement and gesture: men performers learn lightness of gesture, small steps, choose particular kinds of glance etc., like *onnegata* artists in *Kabuki.* This may, however valuable it is for the individual male performer to explore his own 'feminine' attributes, produce for the audience something of a caricature which shuts off a range of behavioural options. The roles women are assigned in the stories of gods and heroes tend to be submissive and/ or supportive, in line with stereotypes of the wife, mother or daughter: Iyer says of the female characters in *Kathakali*: 'their important role in the drama is the delineation of the amorous and the pathetic: women in love and women in distress – the two themes around which the great stories of the world are built' (Iyer 1983, 50). Mahasweta Devi's comment quoted in Chapter 2 (p. 44) makes a similar point rather more acerbically. Finally, in some of the forms which allow room for improvisation, humour and interaction with the audience, women are barred from attending this section of the event because it frequently includes bawdy material. As I say above, much of this is changing. But it is part of the historical structure, a structure which, like counterparts elsewhere, appears to do a very thorough job of marginalisation. Texts, where they delineate women's 'nature' and role, appear to authorise this closeting; the effect however operates as outreach in performance in all senses, limiting their scope both in daily activity and at all levels of the event-structure of performance as discussed in this chapter. *STQ* 14/15 has two articles which recount the experiences of actresses in Manipur over the last half-century: the difficulties they speak of are still found in many other parts of India.

There are of course many excuses, ranging from physical stereotyping (e.g. many *Theyyam* roles require the performer to wear heavy headgear and rush around for long periods, sometimes performing gross or grotesque actions; *Kathakali* actors draw on the martial art of *Kalarippayat* and the form, like the cognate *Yakshagana*, is in part rooted in a military/martial culture) to temperamental unsuitability (women are supposed by nature to be more 'modest'). Most of them come down to a conception of gender roles which accords with the representation of female characters mentioned above. It is fairly clear that most of these assumptions are flawed and/or biased in some degree. What needs to be asked here is why did they arise and what has been their effect in the domain of Indian theatre? Is it the case that only 'man' (as Vatsyayan revealingly puts it) can 'cosmoscise himself'? Are women not regarded as aesthetically and psychospiritually adept enough to enjoy the profounder levels of *rasa*? And doesn't this seem to contradict iconography in which androgynous figures or the celebration of sexual fusion are equated with states of wisdom and 'divine' fulfilment?

Three of the best-known female characters in Indian theatre of all kinds are Draupadi (wife of the five Pandavas), Sita (wife of Rama) and Shakuntala (Kalidasa's protagonist). We might also mention Parvati (Shiva's consort and mother of Ganesh), Radha (Krishna's favourite Gopi), the apparently destructive but ultimately benevolent Kali, sundry demons, jealous mothers, abandoned lovers and other stereotypes. There are also in myth and some transpositions examples of wise, virtuous, devoted and even enlightened females. So the first thing to say is that, in spite perhaps of a tendency for stereotype to predominate, there is a wide range of possible models available. It may also be the case that few women would object to being represented as gracious, intelligent, virtuous etc., so long as it is clear that they are not refused any kind of existence outside these parameters as narrowly conceived.

In spite of these mitigating factors, major questions remain. Firstly, most of the named characters above do not have much *scope* for action: their choices are largely determined for them by men or by the norms of a male-led society. In one (important) sense this is a political issue, and one currently in process of enormous overhaul. In another sense it can be framed in terms of how we understand fundamental drives and faculties. (Remember, the epics deal with 'gods' and 'heroes', i.e. with the highest level of operation possible, with if you like the potential for operation at the height of human capacity.) If deliberation and debate, decision-making and execution, and desire and drive are all in some way seen as 'male' characteristics, the main-springs of both personal and political life may be deposited in the hands of the gender which apparently owns most of these qualities. This might be seen as a serious category mistake: experience of more subtle levels of thought and feeling, where intention and desire originate, suggests strongly that gender is not crucially involved. Of course *what* men and women think, need or want is strongly influenced by their gender make-up as well as by other factors; the fact *that* we think or want and the capacity to do so, on the other hand, is not. (Some research suggests that the forms of thought emerge as more 'right-hemisphere-dominated' in women and the reverse in men; but it is also clear that both genders have both kinds of capacity and that there is no fixed ratio. There is no research I know of which suggests that either sex has a predetermined capacity to think or feel more effectively than the other.)

History, tradition and mythology however frequently erect weighty 'overarching narratives' which, by distributing roles according to gender, valorise distinctions which then become sanctioned and may operate as forms of power-alignment. Power as an externally visible structure is attributed or acquired as a result of an apparent match between function and functionary. Even moderately enlightened societies operate according to this principle, and Indian scriptures claim to be laying the basis for fully enlightened society. The aim is laudable. But if the signs are misread, the function may be misattributed. The signs for power seem to point to characteristics which males tend to display more obviously. However, considered more astutely and from a more formative stage, there is no distinction between 'male' and 'female' operations of thinking (cognitive), sensing (affective) and the initial impetus whereby the latter are translated into (motoric) action. And in terms of performance, the evidence (from within theatre, drama and narrative as well as from without) is that neither sex always does better. There is in fact evidence in the stories contained in *Mahabharata* etc., in spite of them probably having been compiled by men (the claim that the writers were in a heightened state of cognition is however both interesting and relevant here) that whichever sex attempts to grasp power by force, or hold onto it deviously, creates havoc; and that both men and women are capable of perceiving better ways of going about things, however infrequently they manage it in practice. In contemporary experience, a reading of something like Caryl Churchill's *Top Girls* (which explores what they have to do to get there) and evidence from female political leaders in and beyond the Indian sub-continent suggests that they are equally capable of doing just as badly.

In other words, *modus operandi* goes more with role or function than with gender. The way to safeguard against the tyranny of role (or the role of tyranny) may well then be to learn how to step out of it from time to time, which is precisely what Indian (and other) theatre can provide, as Emigh's 'ontological acrobatics' signals.

But this also means that to reinforce the weight of stereotyping may be to disallow such acrobatics, to limit freedom. We can check this against some evidence from texts, by looking in more detail at what happens to Draupadi, Sita and Shakuntala.

Each of these three is first *humiliated* and then *rehabilitated*. One of the central moments in *Mahabharata* is the humiliation of Draupadi by the Kauravas, who attempt to unravel her sari in spite of the fact that she has her period. This aspect of the humiliation does not quite succeed because Krishna has seen to it that the sari is inexhaustibly long. However, the experience is not much less terrifying, and in another sense Draupadi is being used by the Pandavas to establish a motive for revenge. Sita is abducted by Ravana; when she is restored to Rama she is further humiliated because he requires her to take a test/provide a sign to prove that she has not been unfaithful, and even after she has done so he will not live with her for some time. (He is apparently bowing here to pressure from the people, suggesting the weight of tradition.) Shakuntala is similarly not recognised by her husband, who is suffering from the petulant curse laid on him by her father; she too has to provide a sign (the missing ring) before being accepted as wife to the king and mother of his child.

There are lots of motifs here, and lots of possible interpretations. Nor are the traditions which sanction these attitudes exclusively sustained by one or other sex. What I'm going to pick up on is not exclusive, but it could be significant in terms of the psychopolitics of gender. From these incidents it looks as though femaleness might be a threat if it gets out of order. Draupadi may be exposed in her essence as a woman (she menstruates, she is a sexual being); Sita may have been sexually active outside the prescribed domain; Shakuntala may be an 'unlawful' power-seeker who threatens the succession as a result of her sexual potency. In all cases there is a threat both to the individual male 'owners' and to the social order they head. Whatever instance (political necessity, father's curse, requirements of the narrative) motivates the action, it seems as though the woman has to be made to display herself as potentially dangerous in her essence in order for that danger to be circumvented (usually by 'magic' or 'divine' intervention – Krishna's sari, Hanuman's bridge-building assistance to Rama in tracking down Ravana, the finding of the ring by the fisherman). Order has to be seen to be threatened so that it can be restored. That may indeed be a profound psychological and political insight. But why is the threat in these (famous) cases figured exclusively through women?

It does look as though women are seen as dangerous and 'other', and dangerous in their otherness. (If that can be domesticated into motherness, everything in the garden is – hopefully – fine.) They appear to pose a threat by virtue of their sexuality. The women in the stories are not immodest, promiscuous or voracious: but the men fear that they might be or might have been. Note that it is not the nature or degree of the women's desires which is problematic – each of them in fact expresses the wish to be reunited with her husband (or husbands in the case of Draupadi). Rather it is the potentially excessive nature of *male* desire, or perhaps better, of desire in a male-ordered value system, which offers the threat and is then off-loaded onto the other, the woman. The women can only be readmitted to the male order of things after they have given a 'sign' (in Draupadi's case a protective sign is conferred upon her).

As women, it seems, they evoke in men the fear of loss of control; they are physical, sexual, they are objects of desire, which can only be controlled by being possessed, domesticated, harnessed. They represent the realm of the flowing, the uncontrollable, that which escapes boundaries; of physical matter and hence of mortality (troubling to heroes and gods in a world where everyone is concerned about immortality and constantly performs austerities in order to have it granted them). Their being escapes language in its overlap with the wordless darkness of desiring, of recognition of loss and desire for reunion, of birthing and dying. Hence the need for the sign, the 'password' back into the Symbolic Order of a linguistically sanitised universe. They are the chink in the (Brahminic) armour. There are many instances in the epics of sages, saints, gods etc. being 'tempted': by women, of course, sometimes 'created' specially for the purpose, to show that what is really being tested is the resolve of the male protagonist: 'woman' here is not a real person with her own agenda, any more than Draupadi, Sita and Shakuntala are in the incidents under discussion, but more a site of male insecurity and anxiety.

This looks like another category mistake: not women, but male fear of the otherness in themselves, is what poses the threat. Neither in their external behaviour nor in their real desires do these women pose a threat: they behave modestly, sensibly, resourcefully. Yet their stories have come down to us in narrative and in performance in this form. And women, by and large, have not had access to perform in their own right either on stage or in the religious and political arena, until the present century. Where they have, the forces of 'order', both indigenous and colonialist, have either suppressed them (the example of the *devadasis*) or marginalised them; they have even regulated them further by permitting only mainly stereotyped representations to be seen, performed either by a defined group of male impersonators whose own sexuality is not threatening, or by an equally circumscribed and corralled group of transvestites: the sign 'woman' is here licensed by (male) prerogative. Moreover, the examples and analysis I have presented, stemming from the central texts of Hindu culture, seem to cast considerable doubt on the convenient (Hindu) scapegoating of colonising Muslim culture as responsible for repressive attitudes. No doubt Islam has played its part, here as elsewhere, in the suppression of women, but it is not the sole player.

Indians not infrequently get annoyed at 'westernised' critiques of Indian culture, and I am not unsympathetic. I only present this one with a certain degree of surprise at the apparent closeness of parallels in behaviour. That women in the performing arts in India have taken it on board is, I think, not in dispute; and some of the discussion in Chapter 5 will pick up relevant aspects. There are also important implications for theories used to approach both Indian and other forms of drama, which I discuss in Chapter 4. Here my focus is to ask in what ways it feeds into the view of performance which this chapter pursues.

I have suggested that performance across the spectrum of Indian forms can be seen to be concerned with providing access to wider possibilities of being for producers and receivers. That claim could be compromised by the rather massive hole I have just excavated in the foundations. Is extension of being only viable for men? (If so, is that because women don't need it, being already whole, or aren't worthy of it, being incapable of wholeness? Either answer is disturbing.) The charge is not limited to the area of artistic performance, of course. But it seems to me that a look at the history and practice of performance raises the issue, and only forms of action in the present can take it further.

Both ritual and traditional forms offer the lesson that an encounter with otherness can be positively and profitably negotiated as a recognition of new dimensions and modes of self, if the ability to play is most fully engaged. Such a shift across the border may however be experienced as threatening to that configuration of selfhood which, not unreasonably or initially malevolently, clings on to the contours of the known, of the defining Symbolic or Imaginary order. This mobility is not merely revealed in and by performance; in a profound sense it *is* performance or the performative, the capacity to fall out of role, to change and shapeshift. The fluid and flexible, that which is less rigidly 'articulate' and whose 'language' is closer to an organic sensing, that which partakes of the business of forming rather than the preservation of the formed, that which is dialogic rather than monologic, that which exists in and as the transitory and the transformative needs to be located and celebrated in all of us. But the task is not easy: it means, to return to Ayyappa Paniker's insight, that the only way to overcome Death (the desperate rigidity of the Symbolic) is to meet it in our own person and our own body. 'Not-not-I'-ness is neither masculine nor feminine, it is prior to both; but the passage to it appears to lead across the loss of the known, and the tendency to build the 'solid' walls higher may take over. In the process, even women may swell the ranks of the exilers.

This whole area clearly has significance for a *politics of performance*, although in terms of the way I have discussed it, it goes somewhat wider. I am not offering a separate section on politics; partly because the implications drawn from what I have just said can be applied; partly because I come back to political theatre and cognate issues in Chapter 5; and partly because some of the material in Chapters 1 and 2 has already addressed questions of 'authority' and some of that in Chapters 1 and 4 is focused towards an ethic of freedom. It will be clear that I regard performance as an active politics, but not one which is encased in any single political framework: it is both politic and politics precisely because it is always pushing beyond frameworks. In the above scenario those limits have not, it seems, always been recognised in full.

CHAPTER FOUR

Theory

This chapter will both discuss kinds of theory which have been applied to Indian theatre and propose its own composite version.

I will group theories and theoretical perspectives used so far under two (loose) main headings as follows:

2. Aesthetics: Semiotics and Reception theory
Performance theories
Theory of Sanskrit drama
Natya Sastra, Vedic linguistics

3. Politics & Ethics: Anthropological theories
Historicist and Marxist theories
Feminist and related theory

The discussion will roughly follow the above order, though there will be some overlap: for instance, 'anthropological' might equally well be linked with performance theory; more generally, all the bodies of theory mentioned have both an aesthetics and a politics. I shall derive from it an argument which proposes that the experience and concept of 'freedom', defined in several different ways and across different fields, is of fundamental importance to the theory and practice of theatre in India (and, by implication, elsewhere). Note that I include in my category of the aesthetic, approaches which deal with both production and reception; and I shall examine all theories as blueprints for and/or accounts of practice. In *Natya Sastra* it is said: '*rasa* is itself *natya*' (Shah, n.d., 21); that is to say [i] aesthetic experience, up to and including the sublime, is *performative, enactive*; [ii] 'theatre' must include the reception process.

THE CHANGING NATURE OF THEORY

The context of the present discussion needs to be evoked: theories of theatre and drama have shifted their ground considerably in recent decades. To foreshorten the issue, 'western' drama theory prior to around 1960 was not particularly dramatic: that is, it used categories and approaches equally, or more, suitable to other literary genres and forms of writing – and for the most part, it treated theatre and drama *only* as writing, in spite of Artaud's passionate denunciations of the purely verbal in the 1930s. Criticism was focused through biography, histories of performance, psychological analysis of character, political or philosophical discussion of content and meaning: approaches drawn in the main from traditional literary studies.

Since the 1960s things have changed. Raymond Williams' *Drama in Performance* (Williams 1968, original 1954) signals the shift, at least in its title; Keir Elam's *The Semiotics of Theatre and Drama* (Elam 1991, original 1980) marks it more profoundly as a change in method. But plays by Beckett, Ionesco, Gombrowicz, Kantor and others were from the 1950s making it difficult to retain only the categories indicated above, because the performance experience which they produced could not be fitted easily into them.

All the theoretical frameworks which followed (semiotics, reception theory, theories relating to acting methodology, varieties of performance theory) have in common an understanding of theatre as interactive dynamics rather than as given and stable text. Taken together, they represent an almost complete *volte-face* of critical methodology, as a result of which western theory is in much better shape to begin to comprehend eastern practice. The phenomenon is taken up again below, and discussed further in Chapter 6 in the context of east-west exchange: as indicated in Chapter 1, certain aspects of 'eastern' understandings appear particularly relevant and attractive during this period.

It will be useful to look briefly at these frameworks, bearing in mind that they may be particularly suitable for dealing with Indian theatre.

AESTHETICS

Semiotics and reception

Semiotics tries to set up a model of 'codes' by which the event is transmitted, to order the complexity of perceptual activity; *reception theory* tries to grapple with how the event is received – what expectations may prejudge or distort it and how they may be circumvented, what psychological changes may occur: what receivers bring with them and what happens to them through interaction with the performance event. (I'm using 'event' here not so much in the sense of 'the show', e.g. 'musical event', which locates it 'out there' somewhere, but more in the sense of an occurrence *in* consciousness with which that consciousness must necessarily engage, be active, and by which it is in some degree transformed.)

Of course the two things (semiotics and reception process) interact and alter each other. We tend to call that interaction 'meaning' or 'knowledge'. But knowledge and meaning are not fixed collections of data, but rather constructive processes, 'information-flow'. What we know depends on the state we (the 'subject') are in and the condition of the phenomena (the 'object') we are trying to assess. Both things are liable to change – they are variable, and they are relative to the space-time in which they are located. So the attempt to understand the way we react to and grasp performance is important in terms of how we understand everything: life can be seen as a flow of performance events which our systems of categorisation and analysis attempt to probe.

Keir Elam is perhaps the first writer, at least in English, to categorise the multiplicity of semiotic codes with reference to drama. Elam reminds us that *semiotics* derives from Saussure's work on linguistics and Peirce's theory of signs, both early in the twentieth century; from the Czech formalists in Prague in the 30s and 40s; and from postmodernist and structuralist theoreticians in France, Germany, Italy, the USSR and the USA in the 60s and 70s. It can be understood as:

(a) *a science of signs*;
(b) *signification + communication (generation + exchange of meaning)*.

Elam's section on systems and codes (1991, 49–88) tabulates and discusses how we read the many systems in performance. He lists e.g. vestimentary, cosmetic, pictorial, musical, architectural codes; proxemics (distance between characters); and further, linguistic codes (dialect, rhetoric etc.); conventions and expectations; cultural behavioural norms; sense of history/theatre history, and so on.

This delineation of the complexity of performance implies both the interdependence of codes and signs within it, and the fact that understanding is a constantly renewed act in which connections are always in process of being made; comprehension requires a 'global' model which can relate the local and the contextual. Theatre is a 'cybernetic machine' (Barthes); and one in which the activity of the 'spectator' (who does much more than just observe) is paramount.

The 'semiotics of performance' then does not just mean a disembodied collection of signs of many kinds; it is the tactile interface of an activity connecting us and the performance and it represents a change of gear in the way we relate to what we are experiencing.

The activity of semiotic decoding ('reading' the signs) creates worlds within the play. These worlds are possible rather than actual (i.e. they are fictional), but the fact that several of them may co-exist serves to indicate that what we call the 'real' world is also simply an agreed interpretation based on certain data received from a particular position. The audience of course brings with it its own assumptions, its cultural baggage, its prejudices, or in Jauss's term its 'horizon of expectations' (Jauss 1982). Worlds and interpretations are in conflict, in the making.

The play world is however 'hypothetically actual', physically shown to audience: unlike in a novel, it is not a 'pretended *representation* of a state of affairs but the pretended state of affairs itself' (Searle, cit. Elam 1991, 111). The dramatic world is dense and layered in that it may contain different modalities: knowledge: *epistemic*; belief: *doxastic*; hopes/fears: *boulomaeic*; dreams/fantasies: *oneiric*; commands: *deontic* (Russell, cit. Elam 15). It also includes different levels of time: the *now* of *discourse time*, the *sequence* of *plot time*, plus *chronological time* (the time supposedly elapsing during the play) and *historical time* (when it is set) (1991, 117–8).

These terms are presented by Elam to identify some of the structuring principles by which the presence of performers and spectators in drama composes complex and active realities.

The implication here is in line with the understanding of reader-activity suggested by Wolfgang Iser: important aspects of it take place in the 'gaps' (between signifiers), which invite 'completion' (Iser 1978). So the activity undertaken in de-and re-coding is diverse, and the kinds of information and meaning constructed are complex. The degree of their interaction requires a highly coherent ('supercharged') kind of mental/physical functioning, the kind in which new *Gestalts* or meaning-complexes are generated, involving for instance alternation between whole and part, 'field' and 'event', and possible only by means of holistic integration of different brain hemispheres. This is more than collation and closer to creation.

One more area which it is relevant to consider derives from linguistics and describes language activity in terms of 'speech acts' (Elam 1991, 156–169); or doing things with words (language as performance). (Elam quotes from Austin and Searle.)

Speech acts can be:

Illocutionary: what is performed in saying something, e.g. asking, ordering, asserting, promising;

Perlocutionary: what is performed as a result of saying something, e.g. persuading, convincing, preventing.

They have a spin-off in 'actioning' (a practice used by contemporary British directors Mike Alfreds and Max Stafford-Clark), which understands all theatrical activity as doing something to someone even if it looks like description or monologue, and in investigating the text/sub-text in order to discover the action of each utterance or segment. We're talking here about pushing the investigation of semiosis further towards the subtle impulses which underlie, precede, generate actions and words. Such techniques are an extension of what Stanislavsky may be implying with reference to working with the 'subtext', attempting to disclose intention and event beneath the spoken text.

This pluralistic and active approach to theatrical acts is relevant to much of the performance spectrum of Indian theatre, both as outlined in Chapter 3 (on traditional performance forms) and below in Chapter 5 (on contemporary practice); it can also be placed against the instructions, suggestions and implications to be found in *Natya Sastra*, which will be discussed shortly.

The whole syntax of performance, from the language of the text to the verbal and non-verbal sign systems and inflections of its transmission, and the whole context of the presentation, is a temporal phenomenon whose complex and multi-faceted causality is traceable to a variety of historically-determined frameworks: including that of the original composition, that of the contemporary audience's horizon of expectation, and that of the performers' individual and collective responsiveness and level of performance skill; many languages or dialects embedded within each other, many strands of social, aesthetic and political attitudes, many varieties of protectiveness and availability. A performance puts all of that in play in dialogue with the meanings of the text and their physical enactment. Any performance is thus both a direct example of intertextuality and an extremely complex event, and just as there are many codes and sign-systems by which that event is articulated, so it is appropriate to employ different frameworks to locate and understand its diaspora of meaning. Meanings are *made*, they are the work of the moment, and they always have to be remade. Anthropology, semiotics, psychology, deconstruction may all help to make, unmake and remake them.

Actor-training methodology

In the west, the work of twentieth-century European *actor-trainer/* directors like Stanislavsky, Copeau, Meyerhold, Brecht, Grotowski, Fo, Lecoq, Brook, Mnouchkine and Barba has placed the emphasis firmly on the inner activity of the performer, on the processes s/he employs to make available the full range of intellectual, sensory and motoric skills which will create the performance-score he or she will contribute to the enacted text. This work has had three main effects on theorising about theatre:

(i) it has foregrounded the performative aspect;
(ii) it has contributed to a reappraisal of the actor/audience relationship;
(iii) it has underlined the status of acting methodology within the spectrum of drama theory.

Concomitantly, it has assisted the shift from 'directors' theatre' towards greater input from everyone involved in productions including actors; it has drawn from and contributed to the increasing presence of the improvisatory, with spin-off effects both in the nature of the performance product and in the economics and logistics of performance events.

The match between the goals and methods of western actor-trainers and what they perceive to be valuable in Indian practice has been alluded to in Chapter I. But it is relevant to note here, firstly that *Natya Sastra* includes highly specific instructions for performers and secondly that actor-training has, at least traditionally, a particular, if also particularly vulnerable, status in India. So performance training in very considerable detail (both the 'mechanics' of gesture, posture, breath control, kinds of facial expression, etc. and hints about the relationship between producing these signs and entering the affective or cognitive states which they articulate) is established as central to the whole business of theatre in a way which it was not in the west until Stanislavsky. And the 'devotional' (*guru/shisya*) mode of transmission signals an exclusive commitment to and thus acknowledgement of the supreme value of the performer's art which frequently goes beyond that even of dedicated professionalism. (In both cases there is some slippage in contemporary India: less rigorous adherence to traditional forms and content of training, more likelihood of reward-oriented activity, especially in tv and films; so to some extent there is a kind of transfer between east and west in operation, where each is adopting some of the other's attitudes and practices.)

Other issues relating to performers figure in the next sections.

Theory and performance

Theory arises from the context of performance. Sometimes it just appears as the playscript (Shakespeare): as a working document responding to immediate requirements. Sometimes it appears in another imaginative guise: Goethe's understanding of drama, for instance, is better extracted from his philosophical novel *Wilhelm Meisters Theatralische Sendung* than from anything apparently more direct (except *Faust* – which interestingly begins with the claim that action precedes or is simultaneous with conception, and refuses to 'end' in that it offers a vision of Faust after death 'still striving'). Where a relatively short time intervenes between performance manual and methodological summary (Brecht, Stanislavsky, Brook, Boal), the active mode is retained by anecdote and suggestions for exercises. Where the time span is longer or indeterminate (Aristotle, *Natya Sastra*) the tone tends to become more like commentary or philosophy – though it should be noted that the *Natya Sastra* is framed very much as a manual. Critics – who until fairly recently were rarely theatre practitioners themselves – inevitably add a layer of analytical dust, and 'theory' ends up becoming something divorced from the act of animating a performance. Clearly this allows all kinds of interesting philosophical questions to be posed at greater length. But precisely the aim of performance is that those questions should be posed *on the spot, in situ*, accessible to the receiver as a complex of semiotic information which is so structured as to cause him or her to perceive its significance in ways which are less available in everyday life. Even for Brecht, theatre is a very carefully composed situation in which alertness and relaxation need to be balanced in order to achieve both attentiveness and critical judgement. For Boal, in spite of his suspicions (shared with Brecht) about the potentially quiescent effects of *catharsis* (promoting acceptance of the *status quo*), the audience needs to be transformed into 'spectactors' by specific games and techniques, so that they can participate in the act of theatre in a manner different from (more dynamic, more alert than) their everyday behaviour.

Schechner (1988) advances two major criteria for performance theory:

(1) repetition;
(2) transformation.

Performance theory is about discovering a model for forms of behaviour which are identifiable because repeatable and developmental because transformatory. This ranges from the 'micro' activity of individual brain functioning to the 'macro' major social ritual occasion (rite of passage). As noted earlier, Schechner draws up an 'event spectrum' and a 'function spectrum' for performance. The former ranges from closed rituals to national festivities, the latter from entertainment to efficacy.

Schechner's anthropology of theatre derives substantially from Victor Turner's investigations of communal events, rites of passage and so on; whereas I focus in this section on his analysis of the *effects* of such events, I look below at some of the ways in which they are framed (i.e. as part of the social fabric). Schechner uses as one major illustration of his theory the annual Varanasi *Ramlila* (Schechner, 1988), so Indian performance modes are important for him. His Turner-derived methodology may already be subject to charges of the colonising perspective: 'anthropology' is defined by Devy (1997, 33) as one of three major strategies of marginalisation of non-western culture, and the most demeaning – he quotes William S. Willis's view that it has been 'the social science that studies dominated people'. The Varanasi case is compounded and complicated by a number of factors, including Schechner's public adoption of Hinduism, which he later views quizzically himself, the peculiar nature of the Varanasi event as the *fiat* or 'gift' of the otherwise extinct Indian aristocracy in the form of the Maharajah of Varanasi, and the effects on its status of the very publicity afforded by Schechner's study. He may indeed be viewing the event as evidence of what he wishes to construct as 'Indian theatre', which, as I have continually tried to indicate, is problematic, as are of course any claims this book may make. None of this however significantly affects his location of *Ramlila* as an example of 'environmental' theatre, taking place to a changing and mobile audience on successive days in different parts of the city; and the event itself, although its significance, like all performative events, is subject to change, remains central to many of the community's perceptions of itself, however problematic they may be doctrinally and/or politically.

Eugenio Barba's 'theatre anthropology' concerns itself mainly with performers, in that it tries to identify 'bios' or 'scenic energy' through an examination of performance technique in traditions across the world – the three principal eastern forms studied by Barba being Orissi dance, Balinese theatre and Kabuki, especially the *Onnegata* or female impersonator role. His *Secret Art of the Performer* (with Nicola Savarese, 1991) implies that cross-referencing such things as postures, stances, gestures, habitual actions, the distribution of weight and the direction and kind of energy can map common factors and approach the 'secret' which endues such performers with scenic presence. The performances of Barba's own company, Odin Teatret, have not always borne this out: indeed the performers have often seemed most comfortable and innovative when drawing on their own (e.g. Danish or Brazilian for Ibn Nagel Rasmussen and Roberta Carreras) traditions and least at ease when trying to incorporate aspects of eastern forms. But Barba's theory (backed by a number of heavyweight Italian academics via Barba's International School of Theatre Anthropology [ISTA]), like Schechner's, both refocuses (and partially distorts) Indian performance for the west, and at the same time offers a useful model for approaching it, provided caution is exercised.

A few other more general implications of a performance-oriented approach to theatre and drama theory are worth mentioning.

We always perform. Our life is a series of dynamic acts. Our 'self' (individual and national) is composed, extended and reconstructed in and through forms of behaviour. If we are to understand how and why we form psychological and social meanings for ourselves, we need to look at how and why we perform.

As we perform, we learn. Learning is always transformation as it is performance. We learn and we are transformed through the interaction of experience and neural stimuli which are affected in quite specific, though complex, ways by the kind and quality of performance we participate in. For Schechner, 'performance training' is a way of learning how to perform feelings (activate and receive their meaning) through verbal and non-verbal (face, voice, gesture, movement) channels which stimulate 'highs' (extremes of brain functioning) to the maximum degree of output and receptivity.

Such transformative intentions are of course also clear in *Natya Sastra*, Aristotle, and Plato; they emerge in the words and actions of, for example, *The Tempest*. Performance is the activation of theory, but it is also the articulation of it. Just as it appears more justifiable to speak of a *performance-text*, so it may be more appropriate to speak of *performance-theory* (and the hyphen is obligatory). Or indeed theories, since Indian theatre, like other forms of theatre, has been and continues to be approached from a number of different perspectives. I look at ways in which other varieties of performance theory can contribute to an understanding of Indian theatre see below.

Theory and Sanskrit Drama

Where, prior to around 1960, Indian drama has been discussed by western critics, it has mainly been with reference to the (relatively few) known Sanskrit texts and in the context of a debate about the presence, absence, or importance of two modes or genres: tragedy, which in conventional understanding does not feature in Sanskrit drama, and the realistic, which is accorded only fringe status. Comparison is usually made with Aristotle and Shakespeare; Goethe, who was appreciative of Kalidasa, sometimes gets a mention, though his dramatic work is not often discussed, and his theory of drama not at all.

I don't want to rehearse these issues at great length, because they figure in many other accounts; but I do take up below the question of tragedy, in order to attempt to balance eastern and western models. Parallels or oppositions between *catharsis* and *rasa* as modes in aesthetic experience emerge in the course of the extended discussion of the latter. However, the point I want to make first is that most of the pre-1960 debates were conducted by people who had possibly not actually seen any Indian theatre in performance and for the most part were certainly not familiar with the performance context in which the limited sample they were dealing with is situated. Chapters 2 and 3 indicate the range of this context and the complicated links between the various strands in it. Sanskrit drama may represent a kind of poetic quintessence (just as Sanskrit itself is for Vedic scholarship held to be a linguistic quintessence); but that in itself might suggest that close examination would discover the embryonic form of *all* modes and genres, and neither the tragic nor the realistic would be excluded – as indeed they are neither from 'folk' forms nor from modern reworkings of epic material. Part of the intention of these reworkings by e.g. K.N. Panikkar is consciously to demonstrate that Sanskrit drama works in performance. The text – performance – reception model from the previous chapter may be appropriate here also.

The term *Natya* refers to all theatrical performance activity:

> There is no knowledge, no craft, no learning, no art, no yoga, no action which one cannot find in *Natya*.
>
> (*NS*, I, 116.)

> *Natya* is not a motionless picture of the Universe but it reflects the dynamic nature of the world characterised by incessant flux of happiness and despair ... The need to reflect that flux ... postulates ... a means of expression which itself will have motion or movement for its nature
>
> (Byrski 1974, 101).

Byrski here (his book is concerned with Sanskrit drama) emphasises the dynamic nature of performance. This is important since Sanskrit drama has to some extent been regarded as a precious but ethereal specimen, a kind of crystallised poeticisation. It is not the only seed form of Indian performance; but even were it to be considered so, it is less easily dismissed than some critics have thought. Byrski further goes on to link this dynamic quality with the issue of 'tragedy' and to begin to outline a structure or 'through line' for Sanskrit drama which suggests that the possibility of the tragic is indeed not merely within its scope but structurally and psychologically essential.

A similarly dynamic model is applied to the *language* of the *Natya Sastra* by Bedi (see below, p. 123), suggesting that performative understandings of theory and of even the most 'fossilised' objects of theory are required.

Sanskrit drama is generally analysed as having five phases, joined by *sandhis* (dramatic junctures): *mukha* (opening); *pratimukha* (progression); *garbha* (womb, inner sanctum); *vimarsa* (pause, silence); *nirvahana* (conclusion); the terms also refer to areas of a temple building. Byrski compares the course of drama to that of sacrifice, or action for a particular end, which passes through: 'desire, effort and continuation of it, disruption and final completion' (Byrski 1974, 136).

Byrski concurs with traditional interpretations of stages one to three ('Eagerness or desire; Effort; Possibility of attainment', 104), but discusses at length the traditional rendering of the fourth stage (*niyatapti*) as 'certainty of success'. Byrski produces numerous examples from plays, as well as arguments for a different linguistic interpretation, in support of an alternative version for which the closest literal reading would be 'suppressed success', that is to say *loss* of certainty, or emergence of doubt. When aligned with other possible models of the stages of development of action (see diagram below), this looks even more plausible, and it largely does away with the recurrent problem that critics have come up against, namely the apparent lack of any conflict or possible tragic vision in Sanskrit drama. Byrski implies therefore that the origin of the problem is linguistic, and Indian critics subsequently felt obliged to interpret the facts (the action of the plays) in support of the apparently authoritative theory, however odd this might appear (it is relatively commonplace human practice, not least in science). Byrski goes back to the texts and indicates that there are many lengthy and important examples of this fourth stage where the heading of doubt or difficulty fits the action far better than an attempt to argue for the notion of certainty of success (Byrski, 104–112).

At what stage does this phase of doubt/*peripeteia*/loss enter? After the project has become fully materialised and its extent realised, at which point the obstacles to its attainment are most sharply in focus, most concretely present. They dominate the awareness, which loses touch with the initial impetus or desire.

In both Indian and western dramatic structure, this essentially psychological or psychodynamic sequence arrives at a position of setback or hesitation after considerable elaboration of the project but before its completion: i.e. approximately three-quarters of the way through. Even in 'folk' forms in India, the biggest battles take place just before the end (just before dawn in a traditional all-nighter).

This stage or situation can also be experienced as loss or forgetting and is remedied by what then figures as revelation, restitution or remembering (*anamnesis*). Dushyanta forgets Shakuntala, or Shakuntala is abandoned by Dushyanta; in Bhasa's *Vision of Vasavadatta*, King Udayana believes his wife Vasavadatta to be dead. The context in which to understand this is given by Drew as follows: 'the purpose of *Sakuntala* is to induce in the audience an agonizing awareness of one predominant sentiment: pathos at the separation of the girl and her lover ... the final scene exists so that the characters may be reconciled to each other and the audience to itself' (1987, 61). The metaphysical truth reflected is that 'the pain and misunderstanding of separation is ultimately illusory, arising from a forgetfulness that there is only harmony' (62). The curse laid upon Dushyanta is precisely to forget this; in other words, it is the everyday situation that we take *maya* for reality. At the sign of the ring (harmony) he 'unforgets'. Udayana, rather like Leontes in *The Winter's Tale*, is treated to an 'unveiling' scene in which what he thought was dead is returned to him alive. In each case the characters have to live fully through the experience of losing, abandoning, being abandoned; similar phases of exile, loss, death of close relatives etc. occur at regular intervals in the epics. The dramatic experience for the audience deliberately includes both forgetting (being fully involved in the pathos) and subsequent remembering.

Another slant on this model is to see it in terms of desire and its deferral/fulfilment, (i.e. a plot of internal drives, creative trajectories, psychobiology and/or systemic dynamics); this could be mapped alongside Stanislavskian intention and through-line, Brechtian *gestus*, Aristotelian plot and action paradigms.

Byrski also applies a process model to plot with reference to concepts and functions of 'act'/action/actor. His discussion of plot in Sanskrit drama (1974, 103ff) interestingly suggests that the five divisions enunciated by *Natya Sastra* under different subtitles can be most directly applied to the nature of action itself. Plot thus becomes the articulation of the path from intuition through desire to achievement, and is applicable not only to the sequence of the play as a whole, but also to individual actions within that sequence and to the way in which each actor carries them out. We are moving here in the same area as Stanislavsky's investigation of objectives and super-objectives, and of the role of through-line and obstacles in the process of carrying out an intention. We are also close to the (post-Stanislavskian) technique developed by e.g. Max Stafford-Clark and Mike Alfreds of 'actioning', linked to Austin's speech-act theory and aiming to explore the sub-textual dynamics of each utterance in terms of its active dramatic force (i.e. each line of dialogue is analysed as an action: 'what am I *doing* here to whom?' is the question which the actor has to ask). Another parallel is psychological investigation of the nature of desire (e.g. Kristeva, Lacan), which I discuss further below. Each strand of text is thus revealed as an act, and this microcosmic sense of act is reproduced in the sequence of parts or 'acts' of the play. This essentially holographic model of a play helps to bring to light the organicity and dynamism of performance.

Byrski glosses it as follows: 'this concept concerns an "actor", i.e. expresses the course of action from the point of view of an "actor" or doer. Each action consciously undertaken by its "actor" has to be carried through these five stages. They, of course, may be of different duration and importance. Nevertheless, for a doer, there will always be a moment at which there is a desire born in him to do this or that. Next comes concrete effort to achieve the purpose ... followed by the possibility of success. Yet before the final victory there is always a stage at which there is an actual attempt of an adverse force to disrupt an action, or at least, as *Natya Sastra* says, "a possibility of such a disruption present in the mind of an actor". Thus an action stripped of all its specific distinctions, of all its side-effects and accidental complications is reduced to a concept of pure action. Such a concept borders on physics and reminds of the vectors of force ...' (Byrski 1974, 113).

If the structure of the drama enacts the course of desiring, so may the content (desire for 'victory', successful outcome, alliance, restoration of what was lost). All these can point beyond themselves or work as a code for the goal of completion, wholeness, comprehension. There are further parallels with Shakespeare's *The Tempest* and *The Winter's Tale*: these plays close with scenes of 'magic' restoration, for which preceding loss is the catalyst, and which requires protagonist and audience to move beyond what seems credible ('it is required you do awake your faith': *Winter's Tale* V,3) or what is contained in systems familiar or unfamiliar ('I'll drown my book': *Tempest* V,I).

In western tragedy the protagonist usually achieves this soaring insight 'too late' (Lear's rediscovery of his full humanity, Hamlet's cleansing of the sores of state). There are several causes for this:

(i) lack of understanding of the nature and implications of the initial desire/project (*Lear, Hamlet*);
(ii) failure of initial project (*Othello, Macbeth, Coriolanus*);
(iii) disastrous distortion of original project, usually through 'external' – political, moral – influences *Troilus and Cressida, Romeo and Juliet*, parts of *Oresteia, Anthony and Cleopatra, Julius Caesar, Andromaque, Le Cid, Phèdre*).

In all these situations 'disruption' occurs and the protagonists, unable to surmount the confusion of personal and public drives and duties, end as emblems of loss, disaster or failure; the works themselves nevertheless leave behind a hint of better things, an image of completion ('perfect' love, wise statecraft, valour). The 'real' outcome serves to point up the sense of loss precisely because the protagonists look capable of more; the frequent conventional closure scene often contains a wry admission that 'we shall not see their like again'. Significantly, what they aim at involves always some form of extension beyond or redefinition of the intellectual or emotional confines of the 'single self'. The reasons for their failure are too complex to go into here, but it is important that even that loss points beyond itself; otherwise it would not register *as* loss in the minds of the receivers.

Here is a scheme, incorporating a number of different angles, disciplines and cultural models, which offers some parallels to Byrski's model:

para > pasyanti > madhyama+ > vaikhari+ > utterance

arambha > yatna > praptisambhava > niyatapti > phalagama

beginning > effort > poss.attainment > doubt* > attainment

goal > departure > tests > battle/woman > achievement

conception > separation > individuation > angst > union

desire > intention > action > resistance > fulfilment

intuition > expression > embodiment > obstacle > realisation

formtrieb > idea > materialisation > resistance > completion

impulse > initiation > quest > loss > restoration

annunciation > embodiment > acts > mortality > salvation

(Derived from *The Bible, Faust, Mahabharata, Ramayana*, Jung, Sanskrit linguistics and philosophy, Schiller, Aristotle, Sanskrit drama, quest narrative ...; * indicates Byrski's term; + indicates that at these levels of language there is a gap or lack of complete integration between sign and signified.)

This suggests that the basic structure recurs in many forms. Naturally in actual experience, time-scales and rhythms differ, events sometimes appear insignificant when they are the reverse, and so on. But it seems possible to trace a similar pattern for the operation and progression of intention towards outcome.

Often in western forms the outcome is distorted, postponed, or only supplied as a kind of conventional closure – which nevertheless signals the desire for both aesthetic and psychological completion, for a state of balance or wholeness, even while it articulates the belief that it is unlikely to prove available because the protagonists (i.e. human beings) are not up to it or some external forces (gods, fate or history) will not permit it. What appears to dominate is a confusion of needs and wants, a misreading of the personal and the political and/or their interface, a lack of ability fully to frame the parameters of desire. Entropy, absurdity, mischance, and chaos reign.

On the other hand this may indicate that most desires get diverted, blocked or transposed, so that even when they are fulfilled they're not quite the same as when they started out: Olivia gets Sebastian, not Viola; revengers get revenge but also invite it; the 'I' which formulated the original desire is no longer the 'I' which enjoys its fulfilment because the journey of the play intervenes. Homecomings are not always what anticipation constructed them as. On the journey, the desired, the desiring and the desirer undergo radical transformation.

Indian aesthetics and psychology does not seem to see the problem in quite the same way. Protagonists get it wrong; even the gods are frequently not up to the mark; there are plenty of wars and other disasters. So it is not a question of a simplistically idealistic vision of human action. But, just as the aesthetic prescription for *rasa* targets a state of completeness of perception and apprehension beyond everyday parameters, so the forms of theatre which seek to produce that state take a different perspective in both structure and content: loss, misapprehension, doubt and destruction are not only, and not finally, what they seem to be: they are also Shiva-like agents and impellers of a further stage. Vedic linguistics identifies levels of language and possibilities of experience which are prior to fixed codes (see below), so falling into loss and doubt need not be only falling back into the undifferentiated; and Vedic aesthetics proposes a stage which, as amalgam of all possible codes, bursts through them into the real, into unmediated total experience: the theatre of origin, the theatreing of becoming.

This investigation of the forms of desiring makes it possible to trace similarities, though not identities, between Sanskrit, Greek, Shakespearean and other forms, as well as in methodologies of acting which work through the structure and course of intention and execution. Both Stanislavsky's model of (intellectual and emotional) intention and Grotowski's and Barba's work on physical dynamics identify a stage of resistance which is in fact crucial to the actor's further development of the psychology and physiology of character. As Chapter 2 has indicated, there is also a structure of desire underlying narrative, which plays an important part in impelling the outgrowth of performance.

At the same time I want to qualify what might appear to be a tendency to 'universalise' a formula. Firstly, the parallels suggested in the table above are similarities, not exact parallels. Secondly, several other plausible schemes exist. Thirdly, some Indian plays, contemporaneous or prior to Sanskrit drama, offer a different model, as do many plays from other traditions. The purpose of pointing out parallels is not to claim homogeneity for all drama, but to indicate one important dynamic which drives significant parts of it.

For instance, Chandrika outlines a structural model for drama containing ritual elements, including Bhasa, but also Eliot's *Murder in the Cathedral*, Sophocles' *Oedipus Rex*, Shaffer's *Royal Hunt of the Sun* and Panikkar's *Karimkutty*, which has four stages:

annunciation > advent > sacrifice/ > rebirth/
                          death/   > resurrection/
                          crucifixion > canonization
                                    (Chandrika, 1993, 110).

This scheme is slightly different from the one I outline above: there is one 'missing', but not crucial, stage, which is effectively an extension of Chandrika's 'advent' into Byrski's 'continuation of effort'. We seem to have here an extension of the argument linking ritual and tragedy, of which the most famous western example is the 'Cambridge anthropologists'' thesis about the origins of Greek drama. Schechner for one is dismissive of this as theatre history, but admits that he has drawn on it in performance. So it may 'work' in practice: Byrski's comments about action suggest this.

Before going further with this issue, here is a brief look at some other models. Schechner advances a triangular or pyramidal model which fits much tragedy, but balances it with an 'open-ended' version which seems more appropriate to post-Absurdist theatre; Japanese *Noh* also works with a three-stage model (*jo-ha-kyu*) which relates to breath, phases of action and macro-structure; Turner proposes the four stages of breach–crisis–redressive action–reintegration, relating this specifically to drama having a social function. The differences in the models derive mainly from slightly different computations of the initiation and duration of phases. They all try to account for *process* features and they all perceive the energy which drives the events forward as passing through a phase of containment or loss, followed (actually or potentially) by restitution. In post-Absurd theatre and in some tragedy (for instance *Titus Andronicus*), not much beyond loss or chaos seems to be available, but I will pick that up later.

What Byrski is proposing, and I am following up, is a way of linking internal process and structural function. Schechner points out that Turner's model (and by implication, others) is contained and underpinned by another level of structure, that of the performance event. The gathering/performing/dispersing rhythm of the event is 'solidarity, not conflict' (Schechner 1988, 168). So whether we are talking about ritual, 'classic' tragedy or even open-ended 'loss' of all secure parameters, the event itself represents a structure of recuperation, parallel to Prospero's appeal to the audience at the end of *The Tempest*: 'And my ending is despair/Unless I be relieved by prayer[…]/Let your indulgence set me free'.

The tragic 'ennobles' in some sense. We are, because both involved and distanced, offered a frame by which not merely to see but also to understand. Even in the abyss of horror (*Titus, Macbeth*) or the blankness of desolation (Godot doesn't come, humans go round and round the same cage), the play itself is this frame. Maybe we cannot 'understand' in any conventional sense. But we have to try, being human. We have therefore to pass through the state of not understanding. The experience of loss (for the audience) is a necessary impetus to access a different mode of understanding. All Symbolic comfort is left behind and only the real remains. A model which encompasses the 'inner' action of the play, its overt function (ritual, socialisation, education, uplift), its dramatic or dynamic structure and its event-structure allows us the chance to take that step beyond knowledge and understanding of an everyday kind. Paniker's remark about the (ritual) performer quoted in Chapter 2 is relevant to the play and the event too: if you could do it yourself (in the 'normal' course of your daily life), you wouldn't get someone }

go somewhere} else to do it.

This discussion suggests both that Sanskrit models, in line with Byrski's argument, include the possibility of the tragic, and that taking this awareness into consideration locates both the aesthetics and the practice of Sanskrit drama as capable of making a significant contribution to debate about dramatic form and its effects. I am to some extent here eliding/'tragedy' and 'conflict', since I see the potential or actual existence of a tragic perspective as necessarily engendering a conflict or dialectic of viewpoints and outcomes; conflict on a more mundane level is present in the sequence of events – misunderstandings between lovers, curses by relatives etc., – although in the overall scheme of things it can be said to serve a positive function by signalling a need and/or desire to deal with issues which might otherwise have remained unspoken.

One indication that Indian theatre does not consider the exploration of such difficult or oppositional modes irrelevant is in the frequency of stagings of, for instance, *King Lear* and *Macbeth*. The latter particularly seems to have a central place in Indian stage history (see also Chapter 6). Within its own ancient repertoire, the Tamil classic *Shilappadikaram* (The Ankle Bracelet) ends, not with resolution, but with the cursing and destruction of the city of Madurai by the anguished heroine, whose husband has been unjustly executed although he has been unfaithful. This work probably predates Sanskrit theatre; its major focus on a female protagonist is echoed by the 'sequel' *Manimekhalai*, which centres on the daughter of the dancer for whom the wife in *Shilappadikaram* has been deserted. The protagonists' experience in these plays passes through abandonment, desolation and violent reaction comparable to that discussed in *Medea* as created by Samarth (see below, pp. 138–9); like Beckett or Ionesco, it involves an anatomisation or explosion of the Symbolic.

The *Natya Sastra*

In Chapter 1 some account is given of the *Natya Sastra*, a comprehensive theory-cum-manual to which all Indian performance aesthetics and reception theory refers back. Details of what the *Natya Sastra* covers can be found in Meyer-Dinkgräfe 1996 and Kale 1974. Meyer-Dinkgräfe indicates that western practitioners like Grotowski, Barba, Schechner and Brook have also derived much of their understanding of Indian forms from direct or indirect contact with *Natya Sastra*. The work thus remains central to approaches from whatever direction to Indian theatre of all periods. I take up below aspects of Meyer-Dinkgräfe's discussion of the experience of actors and audience, and of the modes of consciousness necessary to sustain these.

There are two original versions of *Natya Sastra* and many variations. Version 1 has 12,000 *slokas* (verses), the other 6,000. 1 was first edited fully in 1894, 2 in 1929, and there is an edition containing all variants (Baroda, 1926–1964). The original dates in all probability from before 300AD, certainly from before AD 1,000. It is attributed to Bharata: maybe one or more authors, possibly a tribe or clan name (for actors?). The most readily available English version is the literal rendering edited by Manmohan Ghosh (Ghosh, 1951–61).

The statement that the *Natya Sastra* contains everything is a frequent Vedic scriptural claim (*Mahabharata* is said to contain everything too) but the claim has some justification given its extensive scope and, like other Vedic texts, the writing is always nugatory and allusive: they aim (*Natya Sastra* explicitly so) to take the reader/receiver to a state in which s/he is operating at subtle interpretative levels where meanings proliferate and possibilities of interpretation abound.

The detailed instructions on such things as the eight *rasas*, the various *mudras* and body positions, on decor and costume, voice-production and rhythm and so on take up many chapters in the *Natya Sastra* and have been summarised and repeated quite frequently (e.g. in Iyer on Kathakali: Iyer, 1983; Kale 1974). Taken together, they indicate a comprehensive and precise awareness of how theatrical semiosis in all its forms creates imaginative worlds, predating Keir Elam's *Semiotics of Theatre and Drama* by at least one millennium.

Here it will be helpful to recall two main points:

(i) the centrality to the *Natya Sastra* of the theory of *rasa*, which views performance as an attempt to cultivate the receptive faculties of the receivers; 'rich' performance activates a whole range of channels of response whose aim is a condition of *samhita*, or wholeness.

(ii) the *Natya Sastra* is known as the 'fifth Veda' which unifies the other four; it has a venerable and indeed sacred status within the field of Indian thought.

The second point is interesting in that a theory of *performance* commands such respect: in common with philosophical under-standings of *maya*, the transient is not seen as irrelevant or inferior, but rather as the manifestation and forming of creative intelligence. India therefore traditionally accords to performance a precise recognition of its profound value which is, for instance, lacking almost entirely in Islamic societies and frequently downplayed in Christian ones.

As I put it in Chapter I, performance is understood as an individual and communal act which aims at the transcendence of everyday limits of consciousness by the precise cultivation of holistic functioning of multi-channelled awareness. Hence the interest from western practitioners; hence also the need, in contemporary India, to match the tasks and possibilities of performance in the current situation to a sense of its purpose as proposed by *Natya Sastra*.

Rasa, soma, 'neutrality' and performance

Central to the *Natya Sastra* is the concept of *rasa*, usually translated as essence or flavour. The aim of performance is to create *rasa*: so it is more than a concept, it is a psychophysiological condition in performers and receivers which marks a transformation of behavioural state. The 'taste' or 'flavour' is the intuition of wholeness, the aesthetic experience of not merely receiving a given configuration but actively participating in its creation, in the enactment of meaning. Here 'seeing is an activity in its own right ... theatre has no meaning without the perception and imaginative intervention of the *sahridaya* ("of open heart"), whose sensibility has been trained not just to receive the secret messages of a performance, but to participate [in] (and thereby create) its phenomenological immediacy' (Bharucha 1993, 44). Borges, probably quoting several other people, locates the aesthetic experience *per se* as the moment in which we experience 'the imminence of a revelation which does not occur' (Borges 1962, 223), implying some kind of dual vision, of seeing both the veil and what might be behind it.

There has been considerable debate as to whether performers as well as receivers access some or all of this condition: *Natya Sastra* itself can be read both ways, and Meyer-Dinkgräfe draws on this ambiguity to illustrate one case of the paradox he views as central to considerations of the effects of performance. I discuss this dual condition below; however, in view of what I suggested in Chapter 1 (about self, other and freedom) and of descriptions of performance practice in some traditional forms in Chapter 2, it seems highly likely that a similar shift of functioning occurs in both parties.

Pramod Kale, in *The Theatric Universe*, indicates the relation between *rasa* and *soma* (Kale, 1974, 81–2). In the *Vedas, soma* is often described as a 'libation' and has generally been assumed to be some kind of intoxicant derived from a plant (it's always present at ritual invocations of divine forces and plays a major role in the achievement of the desired goals). According to the *Natya Sastra*, drama is the highest form of offering to the 'gods': 'the person or persons who present a good performance as an offering will be blessed and attain to the highest bliss'.

Throughout this book I adopt an attitude to statements like this which is consistent, as I see it, with an understanding of *rasa* and of the aesthetic function of art in Sanskrit tradition. But it should be made explicit here. Whenever references are made to 'gods' and 'divine' attributes, I interpret these to be related to specific modes of functioning, kinds of experience and ways of achieving such modes and experiences. That is to say, they can be understood as experience of certain conditions of consciousness available to human life; to experience 'bliss' (and the Sanskrit term *ananda* refers equally to aesthetic and spiritual delight) means therefore to be in a specific state or mode of functioning. The integrative and coherent mental, physical and psychological functioning which enables maximum efficacy in the production and reception of drama is one means to instigate such a state.

The more common interpretation ('intoxicant') is rooted in a view which regards everything in external terms and attempts to explain 'sacrifices' away as 'primitive' demonstrative behaviour aimed at communicating with gods thought to reside 'out there' in the universe, be it as creative instances or as natural forces. This model itself rests on the unproven, though usually in western tradition unquestioned, assumption that inner and outer worlds are entirely distinct, that subject and object can be fully distinguished from each other, and that practices which seek to explore the ground between these realms can safely be relegated to the category of the primitive and the irrational – where 'irrational' itself becomes a derogatory term and indicates that forms of consciousness which might not fit the current criteria of rationality are considered inferior.

It should be obvious from what has been said so far that neither Indian performance nor Vedic aesthetic theory necessarily subscribes to such views. It makes more sense then to look for possible alternative understandings of the state represented by the terms *soma* and *rasa*. There is in fact at least one major parallel in western performance history: in Dionysian cultural and ritual practice the performer was said to be *entheos*: not just 'enthused' or 'intoxicated' but 'in the state of a god'. (Other parallels exist in accounts of the nature and purpose of shamanistic performance.) *Soma* is also sometimes rendered as 'the glue of the universe'. In other words it promotes a 'divine' state of ease in which all connections are available, it is a sufficient condition for perceptual activity in total openness. In this it is similar to the preconditions of *poesis* sought by many artists and may link to the states of psychic or physical 'overdrive' or 'flow' experienced by performers in many fields. Kale implies that *rasa* and *soma* indicate a state of bliss (*ananda*), as the *Upanishads* would put it. Hence also *soma*'s oft-indicated role (especially in the *Rg Veda*) as progenitor, basis of fertility, source of milk, curds and honey, provider of cattle (female) and horses (male), riches and strength.

It's important to emphasise the psychophysiological dimension of these concepts, because not only have they been largely invisible to western thought due to its resolutely Cartesian bias, but Indian scholarship has also largely succeeded in burying them under mountains of abstract philosophical commentary. Ritual, invocation and sacrifice are *performances* designed to achieve specific results for celebrants and participants. To look at them *as* performance is to relocate their essentially physical and practical function. They are practices intended to shift the metabolism, the physiology, and hence the perception of reality, into a style of functioning other than that operating in everyday behaviour, in order to attempt to bring closer together the mode of functioning of individual(s) and the complex of forces in which they necessarily operate. To alter the dynamics, if you like. In order to assume that this is possible it is necessary to bypass any rigid separation between mind (consciousness) and matter. Some twentieth-century physicists and biologists would not see particular problems with this (Einstein, Heisenberg, Schrödinger, Planck, Capra, David Bohm, Wheeler, Sheldrake, Prigogyne, Watson), although the legacy of nineteenth-century scientific conformism certainly does.

'Sacrifice' as I interpret it means engaging in a process which quite precisely edits out (gives up) the egocentric individuality, the frightened clinging to the frontiers and frameworks of the exclusively logocentric. It is an opening out to the unknown, to being as possibility, not as repetition. It is, as Copeau, Johnstone and Lecoq, among others, have realised, of prime importance for performers who wish to remain inventive and receptive to their co-performers and their audience. (See also Chapter 5 for some further discussion of the goals of these and other western theatre workers.) *Soma, rasa* and sacrifice are not exclusively esoteric concepts but rather key terms in an understanding of the dynamic of performance activity.

Antonio de Nicolás' profound investigation of the psycho-physiological demands embedded in the *Rg Veda's* structure, voices, rhythms and images discloses an underpinning practice of 'sacrifice', which he elucidates as a readiness to give up all recognised and comfortably inhabited structures and systems of thought and behaviour, to be prepared always and at any moment to shift out of idea into the immediacy of the moment in which consciousness and being are yoked: in terms recognisable to all performers in any field, to 'inhabit' that moment as the only one in which full being is available and in which, therefore, all possibilities of becoming reside. This closely parallels Ayyappa Paniker's perception, quoted in Chapter 3 (pp. 124–6) that the folk form Patayani presents just such a sacrifice and consequent relocation of 'self' beyond ordinary parameters. The same function of metatheatricality is identified by Nair and Paniker with reference to Kathakali ('multi-transformational acting') and related also to the audience in Sudhana Gopalakrishnan's comment on Kathakali, Kudiyattam and the role of the Sutradhara as foregrounding metatheatric devices which 'account for the "multi-consciousness" of the audience' (Gopalakrishnan 1993, 54).

The *Natya Sastra* indeed sees this state as a requisite not only for performers but also for audiences. Art is not diversion, escape, amusement: it is a means to wholeness of vision and to the integrated function of perception in more than ordinary modes.

Performances are in part, efforts to speak ourselves; yet also to overcome a sense of distance from ourselves which language tends to erect, by 'returning' to the immediacy of physical sensation. How can we get back to ourselves? If I want to perform, I want to be myself through performance. But performance is not a static situation. So I cannot ever be a singular entity through it. Maybe that is a kind of being of self, however. It could be called acting, and an actor is in one sense someone who can be many people, many tendencies, many voices, many physical and emotional rhythms and tones; it could also be the task of the spectator, who has to enter into and understand all the figures on stage and the totality of the significance of their interactions. Which therefore also means that I need to be able to access as many of the available states or modes of consciousness as possible, because although plurality, in terms of a multiplicity of personae or intercutting points of view, has a value in itself, expansion in a different plane opens up the possibility of multiplication rather than simple addition.

That needs some explanation. If my view of 'reality' is limited (or I allow myself to be convinced by dominant paradigms of thinking or language that this is the case) to what I experience in 'ordinary' waking consciousness, I will be able to access and juggle a very large number of phenomena, questions, emotions etc. If however I acknowledge that what I experience whilst dreaming is also real and significant in some sense, I open up another sphere, which may allow me a different perspective on the first one (some things I censor in sphere 1 may emerge in sphere 2 and offer me possibilities of understanding). The parallels between dreaming and art are fairly extensive, so sphere 2 is of general rather than merely particular significance. Indian performance is an even more extreme case of the generally true situation of theatre, which occurs in a 'different' time-and-space nexus, marking thus a transition into the time of sleep and dreaming (waking, sleep and dreaming are the three states acknowledged even by western psychology; Indian models add at least three others).

So performance is also a way of discovering liberation from the narrow confines of a prescribed epistemology, from claims that it is only possible to know and be like this. If this is so, it needs celebrating proudly and fiercely as a political and an individual right.

There is what seems to be a crucial phase or 'passage' in becoming aware of shifts in consciousness and the relationships between 'self' and 'world' which depend upon it. But it has to do with experiencing self as 'other', with loss of known boundaries and hence with a kind of falling out of certainties and systems into the performative now state of not knowing what comes next. If that sounds somewhat Keatsian it's not inappropriate; it is also at the heart of much western exploration of the improvisatory.

Like much that I am talking of, it is not found only or exclusively in India or Indian performance, but both these, as real experience and as image, can instigate it because of the degree of density and richness they embody. Let me offer four instances, each of which relates to an encounter with India or Indian culture.

At the beginning of his *Meditations through the Rg Veda*, Antonio de Nicolás describes his arrival in India as a kind of disintegration. 'The world, as I knew it, disappeared ... There was not even a world; just motion ... It was just like a live performance on an empty stage. But there was "more" performance than there was stage and this "more" flowed and ebbed with the suggestiveness of eternal life' (de Nicolás 1976, xv–xvi).

In *India and the Romantic Imagination*, John Drew traces encounters with the idea of India and the forms of its thought, and frames this account with a discussion of works by E.M.Forster and Alun Lewis. Mrs Moore's experience in the Marabar Caves in *A Passage to India* is a kind of negative Platonic vision; only subsequently is this sucking or booming out of everything she had taken to be sense revealed as the beginning of a new kind of relationship to things. Lewis seems to have intuited his own death whilst in India, and talks of a feeling of being immersed in flux; his last piece however records such an encounter with death as an opening and a liberation. When I first arrived in India (at a stage of mid-life crisis) I felt as though I was being forced to live 'inside out', with the rawness of sensation exposed; I felt myself responding to physical and emotional needs before they made themselves present to me as thoughts.

All these experiences are profoundly disorienting, even painful; they give rise to loss and panic. They are not so far, perhaps, from the nausea of Sartre's protagonist Roquentin at the ubiquitous and indivisible viscosity and flux of existence.

What they do to the experiencer is to crack open the familiar boundaries of conceptualisation and to expose the fragility of the known self. If de Nicolás's metaphor is significant, performance (if fully lived) does that too. My first experiences of all-night *Yakshagana* and *Kathakali* performance was of being subject to an extraordinary, spectacular, largely incomprehensible succession of sensory information through many different channels. I couldn't 'grasp' it in the way I was accustomed (though later of course I found some recurrent landmarks). But during these performances I was also relaxed, in a way in which the panic of my first few weeks in India didn't permit. Hence I was able rather more quickly to allow myself to accept the flow and begin both to enjoy it and to find ways of entering into it.

Although in one sense this account of a significant feature of performance appears to contradict the *Natya Sastra*'s goal of non-involved appreciation, I think that the *Natya Sastra* can accommodate an understanding of certain crucial stages in consciousness on the way towards more completeness. The abandonment of familiar moorings (Forster pun not entirely involuntary) is just such a stage, as Plato also knew. There seems too to be a link here with the visceral quality of performance and reception noted above with reference to *Theyyam*: the popular *Kathakali* version of the killing of Durodhyana by Bhima (involving a lot of red cloth representing Durodhyana's intestines and bordering on the pantomime) signals the troubling presence of blood and darkness as a stage in performance experience, though it may also to some extent sanitise or sterilise its impact. *Macbeth* and *Othello* have both received *Kathakali* treatment: both deal with encounters with the ungraspable otherness within and without, as emphasised by the title of Kurosawa's *Macbeth* adaptation, *Throne of Blood*.

The crucial stage then is what I have elsewhere called neutrality: stopping, shifting gear, getting out of habitual behaviour, gravitating to an underlying stillness or suspension of role or activity as the basis on which or against which other modes operate. The *Upanishads* refer to this as *turiya*. It is a pivotal condition which allows breaking free of the daily body and affords room for inception of different modes of activity. It has been categorised as a 'fourth state' of consciousness underlying the 'normal' daily pattern of waking, dreaming and sleeping: it has also been described as '"pure" consciousness' (Stace), 'consciousness without an object' (Merrell-Wolff) and 'the simplest state of consciousness' (Mahesh Yogi). The term 'state' is however slightly misleading (see also below) since it does not usually occur as a permanent or exclusive condition but rather as a momentary awareness or, where – as in the case of virtuoso functioning referred to above – it is of more lasting duration, it is more like a backcloth to 'everyday' conditions. Actor-trainers have sought to approach it in body and awareness through use of the neutral mask, or to describe it in concepts like Brook's 'empty space' of performance; processes which seek to institute a break from empathetic involvement, a kind of *Verfremdung*, an aesthetic distance in performers and/or receivers, also seem to be moving in this direction.

Such a condition is not so much grasped after as allowed to occur: it is a switching off, an absence of effort, a moving away from the familiar and the known. Invocation, hypnotic drumming, rhythm, the move outside daily activity into dreamtime, a shift of the interpreting mechanism from linear to associative, symbolic, poetic or from ratiocentric to intuitive, may be effective strategies to access it. Stop resisting, hanging on to the known form of identity and behaviour. Become a mote in the dance, a Beckettian emptiness, a hollow sign ready for play.

From here take the stillness and the balance (seen in the *tribhangi*, the basis of *Bharatanatyam*, and in similar physical and mental centredness in many other forms, where control and centring of the breath is also vital) and expose it to action. Keep going back and forward. Eventually the quality of the stillness begins to remain accessible even while action is occurring. Through alternation, action becomes 'double'. In this state, the performer is both involved and separate; the spectator is emotionally in sympathy and yet able to frame the event (*catharsis*). Meyer-Dinkgräfe points out that all the best-known attempts to look at actor-audience-text relationships since the seventeenth century have rested on some form of paradox: i.e. that these relationships crucial to performance seem to require an unusual conjunction of detachment and involvement, control and empathy, separateness and *communitas*, singularity and multiplicity and so on (Meyer-Dinkgräfe 1994). That is to say that current thinking not only sees the dynamics of performance situations as embracing most of the parameters of our individual and communal life, but also that they can be seen to require of their participants a more than ordinary conjunction of functioning which consistently transcends the boundaries of given categories.

Meyer-Dinkgräfe argues that in order to account for the nature of many of these paradoxes a model of 'mind' is required which extends beyond the Western divisions of mind/body and conscious/unconscious; such a model begins to be smuggled in, as it were, from Artaud onwards, in the (not fully acknowledged or always clearly understood) borrowing of Eastern concepts, frameworks and practices. (For a full account of such a model see Yarrow 1986(a) and 1986(b); and Malekin and Yarrow 1997.)

In the freedom of this non-involvement begins the play (even to enjoy a tragedy, for actors and receivers: it provides a fuller sense of self). The stillness is also potential, the balance is the readiness to move: so from it derives the display of possibilities which are not 'normally' available, perceived or understood. Here is the origination of *lila*, the dance of Shiva, the reinvention and recomposition of form.

As this continues so the scope of play increases, as more subtlety and more power of signification is released: more complex levels of textual meaning become available, greater richness of encoded action, more patterns to weave and to perceive. Experience moves more in the direction of the universal, in the sense of incorporating a wider range of meanings whilst still operating through specific verbal, rhythmic, gestural and auditory signals. The power to enact and to encompass this signals a move out of the ordinary. Not just an escalation of the everyday (even if fairly miraculous) multiple processing capacity of the brain, but a shift towards a situation in which perception and understanding are simultaneous and instantaneous. The 'playing subject' (which here means performer, performance and audience together) is the totality of what is occurring in the theatre space: *lila* acknowledged by *rasa*, so that all aspects of action are present to the consciousness of all involved. Metaphors of the theatre as world and of the world as theatre are both relevant from this state.

Ideally, that is. In fact I may have fallen asleep by now, because the kind of functioning this represents is precise and delicate and can be achieved only by a nervous system which is fully alert and elastic, able to sustain a paradoxical and 'stretched' condition uniting great relaxation and subtle focus. The usual process which occurs is that when the requirements become too much, the tired system falls asleep. If however I don't sleep, I am likely to experience something pretty joyful; and if I am not too tired, the process of performing or attending in this fully alive way to the performance may itself institute an increasing sense of enjoyment, not just 'at' the performance but derived from my own feeling of increasing well-being and coherent functioning. In other words, I am being recreated, refreshed, renewed.

Indira Bedi argues (Bedi, 1999) that the *Natya Sastra* can be read in terms of functional linguistics as developed by Halliday *et al*, as consisting of linguistic acts; and that *rasa* can likewise be understood as a linguistically encoded sequence of instructions of how to bring about a desired state, (that is to say, it constitutes a 'language' which works as a functional act). If you concede that the state that is desired (*rasa* in the fullest sense) could be described as highly integrated functioning of semiotic receptors and decoders (where the 'languages' received are understood in a wide sense to be gestural, aural, visual etc. as well as verbal and/or written), leading to a condition in which on the one hand the full range of semiosis is available, and on the other hand the participant/receiver is not submerged by detail but enjoying a sense of aesthetic harmony; then it seems to me that you have begun to lay out an equivalence between language and performance which for its fullest exposition needs the following: i) a model of language which includes not merely the fully articulated but also 'pre-expressive' or sensed levels of meaning; and ii) a model of consciousness which can account for the paradoxical state in which such levels are fully apprehended.

The opening of *Rg Veda* is useful as a demonstration of this possibility, because it can be analysed in terms of such models.

The opening words are: 'Agnimile purohitam': literally 'I behave towards *Agni* ("god of fire") in a priest-like (*purohit*) manner'. In traditional interpretation, I perform a fire-sacrifice; or I perform a *puja* (ritual ceremony designed to produce good influences in which a symbolic flame is used). Clearly both these glosses imply action with the intention of producing a result; and they suggest that *Rg Veda* can therefore be seen as proceeding from, perhaps elaborating or extending, that intention. The interpretations are quite plausible. But there is another level of possible understanding. This involves a different orientation towards subjectivity and objectivity. Instead of viewing the world as 'out there' and seeing actions as something performed to or upon it as 'other' (placating fundamental energies, like fire, for example), it requires a readiness to elide the boundaries between 'inner' and 'outer' and to regard the action undertaken as operating in both spheres simultaneously. In other words, doing something to 'Agni' means engaging with a level at which transformative activity can be initiated (fire is the agent of transformation, of destruction and reordering) – a level which is available both 'within' and 'without'. In this reading, 'behaving in a priest-like manner' can be interpreted as getting on a level with these (divine, or universal) energies or forces. This suggests a physical and psychological state of dynamic equilibrium from which action may result, or indeed 'play' may occur (recalling also Byrski's 'vector of forces').

The *Natya Sastra* is similar to the *Rg Veda* in that it sets out to achieve a result, and that result is the establishment of a particular condition, which in the metaphoric discourse of the period is understood as participation in the 'divine play' of the world. It is in this sense that the *Natya Sastra* is also a '*Veda*', in that the *Vedas* do not simply record the belief in such a condition or possibility, but serve as means to achieve it: the (canted) *performance* of the *Vedas* by *pundits* produces the desired effect as a result of the rhythmic and harmonious qualities of the language – provided it is, as the oral tradition caters for, repeated incessantly for long periods – repetition being a means of producing gradual change in the receiving mechanism.

To arouse one's capacity to operate on this kind of level is probably not far removed from the goal of many writers. Hofmannsthal's writer-protagonist Lord Chandos (in 'The Letter of Lord Chandos') speaks of a condition in which language flows (Hofmannsthal 1952); the French Symbolist poet Paul Valéry thinks of it as the 'state of poetry' (Valéry 1957). Quantum physicist David Bohm speaks of 'implicate orders' of matter which contain the blueprint for the more 'explicate' (Bohm, 1980) and speculates that they are not separate from but contiguous with the forms of consciousness which comprehend them.

These situations appear to be at the junction of matter and consciousness, the 'inner' and the 'outer'. Most systems of linguistic categorisation in general use begin with utterance. Common sense, however, suggests that something precedes this which is still an operation with or in language. 'I know what I want to say but I can't put it into words'; an experience which is not just about being inarticulate or having a poor vocabulary, but more frequently reflects a sense that what 'I' am trying to get at is important, complex or profound in some way which as yet refuses to be pinned down in words. And if the experience is followed through with patience, what often emerges is something like the writer's shaping of an idea, which seems like a new insight. I think this matter-of-fact experience indicates a level of linguistic processing which many writers are not unfamiliar with, but which is also part of most people's life.

Sanskrit grammarian Panini has a term for this level, and for one further level which perhaps corresponds to an even more 'implicate' structuring: *pasyanti* (the often dimly intuited, felt but not-yet-grasped) and *para* (the potential of all semiosis). (I rather think Julia Kristeva's 'semiotike' is after one or both of these. You can see why if you consider the Hofmannsthal reference again, which indicates something rather different from the discriminative rational level.)

We need these terms because the *Natya Sastra* and the *Rg Veda* are aiming for the maximum condition of receptive and participative functioning. One way and another, they aim to instigate that through language as performance – including the non-verbal senses of 'language'. What they are after is activation of the full range of meaning-creation.

Performance here then is the activation of *desire*: desire understood in a Lacanian/Derridean way as the barest trace of intentionality, and yet at the same time only achievable in full if located prior to expressed language, in the *para* state defined by Panini. If performance activates this situation of desiring production from this level for all participants, it is both an aesthetic and a political act in the fullest sense.

The account in this chapter of the aesthetics of *Natya Sastra* and Sanskrit drama has largely drawn on traditional (Vedic-derived) interpretations. I have attempted however (i) to frame these to some extent by preceding them by a discussion of performance theory, and (ii) to offer ways of understanding some of the traditional formulations in a more down-to-earth way. But a further question needs to be asked about the declared goal of theatre experience as constructed by the *Natya Sastra*: how in terms of our actual experience when present at a performance can we evaluate *rasa*?

The discussion so far has included many references to what may loosely be called 'altered states', though as Meyer-Dinkgräfe indicates, this term is not unproblematic (1994, 65–69). Although contemporary (largely western) theories generally substitute other terms which imply less a fixed state than a (performative) condition, the weight of critical doctrine in the Indian tradition tends to present *rasa* and the associated condition of being a *rasika* or adept as an ultimate and therefore in large measure permanent goal, a sort of elevated status which one reaches and remains in. Like most ideals,

I suggest that this appears a great deal more solid than it really is in practice. In fact it might be said to be a superb example of *maya*. Perhaps the most profound realisation of this comes, not in the work of Kalidasa or Bhasa, but from Prospero in *The Tempest*, when he discards the cloak which has appeared to give him divine powers.

Many Indian theoreticians and philosophers of Vedic aesthetics — not to mention academics and even politicians — give the appearance of believing themselves to have entered such a state permanently. These usually elderly, male, white-clad divinities, who often specialise in what might be called *sloka*-dropping (intoning Sanskrit aphorisms from time to time), claim veneration on the basis of their ability to discourse about such states rather than any evidence that they live them. They represent what Maharishi Mahesh Yogi succinctly described as 'mood-making'.

In contrast, the mechanics by which consciousness may function in different modes, taken together with the remarks throughout the book so far about the nature of performance acts, might suggest another scenario. As noted above, the different stages which signal facets of *rasa* tend to occur initially as momentary flashes or still points; by moving back and forth between these moments and periods of 'normal' perception, the stillness or distanciation is subsequently experienced along with discriminative perception. Background and foreground exist together and either can be brought more into focus. An appropriate analogy (a version of Plato's cave, perhaps), would be watching a performance in which the receiver distinguishes three different levels: in the 'foreground', as it were, are figures operating in localised space-time and performing specific verbal and physical acts; on a second level one is aware that they are not merely particularised but also symbolic, archetypal or generalised representations of human characteristics or modes of behaviour across time; 'behind' both of these is an unmoving backcloth against which their movement is visible (if it were identical with that movement in colour and form they would be invisible).

What happens here is then something like a condition of porosity in which different kinds of functioning and different qualities of awareness co-exist. As with driving a car, awareness is enabled to shift gears because the driver has discovered how to move through neutral; but neither the condition of neutrality nor that of overdrive are permanently engaged. Everyday operations are still required (and you can't get into overdrive except by passing through the other gears ...). Performance can be a useful way of instigating what is itself essentially a (supremely) performative faculty. Seen in this light, *rasa* does not appear quite so ideal or esoteric as some commentaries suggest, and it is clear that it can have benefits which are applicable to whatever mode of reality one is currently constructing.

The experimental South Indian dancer Chandralekha, says Bharucha, emphasised 'the liberational possibilities of *rasa* through its capacity to "recharge" human beings' (Bharucha 1995, 129); he views this 'drive towards "regeneration of the human spirit"' as 'nothing short of radical' in a period in which 'the human body is a target of attack'.

ETHICS AND POLITICS

Introduction

Those theoretical approaches which dominate contemporary critical practice — Marxist/historicist/post-colonialist, theatre anthropology (Barba), anthropology of theatre (Turner/Schechner), feminist — position themselves partly or largely with reference to the politics and ethics of performative events and their function in social dynamics (see also below, Chapter 5). But, given the nature of the contemporary debate in India about theatre, culture and politics, they need also to be placed alongside and considered in the light of the aesthetic tradition which has been outlined. Whether or not contemporary practice consciously sees itself as operating a more dialogic relationship with traditional values, it remains engaged in extensive and intensive debate with them. Although it is focused on ethics and cultural politics, this debate rarely loses sight of the ways in which Indian performance is rooted in the traditional — including an ongoing debate with *Natya Sastra* — and has in the contemporary situation to find ways of re-energising it. It thus remains committed to a view of performance as efficacy rather than simply entertainment, and it cannot avoid — though it may reframe — the question of what *rasa* might mean for audiences. Many practitioners and commentators who most explicitly locate themselves within traditional practice (K.N. Panikkar, Kapila Vatsyayan) do indeed continue to support the view that the aesthetics of performance produces such an extension of experiential capacity, and their attitude is paralleled by western practitioners like Barba ('presence', 'extra-daily' energy in performers, giving rise to heightened communicative ability) and Schechner ('states of arousal' in receivers).

It is more problematic, but not necessarily incomprehensible, to suggest that, for instance, Boal's 'spectactor' – to some extent like Brecht's ideal spectator – is also in a somewhat special or more-than-ordinary state. If so, the claim could be extended to recipients of development theatre, processional events, 'environmental theatre' (Schechner) and so on. It is a claim which needs to be checked against the discussion of the mechanics of *rasa* in the preceding section. Clearly there are some senses in which the perceptual behaviour of participants is affected, since that is precisely the goal of many such modes of performance practice; it is also the intention that behavioural change should be relatively permanent (i.e. that they are 'transformed' rather than merely temporarily 'transported'); and although the aims of such change are pragmatic rather than esoteric, they still need to occur on the basis of some (at least theoretically) identifiable psycho-physiological modification. Whatever the subsequent direction, Artaud's model of affecting the physiology of groups (which are of course necessarily composed of individuals) still holds. Shelley makes a similar point when he identifies the plurality of expression in drama as most conducive to 'social good'. There are processes of aesthetic transformation at work for audiences of Weiss's *Marat-Sade* and Brecht's *Galileo* just as much as for *The Tempest*, and in none of these cases does the aesthetic negate the presence of political issues or vice-versa; the same argument applies to any rendering of an episode from *Mahabharata*, a reworking of folk material like Girish Karnad's *Nagamandala*, or street theatre in Bengal or Kerala.

In brief, my argument here is that the aesthetic is personal and hence also political. In this context, what does a political act do?

– instigates individual transformation;
– produces attitudinal shift (in individuals and groups);
– changes the self/world/reality configuration;
– revises the self/other dynamic;
– provides an impetus to action (verbal or direct);
– opens up alternative goals for individuals and groups;
– empowers by locating potential for initiative.

Since these outcomes are fundamental to ethical and political action for individuals and groups, if performance manages to achieve all of this, it is well on the way to producing some results. It has been my contention throughout the book so far that a proper understanding of the processes of performance, as evidenced in and through the workings of Indian theatre, suggests that its effects lie precisely and powerfully in this domain. That, of course, is why it (Indian theatre and the mechanics of performance) is worth exploring.

Anthropological theories

These have already been quite extensively discussed above with reference to their contribution to theories of performance and reception. But of necessity, anthropological approaches are framed by socio-political phenomena. The possibly suspect concealed political slant of such theories has also been indicated.

In spite of problematic results, one thrust of Barba's work is to suggest a set of universals located in modes of preparation for performance or in physical aptitudes and gestural/postural practice. It seems to me that he is trying to locate such phenomena one stage too 'late': that is, he needs to be looking at something corresponding more closely to the *pasyanti* level of language discussed above. As soon as you get into traditions of physical preparation, training, stance etc. you are in the realm of the culture-specific. There are of course interesting parallels or analogies to be observed here, but they are not identities and they are not necessarily directly assimilable or translatable across cultures. Barba's English, Danish or Brazilian performers, although skilled in their own right, do not have a residue of physical memories of the same kind as Japanese or Indian performers, and his attempts to locate such a residue 'beyond' inculturation have proved surprisingly ineffective. So this admirable or politically correct (depending on your viewpoint) search for homogeneity founders at profound, perhaps almost autonomic, levels of behaviour. But a politics of universality has to start 'before' or 'prior to' this. It has to start in the realm in which the self is also other, i.e. before any kind of learned response, in a state or condition of non-differentiation. I've indicated at some length what that is above. It is the only realm of homogeneity for human existence. Beyond that, any move towards any kind of expressed form necessarily takes on the colouring of time, place and genetics.

So Barba's attempt at a politics of theatre which transcends the accidents of time and place is not entirely successful. That is not to say that it is not successful at all, however. Many of his productions and communal events have been exciting, provocative, liberating and courageous. But it does mean (since this book is about Indian theatre, not Barba's theatre) that his perceptions are partially rather than fully applicable to the performance modes which Indian theatre displays. He derives from it something which has considerable, but nevertheless limited, success in achieving his own vision of what theatre can do. That partial success does not necessarily illuminate the processes and outcomes of Indian theatre any better than indigenous commentators like Paniker and Varadpande have already done.

Schechner situates performance events along a spectrum (the 'fan' and the 'web') which ranges from public and private ceremonials to the management of crisis. Though, as discussed above, he is also interested in the ways in which individual response occurs and in the effects it produces, this framing locates performative events within the social sphere and as agents of social stabilisation, renewal or transformation. They thus take on an important political dimension. Although his anthropology may in some ways peer down at an interesting sub-species, in spite of his conscious attempt to ally himself with it, it does provide a useful tool by which to categorise kinds of performance, particularly in the more contemporary period. It also usefully underlines the fact that performance, as a public event, is necessarily political in a number of senses, and that by virtue of its 'special' time-frame, it constitutes an occasion for commentary or reflection upon the institutions of society as opposed to a passive acceptance of them (even, perhaps, when the overt purpose is precisely that of confirmation or reinforcement of behavioural or attitudinal norms: do processions of royal personages confirm or offer opportunity for reflection upon the status and value of royalty as an institution?). Performance is thus seen either as a form of reinsertion within or of distancing from the 'given', indicating its potential as a means of renewing personal or communal identity. Indian performance has always acknowledged the legitimacy of both these outcomes. Kavalam Panikkar's consciously 'intracultural' investment in Keralan performance forms (see Chapters 2 and 5) can be seen to take on 'an added political significance in that it is giving currency to inherited culture' (Singleton, n.d. 2).

Schechner's approach is helpful; it also accommodates with, but is not restricted to, those outlined in the following section.

Marxist and Historicist accounts

The work of Utpal Dutt, Rustom Bharucha and others (inspired by, though not confined to, the operation of IPTA – see below, Chapter 5, pp. 178–182) has helped to define a specifically Indian perspective on both the history and theory of Indian theatre in the light of recent (twentieth-century) political and historical events. I am not competent, nor is there space, to go into the history of the communist and socialist movements in India, though this is a fascinating and provocative area for debate, and one with which theatrical practice has been constantly rubbing shoulders in more or less comfortable ways. It was important to establish such a perspective, and to claim for the investigation of Indian performance forms a space distinguishable from the (westernised) norm of theatre criticism which traditionally begins with Aristotle and refers back to his (presumed) criteria. I hope I have already indicated that such a restrictive focus is, both historically and aesthetically, inadequate when looking at the history, variety and aims of Indian performance. I also hope that my suggestions have in some measure cast the net wider than an assessment grounded solely in relation to the determinism of time and place.

All the same, time and place are important. Chapter 5 provides a brief account of the emergence of contemporary trends from the latter days of colonialism: what is happening now is still in large measure fuelled by the need to define an 'Indian' theatre. 'Post-Independence India ... has witnessed those deviant practices of resistance become the dominant ideological performance practices of modern India' (Singleton, n.d. 1). And the forms of theatre, like those of all artistic expression, both reflect and dialogue with the underlying parameters of social and political life. The recent history of Indian performance is in many ways the story of 'différence' or differentiation, of asserting an identity against attempts, however apparently innocuous or well-meaning, to recuperate it either into homogeneous categories of 'Indianness', or into the story of 'world theatre' (the recent battle of encyclopaedic formats between e.g. Cambridge U.P. and other presses in this domain is worth a thought here: what kind of activity does it represent, and what if anything has it got to do with theatrical practice?). History and specificity need to be asserted. But they do not need to be exclusively asserted.

Chapter 5 illustrates several dimensions in which that differentiation operates. It functions as a 'deviant practice of resistance' against, for instance, the following kinds of imposed, officially-sanctioned (Symbolic) order:

aesthetic
fundamentalist

gender-blind
monolinguistic
monotheistic
moralistic
nationalistic
traditionalist

Theatre practice provides a voice, a form of expression, creative opportunity and an alternative vision in face of the silencing or (physical, financial, educational) exclusion of caste or ethnic minorities and underprivileged groups ('scheduled castes', Manipuri or other 'resistance' groups in disputed territories, women, sex-workers); offers a forum where debate is practised rather than silenced (in villages and urban slums, about gender roles, outcasting, discriminatory practice); provokes questioning of received attitudes; articulates the possibility of challenging political policy; stimulates intelligent exploration and celebration of regional and local languages.

All of these (and more) things are happening currently. Resistance occurs against the background of events in (so-called) 'real' time: as performance, it does however push against that time, against the unquestioned acceptance of its contours as the only ones possible: as Andrew Marvell puts it, it offers a chance to make time run rather than stand still. Understanding of theatre activity in a contemporary historical perspective is therefore vital. What, specifically (but not only) in the Indian context, is also vital is the ability to balance against this (linear) model of time and its deterministic functioning, an understanding of the ways in which that time-experience can precisely be stretched and shaped as additional vectors. That understanding is found throughout Indian performance history and is explained in several places in the preceding chapters. The activity of engaging with it is itself a form of rewriting 'history', both in the sense of a linear sequence of events and of a spectrum of interpretative strategies grounded in an extended range of consciousness.

It is this wider sense of the historical that seems to me to emerge from a close involvement with Indian theatre, and to be necessary for its full comprehension both as a phenomenon with a development through historical time and as a practice of response within the contemporary context. This sense, incidentally, accords a legitimacy to Indian understandings of 'history' which most non-Indian, and not a few Indian, writers have underplayed or rejected.

Feminist and related approaches

The relevance of a considerable number of theoretical approaches, both 'traditional' and contemporary, indicates both that Indian theatre offers itself as an extensive field for study (or play), and that in this as in other areas theory itself is in process of (historical) change: just as Indian theatre is a plural and not a singular, so its theory is both plural and still in the making. In the deliberate plurality of its method, this book intervenes in that making. Some of the approaches discussed above are longstanding, others of much more recent date; there are others which have yet to catch up, as it were. I will look to some extent at economics in Chapter 5; in Chapter 6 I will contribute a stir or two to what might be called the currying of the multicultural.

I don't think there is a feminist theory specifically applied to Indian theatre; at least I haven't discovered one. There is in fact relatively little writing about it by women. One major exception is of course Vatsyayan's book, though that is not in any sense feminist. Out of 32 writers in Lal's collection of essays (Lal 1995), only three are women. I refer below and in Chapter 5 to articles by several others, and there are many interviews with women performers and accounts of areas of their work in *Seagull Theatre Quarterly*; as Chapter 6 also shows, participation by women at all levels of current performance activity is considerable and significant; but the total proportion of written material is still not large, and none of it produces a theory specifically focusing on the presence or otherwise of women. I have begun some moves in that direction in Chapter 3, pp. 86–94, where I look at some aspects of the place of women in performance. The reason why I extend that discussion here is precisely because, as I hope some earlier material will have at least implied, it provides a further angle on how and why traditional understandings can be matched to contemporary practice.

As a lead in, a glance at other kinds of performance theory may be useful. Above, I looked at ways in which 'anthropological' theories specifically explore performative situations as events happening to performers, and to individuals and groups of receivers at a particular time and place for a particular purpose. What is highlighted here is the enactive and, at least potentially, transformative quality of such events. Other performance-related approaches bring out the 'happening' status of events, extending the performance spectrum to occurrences in the visual arts (live exhibitions), and locate events of all kinds as 'representations' within or against the cultural matrix, emphasising the constructed nature of all cultural signifiers. In other words, they emphasise ways in which all aspects of performance (all semiotic encodings) signal particular culturally-determined perspectives on roles, attitudes, behaviour, and so on.

As such, they frequently deal with what happens to bodies in performance (some performance art deliberately transgresses what convention determines as acceptable in this respect, for example in an attempt to foreground preconceptions about gender and sexuality). Writing about performance of this kind and in this way is an attempt to deconstruct habitual stereotypes; it sees performance as a strategy of resistance. Such resistance may take the form of graphically demonstrating ways in which the body is aggressed or demeaned by 'accepted' perspectives, and in the process reduced to the status of an object. Where the body in western culture is concerned, Pradier's analysis of performance history since Greek times suggests that the combined predominance of the anatomical, rational and Christian gaze has served to lock it up or reduce it to a set of parts: 'la fragmentation née de la rationalisation scientifique de l'examen du charnel a eu pour effet de contribuer à réduire l'imaginaire' (Pradier 1997, 332). Thus not only is contemporary 'resistance' a significant intervention in western understandings of the mind/body spectrum, it also offers the possibility of restoring an organicity which generates imaginal rather than Symbolic modes of apprehension.

There is no doubt that, though in very different ways, some contemporary performance work by women in India, which I discuss below, addresses similar issues, and does so through very specific focus on the body of the performer in action. However, I do not want to limit the discussion only to this work. I include it within a consideration of how women have been viewed in Indian theatre, and of how a more fundamental interpretation of traditional criteria suggests that they could well have been (and hopefully now are being) both constructed and constructive in other ways.

It is appropriate here to recall the analysis in Chapter 3 of the ways in which traditional forms have suppressed, marginalised and regulated the representation and participation of women, to such an extent that, I suggested, the term 'woman' becomes both a site of male insecurity and a sign licensed by male prerogative. If that situation is beginning to change, it is for many reasons:

(i) General perceptual shifts due to political and socio-economic transformations, including e.g. women Prime Ministers in India, Pakistan, Bangladesh and Sri Lanka, women in business, education, the media etc. (in part influenced by western feminism, but more fundamentally, evolving a model appropriate to the Indian context).

(ii) Aspects of the history of women in performance noted in Chapter 5, e.g. the history of Gul Bardhan, the role of women's groups, increasing emphasis on issues of marginalisation and de-voicing. Major recent landmarks here are Mallika Sarabhai's one-woman performances *Shakti: The Power of Women* and *Sita's Daughters*. Acclaimed both in India and abroad, they raise provocative questions about the perception of women throughout Indian history and, in the form and the person of the performer, foreground and claim a new status.

(iii) Increasing visibility of women in other art-forms, e.g. painting and literature; much greater availability of e.g. fiction by women, in part due to the existence of women's presses within India and elsewhere.

To this should be added the understandings of function and form of performance practice outlined above. All the very extensive work indicated above under (i)–(iii) is essential in opening up the space for women to perform as and for women, and as full participants in a (so-called) democratic society. It also forms the basis for a revised theory of their role.

It is worth considering then why this has not happened previously and what might occur if it were to happen.

Male insecurity, male regulation of female status and activity is one dimension. It has its root in fear; and fear leads to violence, to the subjection of what is, probably subconsciously, perceived as threat. I think it is helpful here again to use Lacan's concept of the Symbolic Order, which corresponds to those forms of organisation which confer on the dangerous flux of experience a graspable, supportive shape: language – particularly written language, logical conceptual operations, the erection and maintenance of definite and enclosing boundaries to self and its immediate environment ('my' world). These kinds of operation are not of course exclusive to the male sex, but a certain kind of 'maleness' seems especially prone to them. Borges' laconic and speculative account of why Emperor Shih Huang Ti built the Great Wall of China at the same time as ordering the burning of all books prior to him unpicks some of the underlying motivation: 'the wall in space and the fire in time were magic barriers designed to halt death' (Borges 1962, 222).

What is feared is, ultimately, that 'otherness' which threatens to invade, to sweep away the boundaries of the known. As Klaus Theweleit impressively documents in his two volume *Male Fantasies*, it is a fear which fuelled much of Nazi behaviour towards Jews, homosexuals and women (Theweleit 1987). If the contours of the Symbolic are threatened, 'everything' is at risk, as Lear discovers when his two elder daughters shut him out in the storm. The psychopolitics of 'othering' derives from an inability to allow that other the space or the right to exist.

Sarabhai's 1995 (and later) performance, *V for ...*, focuses on violence, on what it is and what it does to people. Violence, either within the individual or as external force, restricts: it closes off freedom, constricts movement, cancels out possibilities. Its roots may lie most profoundly in the fear of loss of that which is seen as constituting identity: power, image and role; attributes and possessions; personal and cultural status; a place to be; meaning for oneself and for others. That sense of threat or fear of loss, expressing itself also by categorising groups or individuals who apparently represent that threat as 'other', is common to all of us; it is not gender- or culture-specific, it goes deeper than that. In many cases it is apparently insuperable, however much well-intentioned helpers attempt to rearrange the environment, because it touches profound levels of our human insecurity via-à-vis contravention of the Symbolic order. Male insecurity is thus a special case of a more general situation.

It looks however as though within the process of preparing and performing there is a state which works in the opposite way, and which Sarabhai consciously aims to activate. This state frees from fear and restriction, it discloses a more extensive sense of self and its powers, it opens up mind and body expansively rather than closing them down protectively or aggressively, it can lead to what John Martin (who has worked extensively with Mallika Sarabhai) calls 'a feeling of latent energy, latent action and the thrill of being in this state' (Martin 1997, 57). As in many of her performances, what is transmitted to the audience is an experience of intense energy, vitality and warmth which is both stimulating and cohesive and hence functions as a positive force for assessment and action.

Mallika Sarabhai sees her role as an artist who communicates, and she defines the underlying impulse to create/communicate as *anand.* (Joy or bliss are the most usual translations: *anand* is part of the compound *sat-chit-ananda*, which indicates a condition of totality of consciousness in which individual being is in tune with the full extent of its potential, as awareness without object or content, as expression of that which is. It is a condition which is most fully entered through the strait gate of stillness, equipoise, neutrality; which opens beyond everyday modes of functioning.) *Anand* here is a state from which creative activity most generously arises, and which it inspires in performers and receivers, often as 'flow'-experience. *Sat-chit-ananda* is, precisely understood, a condition beyond or prior to activity: it is the consciousness of being as joy, but entirely potential. However, within this non-active condition, it is the joy aspect, the tickle of delight as it were, which acts as an as-yet-unmanifest impetus to expression. This condition is both impetus and outcome, it is what drives one to create and what one gets out of doing it (and thus wants to go on doing it again). Sarabhai works both as a 'classical' dancer within the traditional aesthetic *and* as an innovative, contentiously polemic issue-focused performer, both as solo performer and as part of a company. So the experience of *anand* is apparently not determined by the parameters of the performance *product*; it is something which occurs at a crucial level of the *process*.

It is striking that the same term, *anand*, is used to describe the most identifiable experience reported by women sex-workers engaged in the production in Calcutta of a play expressing aspects of their situation (see *STQ* 9, April 1996). Although the term here clearly means 'fun' or 'enjoyment' in the first instance, it has more profound overtones and a more everyday alternative is available if all that is required is 'fun'. The sense they are reporting is of pleasure in coming together, creating something together, and this activity is rated as much *more* 'fun' than e.g. watching tv. Anjum Katyal's Editorial to that *STQ* number translates it as 'joy', and links it not just to fun but also to healing and empowerment. 'Joy. Healing. Fun. For women who are denied one, a voice. A sense of power. Visibility. Recognition. A space she can claim; a space where she is listened to' (*STQ* 9, 2). There is a liberation here both from the desperate condition of everyday activity and from the forms of (bodily, verbal) behaviour which structure it, a move into a condition in which the performers can in one sense stop being 'themselves', in another sense discover the possibility of being more than that by playing other roles, and in a third sense become more conscious of both aspects through the distancing effect of playing themselves and others.

In *The Playful Revolution*, Eugène van Erven quotes Bulhan on Fanon: 'true liberation requires the *simultaneous* transformation of the oppressed individual *within* an oppressed group and of the social conditions that caused the individual's distress in the first place' (Van Erven, 11).

Both Sarabhai's and Katyal's uses of *anand* imply that some more extensive faculty is energised in performance, and that this faculty is empowering and enlivening. Bharucha, discussing Grotowski's paratheatrical work, which aims at a sense of communion, notes that Grotowski speaks 'cautiously' of '"lack of anguish" ... which I would prefer to call "joy"' (Bharucha 1993, 53). I can be more (than my egoic self, than my socio-economically-defined or prescribed self) when I perform, and if I perform from there I can assist others to locate that liberating capacity within themselves too. One of the women in the Calcutta play said: 'This is something for myself.'

Keralan playwright and director Kavalam Panikkar defines one of the goals of performance as the achievement of *thanathu* ('our own'), which he glosses as a quest for the 'extreme point of imagination' and as 'the discovery of the self, including the supreme self' (*STQ* 7, 58). Performer and director Alaknanda Samarth, writing in *STQ* 6 about her performance of Heiner Müller's *Medea* in conjunction with visual artist Nalini Malani in Bombay in December 1993, says that the rehearsal process put her in contact with 'a state of mind/body brought about by new ways of seeking (repeating/rehearsing) leading to change in internal structures not propped up unilaterally by nation/territory or geographically sited cultural memory or practice' (Samarth, 58). Samarth further defines the need 'to go beyond Stanislavski, and in so doing, restore/reinforce, re-invent our own Indian approach and understanding of the non-psychological, non-individualistic alignments in actory codes, an understanding of the *pause*' (60). She too signals, along with Panikkar, the mechanisms by which performance liberates and the extent to which these mechanisms are located within Indian traditions.

An important marker is for women to stop 'casting themselves', as victims and thus internalising the situation of oppression and marginalisation. But finding the courage to do this is much easier in situations which are supportive (working with others), or protective (performance provides a framework, a time and space which is not the everyday, but in which the everyday can be faced). The energy which derives from this special situation is a major factor in the move to reassessment.

Sarabhai, in *Sita's Daughters* and *Shakti*, signals the recognition of entrapment and the consequent possibility of liberation: in character as Draupadi and Sita — manipulated and idealised — and as schoolteacher rape victim — used, discarded and de-voiced: all of them acquire a voice and refuse expected compliance; and as performer, in charge of her own material, which significantly rewrites the cultural 'heritage'. Samarth, as Medea, internalises and traverses the Kali-zone of vengeance born of repeated rejection: negated in her allotted role, discovering across profound transgression an alternative form of being as character, and across the loss of self, an alternative modality as performer. These performers signal and celebrate dis-engendering, the refusal of the imposed label 'woman' and its baggage of expectations. In so doing they open up a space beyond imposed gender, from which a re-engendering could occur. As woman: as soon as performance activity starts, it operates in and as body. But it is a reclaimed body; resurrected, perhaps, after the death of the old Eve: one which, in performance, can radiate a vibrant and celebratory charisma.

For Chandralekha, dance performance involves celebration of the feminine as primal creative power, which she insists must be negotiated and internalised in the body, not simply claimed as concept; at the same time it promotes a validation of the male/female dynamic through a 'daring' vocabulary of movement and position, a parallel to the use of traditional theatre forms to physicalise as well as verbalise taboo issues by e.g. Karnad and Kambar. Note also Chandra's view that 'femininity' is not biological (Bharucha 1995, 253) but rather a form of creative energy: the practice of creative acts takes one in the direction of balance or androgyny (cf. Chandra's use of the androgynous *ardha-narishwara* icon in her exhibition for the Moscow Festival of India).

Samarth speaks of 'going beyond Stanislavski', into the 'non-psychological, non-individualistic' which, across 'the pause', underlies the way an actor expresses. Beyond individual psychology, beyond the egoic: acting starts anew from here, prior to preconception, learned response, cliché, habit. Also, therefore, beyond gender and into the space of gendering. The value of restoring, reinforcing or reinventing this 'Indian approach' is that it acknowledges this dimension, it has words for it, just as Panini has for what lies 'beyond' speech.

Extension of self leads to relocation of where 'I' might 'begin' (see above, Chapter I); together with the quest for 'the extreme point of imagination', it predicates a redefinition of the origin, structure and outreach of desire. That which fears the loss of the known, constructs desire as a means to replenish its defences: to 'man' the barricades, to erect barriers against death. Although the act of desiring here goes beyond that fear which excludes or excommunicates otherness altogether, it ultimately tends towards the same goal: annihilation. It seeks to acquire, to enlist and incorporate the other, to neutralise its otherness by rendering it part of the protective structure: I want you because I can then control the you-ness of you. Desire here projects the need to reinforce, to stabilise, to confirm and conform, to buttress the recognised image, the safe, defendable, circumscribed territory of the known. It wants more, but more of the same. It reduces 'other' to 'same', as (for instance) does one approach to multiculturalism (discussed further in Chapter 6), which promotes homogenisation as a national/cultural good rather than encouraging diversity.

In and through performance, however, desire can operate 'otherwise'. My discussion in Chapter 1 indicates ways in which degrees of 'not me/not not me' may take performers and audience beyond their everyday contours, where otherness is enriching. It happens by passing into the unknown, into the fear and out again. In performance, I have to be open: to the personae I may take up, to the audience, to my fellow performers. I may enact all possible varieties of closure, but I am also more than these. Desire functions not to close off but to open out; it is the (Agni) flame which burns off the inessential and frees up the power to inhabit many forms.

That is its direction. Its origin here is less in need or lack (classic western psychoanalytical premiss) than in the recognition that, although a passage through loss is involved, the reward is *anand*, the exhilaration of playing in new dimensions. It's only a slight shift of emphasis, but its psychological implications are enormous: I want more because I am lacking or I feel insecure; I want more because I enjoy the resultant empowerment. The first version constructs the subject as deficient and promotes anxiety; the second perceives it as a stretching towards fullness and promotes excitement. (It seems to me that there is a plausible parallel here with models of *jouissance* in western psychoanalysis as formulated by Kristeva and Cixous: the 'male' version seeks closure, the 'female' welcomes openness and play, though the terms need to be read as not too rigidly genderised.)

As in the quest-model discussed above, the experience of loss is understood as part of the trajectory of desire, not as its primary source. Hence the moreness that is sought for is driven not so much by a need to plug a gap as by a preparedness to accept the new; its nature is not defensive but expansive.

At the risk of being reductive, Freud might be said to consider that desire is the expression of the need to be a penis, whereas Lacan suggests it is the need to function as the Phallus. In both cases admission to and preservation of the Symbolic subtend it. Where however the experience of going beyond the Symbolic results in pleasure, enrichment, joy, another kind and quality of desiring becomes available. Desire not for entry to the club of the Symbolic, but rather for the freedom to play on and across its borders and hence to activate an extended range of creative response.

Musing on the sexual ambivalence of *Krishnattam*, where the style and the viewpoint is feminine (Radha's and the *gopis'* love for Krishna) and the actors all male, Bharucha finds in the ambivalence or liminality of this 'male' experience of 'female' desiring something of 'the field of desire in which Krishna plays' (1993, 188). I likewise want to make it clear that the gendering of desire is neither irrevocable nor unequivocal, and that Krishna's playing is precisely what Indian theatre allows us all to participate in. There may even be room here for the new Adam too.

Indian Theatre in the contemporary world: cultural politics in India

IDENTITY, DIVERSITY AND CONSCIOUSNESS

I have been a swallower of lives; and to know me, just the one of me, you'll have to swallow the lot as well

(Rushdie 1982, 9).

Midnight's Children suggests, on its opening page, the post-Independence gloss on the old story of the One and the Many: the desperation for an ideal unity in a country which was created from the opposite and which has continued to struggle to unite often violently warring factions within and to assert its national(ist) identity against real or imagined external threats.

A – very – brief synopsis of some of these threats for non-Indian readers would include:

(i) Pakistan, China, Sri Lanka as sources of terrorist infiltration and 'destabilisation';
(ii) separatist movements, suspected of being supported by 'external' powers like those mentioned above, in Kashmir and Punjab;
(iii) 'Naxalite' or other indigenous resistance movements
    especially in north-eastern states (e.g. Assam, Bihar, Manipur) where direct military rule by India has been in force;
(iv) internal conflicts between religious (Hindu-Muslim-Sikh), caste or ethnic groups.

Non-Indians may, given the absence of reporting in western media, be unaware of the number, extent and complexity of these situations. It would be no exaggeration to suggest that over the last few decades at least 100 people have lost their lives *each week* in these conflicts. All of them in one way or another affect theatre, as general political background, as specific thematic detail, as major economic determinant or as context of sanction or repression. They feature below in discussions ranging from the content of Mahasweta Devi's plays to the cultural situation in Manipur. They are a major factor in the 'self and other' politics of the contemporary theatre situation.

Rushdie's (distanced, though during the *fatwa* hardly inviolate) postmodernist exuberance makes of the plurality of Indian identity an impetus for generative narrative, aptly inheriting the structural potential of the epics and interpreting, but also quite consciously and ironically 'devaluing', the profundity of the Vedic formula. The issue cannot be other than problematic in contemporary India; but it also cannot be avoided. This chapter considers contemporary (1990s) practice in India in three contexts: that of the recent past, that of current political and social reality, and that of inherited assumptions about and forms of performance.

Debate about theatre in India in the past two decades has been dominated by issues of identity. There are several strands to the debate, in addition to or alongside the one/many issue; crudely stated, they are:

(i) the attempt to detach theatre from colonialist models;
(ii) the relationship between traditional performance forms/origins and contemporary needs;
(iii) nationalism versus regionalism.

All of these shorthand formulae conceal further levels of contention and complexity. However, they do indicate an important way in which theatre, and debate around it, has functioned as a highly conscious aspect of a general process of cultural and political questioning which has been going on since 1947. My purpose is not to try to sum up or indeed enter that process in detail. Rather, it is to suggest perspectives in which concern with identity links not only to the content or issue-related focus of theatre and its place in society, but also to the sort of activity performance is, to ways in which it works, and to what its effects might be. Performance is, in the view of Schechner, Turner, Barba and others both within and beyond the world of theatre, something which both shifts and articulates identity: it has the potential to change its participants and receivers, and it gives them an image of that change. The change is of necessity both external (operating through the network of relationships human beings engage in, including social and political structures) and internal (operating as shifts in individual consciousness and in its modes of understanding self and world). There are people working in theatre in India who are quite consciously concerned with change in both these dimensions.

Recent theatre-related debate in India has tended in part to favour a largely Marxist version of consciousness, positioned within the post-colonial context (for example, Utpal Dutt, some of the writing of Bharucha and much of the debate reported in six years of the Calcutta-based *Seagull Theatre Quarterly*); perfectly reasonable on many levels as a strategy to counteract e.g. Schechner's or Brook's alleged cultural piracy or modern Orientalism, or to support various kinds of 'consciousness-raising'. Indian theatre, like the notion of Indianness, is debatable and debated, part of an ongoing cultural crisis which is extremely complex and involves much more than theatre. However, although reference to this framework and definition of consciousness as operating within it are quite legitimate, to refer to it only in these terms limits consciousness to something purely operated on and operating within historical time and space, and turns the debate into a form of cultural politics which may exclude insights about consciousness operating within aesthetic experience which have their roots in Indian tradition, as outlined in Chapters 3 and 4, and which seem also to relate to levels and forms of experience available now.

One thing to take from that discussion – as conducted, for instance, at numerous colloquia and in the pages of the *Seagull Theatre Quarterly* – is a desire to contribute to the making of theatre, whatever the form and the context, which draws on a fundamental sense of personal and cultural identity, is appropriate to as many as possible of the parameters of the contemporary (e.g. economic situation, kinds of audience, language) and which at the same time respects and makes use of models of performance which are not either simply colonial derivatives or simply reactions against derivatives. There is here a richness and a complexity both of theatre forms in the making and – at least implicitly – of ways of understanding the consciousness that creates and receives such forms. In other words, the overall picture presents a generosity of construction towards 'theatre' and 'consciousness' which may not always be apparent in individual aspects of the debate.

Practice reflects that diversity. Since Independence, there have been several major and numerous smaller units engaging in various forms of 'action' theatre, including IPTA (Indian Peoples' Theatre Association) from 1943–64, Safdar Hashmi's Janam (People's Theatre Front) (1973–89) in Delhi, Badal Sircar's Satabdi (Calcutta), R.P. Prasanna's Samudaya (Karnataka, 1975–mid 1980s), KSSP (Kerala), ARP (Association of Rural Poor) in Tamil Nadu and K.V. Subbana's Ninasam (Heggodu, Karnataka, from 1949). Other theatre workers/writers/directors lead groups and/or schools which use a mixture of traditional form and contemporary focus: Kavalam Panikkar's Sopanam in Trivandrum; Rangayana, founded by B.V. Karanth in Mysore; the Calicut University School of Drama in Trichur and so on. Most of this is scarcely known outside India, but it forms a mosaic of committed and often exciting work pushing at both aesthetic and socio-political frontiers.

Richmond, Swann and Zarilli indicate that changes are taking place in many forms in response to changing social and behavioural norms, cultural expectations etc. State financial aid has in some cases made training and employment more available but has also challenged the dominance of particular castes or groups; many artists have devised variant or composite forms; others have promoted the use of traditional forms to respond to contemporary social or political issues.

Sumitra Mukerji points out that since there is no pan-Indian theatre, the term 'intercultural' applies within India too. Contemporary theatre continues to span folk/classical and traditional/modern categories, and 'manifests the modern Indian nation's cultural heterogeneity rather than homogeneity' (Mukerji 1994, 3).

Authors and directors such as Habib Tanvir, K.N. Panikkar, B.V. Karanth, Ratan Thiyam, Badal Sircar and Girish Karnad display a complexity and variety which reflects 'distinct and disparate developments, both in terms of performance aesthetics as well as the politics of representation and individual ideologies that shape their creative concerns' (1994, 3).

Questions underlying this situation include the following: What is the role of 'traditional' theatre (folk/classical) in the political and cultural debate in India today? What does a theatre whose origin is in myth and ritual have to gain/lose in an exchange with Western cultural models and practices? What adaptations and transformations (e.g. into street theatre, community theatre etc.) are occurring? What are the parameters of performance in India today, and what are their practitioners trying to achieve? What lessons do India and the West have to learn from each other in terms of theatre practice? Does performance have a status (deriving from its ritual function, the way it brings groups together to confirm and underpin traditional behaviours) which nevertheless also allows it to be a place or moment of challenge, a manifestation of crisis and questioning? Is performance, because of the 'framed' or heightened reality it consciously and implicitly aims at, also a crucial mode of such questioning? How does 'performance' (which includes the build-up, the framing of the event, and the 'cooling-off', for performers and receivers) relate to 'ongoing systems of social and aesthetic life' (Schechner)?

Mukerji's article charts other important dimensions which will be picked up later. The following sections indicate some categories, both historical and formal, into which this diversity of theatre activity (post-Independence, and particularly in the last two or three decades) falls.

CATEGORIES OF CONTEMPORARY THEATRE ACTIVITY

Colonialist hangover or acceptance

This includes western realist models, 'fourth-wall' Naturalism, and proscenium arch theatres; it is largely by and for the urban middle-class. *Parsi* theatre (a combination of Western and Indian forms) is still to some extent in evidence, but even entertainment theatre is now more completely 'Indianised'. Additionally, whereas the 50s and 60s saw dutiful or fashionable, but not very clearly understood, imports of forms like the theatre of the absurd, it would now be truer to say that the significance of such forms in the Indian context is more critically appreciated. They may have been assimilated into contemporary Indian writing for the stage (e.g. in the case of Sircar and Karnad); or where performances of western plays are given, they have often been highly competent and perceptive (e.g. a production of *Waiting for Godot* directed by Benjamin Gilani with the well-known actor Naseeruddin Shah, which I witnessed in Ahmedabad in 1991 and which has been frequently revived elsewhere). Some aspects of this kind of theatre are discussed below in sections on theatre in regional languages, particularly with reference to professional, semi-professional and 'alternative' theatre in for instance Mumbai (Bombay), Pune, Calcutta, Delhi and Imphal.

To this should be added the considerable Indian 'Shakespeare industry': in spite of moves to include much more Indian writing in

English (now more widely available in print) on English literature courses, many colleges and Universities still retain a strong emphasis on Shakespeare. College productions are not infrequent; here and elsewhere, however, the trend here too is towards an assimilation of Shakespeare with the Indian context, as witnessed in shifts in production style at the prestigious St. Stephen's College, or in recent Kathakali versions of *Othello* and *Macbeth* in India and on tour; I also directed an 'Indian' version of *King Lear* which played in Ahmedabad and Delhi in 1998.

There is also considerable activity of an amateur kind. Much, though not all of it, is based in schools, colleges, urban environments or social groups. There are for instance regular college drama competitions in many places; the well-funded annual National State Bank Drama Competition; and similar competitions sponsored by other institutions throughout the country. State competitions in Maharashtra have provided the forum for several significant new plays; around 500 plays a year are staged with some 15,000 participants. There is also, as in other states, an intercollegiate competition for short plays. Bombay and Calcutta, in particular, have large numbers of amateur theatre groups. Quite a lot of people are out there doing theatre with enjoyment and commitment. Much of it uses loosely 'western' or realist models, but it is written in Indian languages by Indian writers and deals with Indian problems and perspectives. It's not always great theatre, though it is often competent; it doesn't provide funding or employment on a permanent basis, but it pays its own way. It is at least a significant footnote to the contemporary scene; and it suggests that 'acceptance' is not always the right term, in that this kind of work, whatever its artistic merits, is now clearly an integral part of the Indian scene.

Tradition as revivalist, nationalist or revisionist programme

This category includes:

(i) Traditional theatre in Sanskrit ('classical');
(ii) Traditional theatre in regional languages: Ratan Thiyam, Kavalam Narayan Panikkar (but see below);
(iii) 'museum theatre': e.g. the role of some Academies and research institutes in documenting and preserving folk forms, partly funded by foreign sources: Ford Foundation at Udupi and Trichur.

All these can be seen as part of the promotion of 'Indianness' as a politico-cultural ethos which has also been carried out via channels such as Doordarshan (the national tv station, previously enjoying a monopoly but now under strong competition from independents and satellite channels), the film industry and political pronouncements. Funding initiatives include supporting institutes to record and document folk forms in Kerala and Karnataka (Trichur, Udupi), support from the Sangeet Natak Akademi for particular companies engaged in this kind of work (K.N. Panikkar's *Sopanam*, Ratan Thiyam's Manipuri *Chorus Repertory Theatre* assisted to produce versions of Bhasa and sections of *Mahabharata*); the role of the Indian Council for Cultural Relations, supporting this kind of work within India and as cultural export, and the work of the Indira Gandhi National Centre for the Arts (headed by Kapila Vatsyayan, engaging in documentation, publication and resourcing). Festivals of India, which promote showcase art, and treat art as a national icon or export commodity, are a significant aspect of this inculturation programme, which is strongly influenced by political economics.

Rustom Bharucha (in Lal, 1995) underlines the political choices guiding assumptions about the 'integrity' of Indian cultural forms, a view which he suggests is 'illusory, if not downright false' (Bharucha 1995a, 41). He analyses the 1988 Haksar Committee Report, produced for the Department of Culture, which although largely neglected since its production, highlights many of the generalised assumptions at the root of cultural policy from the 1950s, including the founding and funding of the 'Akademis' and other Government institutions. Not only did the designation of the Akademis institutionalise tendentious differentiation between literature, fine arts and the performing arts, their remit (the 'revival' of culture) significantly overlooked what Bharucha rightly signals as 'the prodigious production of art that survived and resisted colonial rule', including 'the massive contribution of IPTA' (see below), not to mention popular theatre idioms and the role of cinema (1995a, 42–3). In spite of their apparent autonomy, the Akademis have largely failed to fulfil their role as learned societies and have functioned mainly as bureaucratic extensions of governmental policy. The lack of autonomy manifested here is reflected throughout the performing arts scene and sharpened by the fact that 'most Indian artists remain in a hopelessly insecure financial position, receiving neither the support of the state nor the corporate sector' (1995a,

44–5). This situation is an important feature of contemporary theatre in regional languages, which includes both work of the kind outlined above and that which is less immediately reverential towards tradition: further discussion of this occurs below.

It is however important to note also that many artists engaged in 'preservation' (the work of *Margi* in Trivandrum, where *Kudiyattam* is regularly performed even if there are only a handful of spectators or none at all, is a case in point) are not necessarily doing it only or principally in response to such 'nationalist' promptings. They may be wholly devoted to the aesthetics of their art; they may be using it, as Mukerji indicates, to promote debate about traditional values rather than mere passive acceptance. In any case, if traditional forms are to remain as a *resource*, to be confronted, challenged or worked with, they do need to be preserved in the first place. This activity goes on even outside India, for instance in the initial manifesto of the UK-based *Kala Chethana Kathakali Troupe* to counter what was seen as the threat to the form in India. The company has since moved on to use *Kathakali* inventively within a UK context also.

Mukerji (1994) notes that historically, the 'actual processes of cultural representation since Independence reflect an attempt to gain a sense of identity independent from that of the colonised "British subject", without losing the multiplicity and distinctiveness of the various cultures which exist within the country.' The essay further suggests that 'authentic' Indian culture is *not* necessarily 'traditional'; the eclectic/postmodern tendency of the artists it mentions may be *more* representative of modern Indian culture than any '"return" to a single, iconic image of a "pure" Indian tradition': 'the theatre practitioners ... mentioned illustrate this sense of interculturalism within India much better than the official "representatives" of Indian culture abroad, such as our "classical" and "traditional" musicians and dancers (4)'.

Bharucha, in his book on the experimental dancer Chandralekha, suggests that the claims of 'originality' (in the historical sense) entered for the *Natya Sastra* for theatre and *Bharatanatyam* for dance are mythologised, though in different ways: in the case of *Bharatanatyam* by attempts to construct a 'national' cultural scenario, invoking dubious antecedents in the Harappan seal of a 'dancing girl' and claims to 'rescue' the Devadasi tradition by a Brahminical elite (Bharucha 1995b, 39–42). The erection of such symbolic and imaginary 'classical' monoliths devalues 'marginal' forms and traditions and along with them the possibility, explored in Chapter 3, that there might be different paths to achieve similar aesthetic and psychospiritual goals. Different forms may develop in parallel; 'origin' is valuable less as a pseudo-historical prop for claims of 'legitimacy' than as a question about the extent to which any practice engages with the capacity to organise creative acts.

Brian Singleton, writing about Panikkar's work, concurs: 'certain forms of modern Indian theatre are resisting intercultural practices, not by refusal or direct opposition, but by theatrical acts of intracultural rejuvenation, without the injection of a foreign culture as a serum' (Singleton, n.d., 1).

There is therefore room for considerable debate in this area, and the debate is indeed taking place in practice as much as on paper. G.P. Deshpande makes similar points, for example: (i) Indian tradition is eclectic and includes 'Western' models (Deshpande 1995, 3); (ii) what is 'national' is a historical and therefore constantly changing phenomenon (3–4). Ananda Lal's Editorial to a major collection of essays on the last twenty-five years widens the field even further by reference to performance by Indians living abroad and to the growing (but sometimes flawed) interventions by foreign critics in the discussion of theatre in India (Lal 1995, 1).

The continued existence of strong local traditions – 'folk'-oriented in e.g. Tamil, Bengali, Kannada, Marathi, more 'classically'-oriented in Malayalam, more urban in form in Hindi, drawing on a whole range of performance practice, is outlined to some extent in Chapter 3 and discussed further below.

Fluctuations are wide in terms of frequency, degree of professionalism and numbers of performers. In some cases this kind of activity is located more at the 'anthropological preservation' end of the performance spectrum; in others it has been adapted to serve contemporary social and political concerns. There are issues here about the ways in which traditional forms and material function within their local context; they will also be raised in conjunction with the discussion of new/alternative models below. Mukerji suggests that 'cultural identity' is a loaded and suspicious term; Deshpande points out that insertion within *local* cultural tradition and language is a necessary part of 'Indianness' (1995, 6). Both observations underline the local as opposed to 'national' role of performance traditions.

Trends in contemporary writing for the stage

This section necessarily starts with another admission of inadequacy, although one which in the Indian context is not as bad as it might be.

There is probably no single Indian critic or commentator able to read all new Indian writing in the original, since that would require at least fifteen languages. Much writing for the stage is in progress, and quite a lot of it feeds directly into performance; relatively little of it is translated. Lal comments: 'If the Government really believed in propagating unity in diversity, it would have arranged for a plan by which seminal dramatic texts in Indian languages are translated into all other Indian languages' (1995, 3). The material which has been translated – usually into several Indian languages and frequently into English as well (there are some strong senses in which English is an Indian language too) – represents plays which have been acknowledged as of major concern. They have thus already passed a rather more rigorous apprenticeship than much work in 'majority' languages, though the scenario would be familiar to playwrights writing in, say, Welsh or Czech. In recent years the number of such plays available in affordable editions published in India and abroad has increased significantly. The examples I discuss below are drawn from such editions available in English, which is usually not the original language in which they were written, though not a few playwrights (among them Karnad, Sircar, Panikkar) are completely or virtually bilingual. Below I discuss performance practice in the regional contexts, which necessarily includes reference to writing as well: as most of this is only available in the local language, I am however obliged to draw on secondary sources.

Some writers make use of mixed eastern and western models, for example Tanvir, Karnad, Elkunchwar, Tendulkar, Sircar, Panikkar, Omcheri, Devi. Their work has been published in *Enact* (1960/70), then by Seagull Press, then from the 1990s also by more mainstream publishers like OUP India. Mukerji notes that their work is in part 'an attempt to get back to the mass bases of India' (1994, 4–5). Where they draw upon traditional forms, they use tradition as living, vital, based in day-to-day practices; their theatre is also relevant to contemporary urban, social and political issues. Examples of this kind of work have been touched on in Chapter 2 (pp. 55–60) and are considered in more detail below.

One useful recent volume is *Three Modern Indian Plays*, published by OUP India (1989). It contains Girish Karnad's *Tughlaq* (1972); Badal Sircar's *Evam Indrajit* (1974); and Vijay Tendulkar's *Silence! The Court is in Session* (1978).

These plays were first written during the 1960s in Kannada, Bengali and Marathi: they have been translated into several Indian languages since, as well as into English. They follow a largely 'western' realistic format with few if any features of traditional forms; the issues they deal with are set in an Indian context but are not restricted to that. *Tughlaq*, like Karnad's later *Talé Danda* (1989), deals with material from Indian history with parallels in contemporary events: Tughlaq's split self and failed idealism leads to a fourteenth-century power crisis reminiscent of 1960s post-Nehru disillusionment and doubts about national identity, whereas *Talé Danda* is about a twelfth-century movement to promote equality and neutralise caste and gender discrimination whose savage repression by Hindu fanatics reflects on the post-1980s rise of right-wing extremist parties. *Silence* exposes violent desires and sexist trends in the mock trial of a woman for alleged infanticide: both she and her (postulated) child are silenced by the tacit agreement of a bourgeois, largely male group of fellow performers; *Evam Indrajit* presents aspirations for life and relationships beyond the banality of the everyday world and concomitant anxieties about lack of significance. Formal innovation in each play is inspired mainly by 'western' modes, e.g. the setting and framework of *Silence* recalls Pirandello and *Indrajit's* existentialist questioning makes use of a minimalist format in order to cut straight from one scene to another.

A second group of works include Girish Karnad, *Hayavadana* (1971), *Naga-Mandala* (OUP Delhi 1990) [1988]; Habib Tanvir, *Charandas Chor*, Seagull 1996 [1975]; K.N. Panikkar, *Karimkutty, The Lone Tusker* (Seagull 1992), *The Right to Rule, The Domain of the Sun* (Seagull 1989); Satish Alekar, *Begum Barve* (Seagull, 1989); Badal Sircar, *Bhoma* (Seagull, 1983); Chandrasekhar Kambar, *Jokumaraswami* (Seagull 1989).

Other writers include Omcheri (Malayalam), Mohan Rakesh (Hindi) and the well-known Bengali Marxist writer and actor Utpal Dutt; *Enact* (theatre journal) published seventeen full-length plays and many short plays translated into English from various Indian languages between 1967 and 1973.

These plays fuse folk/traditional mythological and ritual material and forms with contemporary language in a conscious attempt to draw on traditional dynamics in a contemporary context. The issues they address (the psychology and politics of sex in *Naga-Mandala*, honesty and corruption in *Charandas Chor*, posturing and viciousness of the local leader in *Jokumaraswami*) are highly relevant in contemporary India, but the narrative derives from traditional tales and epics and the performance includes folk modes of e.g. song, dance and comic repartee.

In many cases plays in both the above categories problematise contemporary issues through the use of both 'traditional' and 'imported' forms. Mukerji notes, for instance, that even though the 'folk or regional-oriented' writers above use Hindu sources (*Ramayana, Mahabharata,* Kalidasa, Bhasa, folk legend) they do not use it 'to promote Hindu hegemony but, often, to critique it' (Mukerji 1994, 6) as indeed do many traditional or folk forms via comic/narrative features. In addition, Panikkar satirises castism in *Ottayan* and *Karimkutty,* and borrows from traditional forms (Sanskrit Drama, *Kathakali, Kudiyattam*) in order to 'problematize the relation between tradition and modernity' (6). Discussion of examples of plays by Dutt, Omcheri and Panikkar is found in Chapter 2 as examples of recent play*texts,* and will not be repeated here.

Tanvir worked with *Jana Natya Manch* (*Janam*) after Safdar Hashmi's death (see below for more detail on Safdar Hashmi). He confronts official versions of tradition and nationalism in working in and with various cultures/peoples and languages. (A similar example is the case of director Bansi Kaul who worked in many different forms and languages, e.g. *Therukoothu, Nautanki, Bhavai,* Malayalam, Punjabi: in twenty years Kaul worked in eighty towns directing in local languages. See *STQ* 4, 43–4). Tanvir's adaptation of *Mrichchakatikam* as *Mitti Ki Gadi* (1954 and after) challenges power and exploitation in the political arena.

Tanvir's association with theatre begins with involvement with IPTA in Bombay (late 1940s), which stimulated his interest in using folk forms: much of his work, in particular with his Naya Theatre, draws on the dialect and performance styles of his native Chhatisgarh. It uses simple staging; he talks of a 'bare, circular platform' (Tanvir 1996, xxv) in a phrase recalling Jacques Copeau's demand for 'bare boards' which launched mime-and-physical-oriented practice in Europe in the 1930s; Tanvir similarly draws heavily on improvisation. After a spell at RADA in the early 1950s, Tanvir returned convinced of the need to work within one's own cultural traditions and context. His blend of local tradition and performance skills, improvisation and scripting, along with a commitment to a project of empowerment of the people, means that his work belongs both to the category of new writing and to that of development theatre: a characteristic he shares to greater or lesser degrees with Badal Sircar, Kavalam Panikkar and some others. Tanvir's best known play, *Charandas Chor,* has been constantly revived since its first performance in 1975, and won an Edinburgh Festival

Fringe First in 1982. His first play, *Agra Bazaar*, was also frequently revived.

Karnad exploits western forms in *Yayati* (1961), *Tughlaq* (1964) and *Hayavadana* (1970); *Naga-Mandala* (1988) echoes models from many places and has been performed in several countries and languages; yet they all blend in elements from indigenous tradition. Rani Dharker sees Karnad's mix of modern staging and folk techniques (including music, drama, movement, environmental staging, direct contact with the audience) as an example of environmental theatre. She compares it to Schechner's assessment of the Varanasi *Ramlila* and suggests it shares with it the quality of 'unleashing the *energy* of folk-theatre techniques' by working, as Turner puts it, in 'liminal areas of time and space [...] open to the play of thought, feeling and will' (Dharker 1997, 120). Karnad's aim is to use all these elements to question accepted values, to 'permit a simultaneous presentation of alternative points of view, of alternative analyses of the central problem. They allow for, to borrow a phrase from Bertolt Brecht, "complex seeing"' (Karnad, *Naga-Mandala*, back cover).

Sircar was born into the anglicised Bengali landowning class which came to make up Calcutta urban intelligentsia after Independence. Existential unease characterises his first play (*Evam Indrajit*, 1962); work with his company Satabdi undercuts the idea of 'national truth'; *Bhoma* (1980) satirises nationalism and patriotism, technological 'progress' etc. Sircar brings '"real" culture' to many via street theatre: 'actors get their energy from the people watching and often performing along with them' (Mukerji 1994,10). The focus of his work is egalitarian, social and critical. His work moves towards open-air theatre (*Procession*, 1973), drawing both on traditional forms of song and on current issues; collage-technique, episodic structure, presentational style all recall Brecht. His book *The Third Theatre* (Sircar 1978) outlines aims and methods: to create a 'theatre of synthesis as a rural-urban link': 'third' means neither indigenous/traditional nor imported. As well as Brecht, Sircar draws on the work of Grotowski, Beck and Schechner: he toured the USSR and Eastern Europe in 1966 and later visited Schechner in New York, and developed his own versions of 'poor theatre', 'living theatre' and so on. He has been an important force in directing, acting and performance practice in India, frequently conducting major workshops (e.g. he workshopped *Spartacus* in Manipur in 1972, an event recalled by many leading figures in Manipuri theatre in the special edition of *Seagull Theatre*

Quarterly devoted to Manipuri theatre (*STQ* 14/15, 1997). Sircar's work, both scripted and co-devised, represents a significant strand in the spectrum from folk to urban, from improvised to scripted, from indoor to open-air, from 'Indian' to 'western'.

Alekar's *Mahanirwan* (1974) foregrounds a shift in attitudes towards tradition, convention and accepted views of life and death, through experimentation with folk elements; his *Begum Barve* presents the disjunction between authenticity and role as a crisis of self-image, played out by two characters who experience themselves as nondescript and a former female impersonator who thinks of himself as a woman. The plays thus articulate identity-related problems of the contemporary world set against traditional frameworks. (Alekar's role as a performance-trainer is noted below.)

At present, plays by women are difficult to locate: none features in the collected editions mentioned above, and, in contrast to women's fiction, which is now available in relative abundance, there seem to be virtually no plays in print. The recent two-volume collection of writing by Indian women edited by Susie Tharu and K. Lalitha features absolutely no drama; nor does the introduction contain any comment on this absence (Lalitha & Tharu 1995). The absence of published plays by women is however signalled by a participant at the 1999 Voicing Silence conference reported in *STQ* 21, 135.

Dina Mehta's *Brides are not for Burning*, which won a BBC prize for radio drama in 1979, was only published in India fourteen years later several stage performances (Mehta 1993) and thus confirms the problems in India for drama both by woman and by es other than English, Hindi and perhaps Bengali. The with is of central concern to the women's movement in politics in general and to theatre in its relationship ; the play, although somewhat wordy and oversensational (ms dowry-death, sexual politics, anarchist violence and marxist critique into two acts) is well-crafted and neither outrageously implausible in its context nor insignificant in its time: it is dedicated to 'all the angry young women, who can be what they choose to be'.

Apart from a single play by Mrinal Pande, focused on a male protagonist, the only other volume by a woman published by Seagull to date is Mahasweta Devi, *Five Plays* (translated by Samik Bandyopadhyay, Seagull 1997). These plays are adaptations by Devi from her own fiction, made originally in the 1970s. Devi, a well-known novelist, interweaves history, folklore and fiction and draws on folk-forms which, she claims, effectively transmit social themes: 'I have a reverence for materials collected from folklore, for they reveal how the common people have looked at an experience in the past and look at it now' (xii). The five plays (*Mother of 1084, Aajir, Bayen, Urvashi and Johnny, Water*) relate to experiences of marginalised, oppressed or underprivileged groups and individuals. *Mother of 1084* details a mother's quest to 'recover' her son (corpse no. 1084), killed as a Naxalite 'terrorist'; *Aajir* is about a slavery-bond which has in fact long since disappeared, but remains in force because its subject still believes it to be so; *Bayen* figures a woman designated as a kind of witch and excluded from family and community; *Urvashi and Johnny* recounts ventriloquist Johnny's loss of his puppet-lover Urvashi's voice from throat cancer (the play was written during Emergency Rule); and *Water* depicts the exposure and subsequent savage revenge of corrupt local politicos and officials, who hive off all the water aid for their own use and then put down the teacher-inspired peasant revolt which leads to the construction of a dam: echoes here of Gerhard Hauptmann's *The Weavers*. *Water, Bayen* and *Aajir* include folk music, rituals and dance, whilst *Urvashi and Johnny* makes effective use of Hindi film songs as the puppet's mode of communication to Johnny; Devi's language is crisp, varied and evocative. In his introduction, Samik Bandyopadhyay celebrates her work as 'novelist's theatre' – 'a theatre that could use the narrative/narration of a text as a component rather than try to use the 'story' merely as the raw material for a play'. Her plays seem to me to employ an appropriate range of performance-modes and registers, which pick up from the energy of her precise and suggestive narratives; she is making use of traditional forms in order to depict contemporary situations across a range of different geographical and socio-political situations. From these resources she creates drama which gives voice and enacts, which textures time, place and the course of action.

Theatre in regional languages and areas: some examples

This brief summary offers another way of cutting the cake in order to indicate the wide range of theatrical activity. Occasionally, mention is made here of work referred to elsewhere (e.g. street theatre, new writing). It selects only a few instances from the fifteen states and languages (not to mention the 100+ dialects and hundreds of local variations). Other areas receive a variety of mentions elsewhere in the book, and Lal (1995) includes essays on most major language areas plus English.

Punjab

Punjabi theatre is currently extant in India, Pakistan, the UK and Canada; there is extensive writing, including several journals; performance is by many mainly amateur companies. It's mainly a twentieth-century offshoot of 'western' drama, with a realistic/ socially-oriented mode showing few links to Sanskrit drama. More recently there have been attempts to incorporate folk material/ elements. Balwant Gargi (playwright and director) became Professor of Indian Theatre at the University of Seattle, producing Punjabi Theatre in the west, incorporating Punjabi folk and ritual elements. Gurucharan Singh (President of the Punjabi Sangeet Natak Akademi) writes and produces work which is anti-communalist (against political movements and parties which support religious or ethnically-biased policies) and activist – using street theatre and popular theatre forms. In recent decades there has been severe disruption in the Indian Punjab due to long-term ongoing political and separatist violence; in Pakistan the situation has always been even less favourable (more repressive) and that tendency is escalating rather than diminishing; outside the Indian sub-continent activity flourishes, though largely at a relatively low level and on an amateur basis.

Theatre in *Pakistan* is currently suffering particularly from Islamicist repression and funding difficulties. The leading alternative group is/was *Ajoka*, led by Madeeha Gauhar from 1983. In spite of repression it has continued to perform, for instance on private lawns, doing plays by Sircar and on the position of women, opposition to fundamentalism and communalism. The group has received some support from SATCO (S. Asian Theatre Committee) between 1992 and 1995, including sponsorship of festivals in Lahore (1992), Dhaka (1993), and Kathmandu (1995). 'Free and unhindered cultural activity is a luxury which a theatre group can only dream of in Pakistan. The State has always considered theatre as subversive ... and the powerful fundamentalist lobby has been openly hostile towards performance. Acting is still regarded as taboo for girls and a waste of time for boys.' (Madeeha Gauhar in *The Indian Express*, 12/2/98.)

Gauhar and her husband Shahid Nadeem founded Ajoka with Zohra Segal's sister Uzra Bhatt at the oppressive peak of General Zia-ul-Haq's regime. They performed Sircar's *Jaloos*; Shahid was jailed for one year, Madeeha lost her University teaching job. Shahid was further sentenced to forty lashes for writing the song 'Insaan abhi tak zinda hai: Zinda hone par sharminda hai' ('The human being is alive and embarrassed at the fact') which became an anthem against religious fundamentalism. Theocracy has stifled a great tradition of folk art and, ironically, left only vulgar commercial theatre.

Manipur

Manipur, in the north-east zone of 'troubled' states, has a substantial performance tradition, a phase of partly western-inspired innovatory practice, and a recent performance history which includes both an attempt to 'Indianise' its activity by according it folkloric status and subsequent attempts to relocate its tradition against all of those influences and seductions. The state has, since the 1960s at least, lived in constant political and social unrest, frequently under martial law. An Amnesty International report of 20 May 1998 summarises the situation thus: 'Manipur, a state in the north-east region of India, has been riven by internal conflicts for decades. The troubled political history of Manipur has been perpetuated by a multitude of factors including anger at economic under-development, drug-smuggling and corruption. Armed opposition groups have emerged, organised on the basis of community affiliations and conflicting demands for greater autonomy and self-determination' (AI 1998). The report also notes that 'abuses of human rights by government forces and by armed opposition groups have become a feature of daily life'. The Armed Forces (Assam and Manipur) Special Powers Act, in force since 1958, confers powers to shoot and kill on the armed forces whilst also providing them with virtual immunity from prosecution.

In *STQ* 14/15 (1997), devoted to an examination of theatre in Manipur, Anjum Katyal's editorial confirms this assessment and indicates its effects: 'a world being continuously ruptured by all kinds of conflict. Violence and anguish are omnipresent; they erupt everywhere' (Katyal 1997, 13). Soyam Lokendrajit describes it as 'this anarchic milieu of violence, terror and lawlessness' in which 'not a single idea remains that has not been perverted, nor any single organisation that has not been corrupted' (Lokendrajit, 1997, 27). This last comment might be read, cynically, but not, given recent political and social history, totally without foundation, as an extreme case of much in India today.

In this situation, theatre activity can take four forms, says Lokendrajit: entertainment (aim: oblivion); exotic classic (retreat or avoidance); workshops and training (promising but prone to inconsequentiality); art imbued with a historical consciousness of the contemporary situation. Clearly favouring the last, he quotes from a manifesto by director Lokendra Arambam: 'To work for change in theatrical expression and to work for change in society is the alternative theatre for the dynamics of social change' (Lokendrajit 27).

Theatre in Manipur has included a powerful strand of 'alternative' theatre of various kinds, dating particularly from the work of innovative directors Ratan Thiyam, Heisnam Kanhailal, Harokcham 'Sanakhya' Ebotombi and Lokendra Arambam in the 1970s; this 'emphasised the exploration of traditional forms' as well as 'engaging with the urgent social issues and problems the young directors saw around them' (Katyal, 6). The work of these directors benefited from interaction with other strands of innovation subsequent to the establishment of the Manipur State Kala Akademi in 1972: Sircar held workshops following a production of *Evam (Ebong) Indrajit* in 1973, leading to a further production, *Spartacus*; Kanhailal spent some time both in Calcutta with Sircar and at Rangayana; Thiyam was appointed Director of NSD; their work received national and international recognition, playing in Delhi, Bombay and London – where Arambam's *Macbeth – Stage of Blood* was performed on the Thames in 1997; but Thiyam describes the recent situation for theatre as comparable to that of Poland under curfew: very active in spite of little scope for cultural exchange (Thiyam 1997, 63).

Their activity, which includes writing and creating, performance training and sustaining theatre companies in very difficult economic circumstances (Thiyam operated a co-operative structure not dissimilar to the simple sharing life-style of Heggodu or, in Europe, Copeau's 'retreats' in Burgundy in the 1930s), already displays a wide range of form and subject-matter. It also 'encouraged theatre workers to get rid of the inhibiting influences of the fixed proscenium' (particularly prevalent in the 60s) and to move towards work which was 'physically more exact and demanding' and expressed 'stark images of the spirit in revolt' (Lokendra Arambam in Lal 1995, 167). This period also saw the beginning of strong influence from NSD.

Additionally, Manipuri theatre possesses a traditional popular form, *Sumang Leela*, – originating in the nineteenth-century – which can accommodate a focus on contemporary issues. Professional troupes (some all male, some all female) play up to three shows a day and plays have 'the courage to challenge the morbid and corrupt system' (Somorendra 1997, 153) and the potential to 'be converted into educative, creative productions aimed at changing attitudes, without losing the high entertainment value' (Moirangthem, 1997, 160). There is also a history of distinguished writers, in particular G.C. Tongbra (1913–96) – also an actor, director, translator, poet and lyricist – whose output runs to around 100 plays, many humorous but focused on contemporary life, and who received many regional and national awards. Whilst drawing on popular genres like 'succulent melodrama' (Arambam 1995, 165) and traditions like epic drama, opera and ballads, Manipuri theatre from the 1950s onwards passes through phases which to some extent reflect the situation in other Indian regions where both rural and urban forms exist, and also mirrors aspects of European theatre history in the period between 1880 and 1950. The increasingly improbable moral certainties of melodrama almost inevitably give way to more searching naturalistic examination of social and domestic life; political insecurity fuels existential anguish which emerges as formal experimentation. This however may itself begin to appear sterile or introverted, and in spite of the 'seriousness, commitment and pursuit of excellence' of directors who in recent years have attempted to develop their own modes in acute awareness of political realities, Arambam suggests that current work has not fully found ways to link art and life.

The spectrum represented here is impressive both in its range and in the commitment and concern for theatre and for its operation in the social context; in this too Manipur serves as an example of much that can be found in India. One director comments that the problems too 'are very similar to the problems elsewhere in India' (getting an audience, paying performers ...) (*STQ* 14/15, 1997, 133). I should point out also that we are talking about a small state, treated for the most part by the central government as though it were 'backward', and containing less than 1% of India's population.

Although Arambam fears that theatre workers in Manipur are in danger of becoming 'pawns in the great circuit of the mainstream' (Arambam 1997, 21), Samik Bandyopadhyay suggests that Thiyam and Kanhailal at least are markers of resistance, even though that 'mainstream' may now take the form of outside funding which imposes implicit adherence to a supposed consensus. What in fact distinguishes the mode of resistance across different periods is a refusal to avoid the 'immediate reality of a Manipur groaning under the assault of violence' (Bandyopadhyay 1997, 73), or, as Arambam puts it, to allow 'the subversion of the naked self' (21). A refusal then to go in for easy options, be they formal, economic or thematic: if entertainment or the exotic classic are present in such work, it is in order to serve the process of confronting the real, not running away from it or covering it up. This criterion (applicable also to much of the work cited above) can be usefully linked to my analysis of theatre's ability to engage with 'the real' (i.e. with what remains when Symbolic Orders and idealisations are suspended) in Chapters 1, 3 and 4. The challenge, as always, is to ensure that, whatever the performers wear or do, theatre is a place where masks come off.

Works which testify to this desire include Arambam's *Macbeth* mentioned above, Thiyam's *Mahabharata* trilogy, especially *Karnabharam* and *Chakravyuha*, Kanhailal's *Pebet* (1975) and *Karna* (1997). Kanhailal says 'I'm trying to ... educate through the emotional experience ... we are trying to reach the root of their senses' (interview with Samik Bandyopadhyay, 1997, 77). An excellent source of further material on Kanhailal is Bharucha's *The Theatre of Kanhailal* (Bharucha 1998).

Theatre in Bengali, Hindi and Marathi

The areas where these languages are spoken include the major urban centres of Calcutta, Delhi, Bombay and Pune. Theatre practice here is more closely connected both with an educated urban audience and with professional or semi-professional structures, including permanent theatre buildings – although there are not an enormous number of these. It is thus in many ways closest to models found in 'developed' (northern) countries, and it has also benefited from more extensive coverage, both within and outside India. Lal (1995) includes sections on theatre in these areas from which much of the following information is drawn: I bring it together in one section however, both in order to avoid needless repetition and also in order to indicate some general characteristics of theatre in these zones.

The ongoing crisis situation in Manipur has given rise to a particularly active response in extremely difficult conditions. No one would claim, however, that life in parts of Bombay and Calcutta is problem-free, nor that the Indian political scene has not witnessed any number of desperate occurrences and provocative situations. Urban 'intellectual' theatre is in many ways particularly well-placed to comment on or highlight them, and much of the work mentioned below is at the forefront of such activity. On the other hand, even this work has a relatively restricted outreach and it is often poorly-funded and beset by serious problems of plant and equipment. Many venues suffer from poor maintenance, and the Bharat Bhavan amphitheatre in Bhopal created in 1982 functioned for less than a decade. The nationally-funded NSD has several efficient venues, but even quite prestigious companies like the NSD's Repertory and the Rep at the nearby Shri Ram Centre are partly dependent on government funding, and most other companies are at best semi-professional. Nevertheless, dedication, commitment and increasing focus on alternative means of fund-raising over the years by groups and organisations such as the Prithvi Theatre in Bombay, Theatre Academy in Pune, and Sudrak and Sundaram in Calcutta has kept theatre of a high standard available.

There is a certain level of interchangeability, in terms of languages, personnel and plays, between the three main cities: for instance, Kironmoy Raha laments the fact that the quality of Hindi theatre in Calcutta is higher than that of most Bengali work, although the quantity is not great (Raha 1995, 123). Plays translated both from other Indian languages and from non-Indian sources have also featured strongly in the repertoire. Delhi has benefited from the presence of NSD and of inventive directors like Alkazi and Thiyam; Bombay has a (fairly erratic) degree of crossover with leading film actors; Calcutta has a strong radical intellectual tradition. Here Sircar's work, though highly significant in terms of its influence on new performance modes and the attempt to bridge the urban/rural divide as well as to reach out to an extended public, has had perhaps less effect on the theatre scene than it has in other parts of the country (e.g. in the workshops he conducted for groups in Manipur, Karnataka and so on which were important markers in the kinds of new work being developed there and in ways of linking tradition and innovation).

Marathi theatre has been characterised in the recent past by an eclecticism of form and content which also seems in many ways in keeping with moves to respond flexibly to the contemporary situation whilst drawing on traditional resources. As in the other areas considered here, directors have worked their way through many of the major plays of western theatre and also imported plays from other Indian languages: Kambar, Karnad, Sircar and Tanvir, to name only the best-known. Marathi writers Satish Alekar, G.P. Deshpande and Vijay Tendulkar have already been mentioned and some of their work discussed above: work which has itself been translated into other Indian languages and performed in major cities, although as already noted the number of occasions on which this happens is still comparatively small. Alekar and Tendulkar, in particular, have written major plays which, whilst intended for proscenium performance, incorporate both formal innovation and traditional performance features. Vijay Tapas proposes that Alekar's *Mahanirwan* and *Begum Barve*, and Tendulkar's *Ghashiram Kotwal*, all written during the 1970s, marked a turning point by breaking expected codes of both form and content and achieving 'an amazing amalgamation of tradition and experimentation' (Tapas 1995, 175).

In contrast, Raha suggests that in spite of a strong tradition of urban theatre and the innovative input of Sircar from the late 1960s, *Bengali* theatre in Calcutta has not really come up with an alternative to 'the blatant commercialism of mainstream theatre and the compulsions of received ideas' (Raha 1995, 123). During the 70s, political turbulence associated with the Naxalite movement (see discussion of Mahasweta Devi and of the situation in Manipur above) inspired work by Utpal Dutt (who ran the People's Little Theatre) and others. Currently, groups associated directly with playwrights (Manoj Mitra's Sundaram, Debasis Majumdar's Sudrak), produce interesting work. In Bombay, Antarnatya has similarly presented new writing and directing work of substance during the past decade.

The Theatre Academy Pune, founded in 1973 by Satish Alekar and others after a dispute over Vijay Tendulkar's controversial *Ghashiram Kotwal*, has since mounted some thirty-five plays by Alekar, Tendulkar, P.L. Despande, Mahesh Elkunchwar and others: it has 'striven to preserve the distinct identity of experimental theatre in Marathi' (*Indian Express* 28/3/1998). Theatre Academy has also performed short plays in found spaces, run workshops and maintained a library, and is associated with actor/director Mohan Agashe's initiative to develop GRIPPS theatre (a German model of theatre for children performed by adults) in India.

Prithvi Theatre Bombay was founded by the celebrated Kapoor family (actor-manager Prithviraj and his wife Jennifer of Shakespeare Wallah fame); it is now run by Sanjna Kapoor. The original aim was to provide a '"space" which will be stimulating and challenging both to directors and actors who use it, as well as exciting and involving for the audience' (*STQ* 18, 1998, 74). In pursuit of this it has mounted workshop performances, attempted to reach out to new audiences by offering diverse kinds of performance at both conventional and unusual times, encouraged new writing via playreading events and run an annual festival from 1984. As Sameera Iyengar puts it, in spite of the hectic nature of Bombay life and the dominance of the film industry, it is imperative for Prithvi and similar organisations to engage in 'the battle for quality – which encompasses the idea of experimentation, change, exposure, constant improvement, productivity, a discerning theatre audience and a committed theatre community' (Iyengar, 1998, 77).

Hindi theatre was given impetus during the late 70s by imports of the kind mentioned above, when, apart from the NSD personnel already mentioned, B.V.Karanth and Habib Tanvir were also active in Delhi (Karanth also directed at Bharat Bhavan in Bhopal). Significant artists were also working in Hindi in Calcutta (Usha Ganguli) and Bombay (Satyadev Dubey). In common with other areas, Hindi theatre has included productions of Sanskrit classics and taken on board the influence of folk forms, particularly in the work of Tanvir. The activity of Hashmi's Jana Natya Manch is discussed below; like that of Sircar's Satabdi and of Sanjoy Ganguly's Jana Sanskriti in Calcutta, it represents an important area of parallel activity. The current situation here too comprises similar factors to the other areas discussed in this section, i.e.:

– eclectic performance models and styles
– increasing technical competence
– problems of funding and support.

Additionally, Delhi, Calcutta and Bombay in particular, because of their provision of publishing outlets, Akademis and institutes for training, education and academic activity, enjoy a relatively high degree of debate about theatre and a relatively substantial clientele of interested or enthusiastic 'extras' (regular theatregoers, people willing to attend workshops and seminars, etc.). Although none of the writers who contribute essays on theatre in these languages to Lal (1995) is entirely sanguine about the state of affairs, there is a sense that theatre activity is, if not entirely healthy or well-nourished, at least potentially capable of maintaining life and contributing to the debate I have pointed to elsewhere.

Theatre in Kannada

One example of theatre activity in the south will extend the picture of the variety of ways it has developed in the recent past: Karnataka.

Whereas in the large conurbations, modifications of practice due to exposure to 'outside' influences, whether Indian or foreign, have been the norm, in Manipur exposure was more sudden, more historically specific and more markedly transformatory. In Karnataka the story is different again. Apart from the curious coincidence that three of the leading figures involved (Karnad, Kambar, Karanth) have names which open in the same way and also echo those of the state and its language, the revitalisation they have initiated has its own specific characteristics which embed it firmly in the life and language of the region. As elsewhere, exposure to the national and international scene plays a part, and those mentioned above plus R.P. Prasanna and K.V. Subbana (see academies and street theatre below) drew on models from western classical and twentieth-century drama as well as on Indian classics. However, their work has been particularly successful in establishing what T.P. Ashoka calls 'a meaningful and mutually beneficial relationship between traditional folk theatre and contemporary theatre' (Ashoka 1995, 143). Karnad's and Kambar's work is sharp, witty, down-to-earth and direct, whilst exploiting to the full regional traditions such as the use of the *Sutradhara*, songs, myth and ritual – which are given contemporary relevance as analogies of sexual, political and social interaction. Karnad's *Hayavadana* and *Nagamandala*, and Kambar's *Jokumaraswami* are referred to above.

B.V. Karanth's return from Delhi in 1972 (he works also in Hindi) gave impetus to a movement launched by Karnad and Kambar's plays of the 60s by establishing 'an authentic and unique mode' of directing (Ashoka, 143) based in a vision of theatre as 'ritual, a festive community celebration' (142). Alongside this vibrant replenishment of the traditional, run the two other major forces discussed below: Prasanna's street-theatre movement Samudaya and Subbana's cultural centre and, later, drama school and repertory at Heggodu, Ninasam. Both these movements result in the revitalisation of theatre throughout the state, as part of social and political life and of the educational and cultural structure of Kannada. Karanth himself also established the theatre institute Rangayana (see below). Ashoka describes Prasanna, who also wrote and directed work other than street plays, as 'unquestionably the first to bring validity and dignity to leftist theatre in Karnataka'; for him, theatre was 'a critical and interpretative forum'. Add to this the considerable success of Ninasam's repertory company Tirugata (which has performed Karnad and Kambar amongst much else), and the continued presence of imaginative directors inspired by Karanth, Prasanna and others, and the spectrum of theatre activity in the last three decades is impressive both for its quality and originality, and in terms of its effects on the cultural life of the state and the perception of the relevance of theatre to that life. The current situation is favourable to new writers and directors, whose work is characterised by 'new insights into history, a subaltern mode of perception, an encounter between the master culture and the subcultures' (Ashoka, 146), thus continuing to situate Kannada theatre at the centre of contemporary debate.

Both the preceding sections indicate the scope of writing and performance activity and the many forms in which it is engaging with the vexed question of identity. It is clear from this, as from much of what has been said before, that the concept, as an aesthetic, a political, a linguistic and a psychological category, needs to be negotiated in the most generous way possible. Indian theatre has long, in its understandings about the sources and resources of creative acts, had the potential to clarify and support this kind of endeavour; the evidence suggests that the process is still going on, in spite of the major difficulties which theatre practice faces.

Drama training and development

One important way of checking on the current and future situation is to examine the provision for performance training. It will be clear that, in the sense of properly-funded and functioning training establishments, the Indian scenario is remarkably bleak. This section breaks provision down into two areas – roughly 'public' and 'private' – though the two categories are blurred and/or overlap. It is also however important to remember that training in many 'folk' forms occurs informally within family or community groupings. Frequently 'crises' may lead to warnings about the demise of local and regional forms; however, as in the cases of *Bhavai*, *Yakshagana* or *Yatra* mentioned in Chapter 3, a variety of factors intervene to preserve or give fresh impetus to them; among these, the use of folk performers in activist or developmental theatre, however problematic, is also relevant (see below).

The National School of Drama (NSD) and other public ventures

NSD (in New Delhi) is the only national drama academy. It has had a chequered history, not infrequently promoted since the 50s as a flagship enterprise when for political reasons it has appeared judicious to be seen to support the arts (at which times an outstanding and/or contentious figure – for example Thiyam, Alkazi, Karanth – was appointed as Director), but in between times struggling for funding, offering only a small number of places (around twenty per year) and perceived largely as a route to film and tv work (the NSD backs onto the Delhi Doordarshan studios). The training it has offered has thus also been inconsistent: sometimes brilliant and challenging, sometimes haphazard. It, and the appointment of Directors and other faculty, reflects the different periods of the post-Independence quest for cultural identity. Hence the selection of outstanding figures, often those who had a proven record of drawing on Indian rather than foreign performance methods, as Director; not infrequently however they fairly quickly became frustrated with the bureaucratic burden of running a state institution. NSD has gone through most phases of the anti-colonialist – intracultural – intercultural debate; some faculty members were strongly associated with IPTA and similar forms of action-oriented theatre; it has attempted to present itself as open to regional currents, for example in the appointment of Ratan Thiyam from Manipur and in the development of extension courses in different parts of the country. It tends still however to be perceived as Hindi- and Delhi-based, and its very success at turning out movie actors may be a wry mark that the 'Indianisation' it has sought ends up by gravitating towards the lowest common denominator.

Both training and productions (by current students and the prestigious attached repertory company) reflect a relatively pragmatic eclecticism which mixes useful ingredients from regional forms and, where appropriate, non-Indian sources. It has tried to evolve an appropriate three-year training which includes basic technical and production competence and acknowledges both Indian and other modes. However, in addition to the language problem, which militates against the possibility of a 'national' theatre, much teaching is currently done on a part-time basis by visiting experts, which works against consistency or the delivery of a coherent model of theatre training.

Reading discussions of theatre training elsewhere in India and talking with those involved, what stands out is the extreme paucity of it and the difficulties this causes. It is subject to whims of funding, heavily dependent on dominant personalities, and leads to few employment outlets. The Bhartendu Natya Akademi in Lucknow, patterned on NSD, 'finds it difficult to run an effective training programme' due to funding problems (Jain in Lal, 1995, 66); theatre training 'virtually operates in a vacuum' (Jain 1995, 67) because there are virtually no employment prospects.

Theatre departments in the higher education sector are few and far between and have suffered similar fates. Good departments doing useful practical work and drawing on local traditions once flourished in Trichur (Calicut University School of Drama); Calcutta (Rabindra Bharati University) and one or two other places; but they are now largely moribund, and the almost complete absence of paid professional work has led to the drying up of applications. The Calicut and Calcutta courses have gone into periods of severe decline. The Theatre Arts course at MK University Madurai has had insufficient applications to be viable in recent years. There are within the history of these organisations praiseworthy attempts both to offer an all-round training in theatre practice, to familiarise students with a variety of models and to do what is possible to support theatre in regional communities; but the difficulties have meant that these have been intermittent and partially successful at best.

Two exceptions are the University of Hyderabad's Sarojini Naidu School of Performing Arts and the School of Performing Arts at the University of Pune recently launched under the direction of playwright Satish Alekar (who turned down the offer of the Directorship of NSD in order to start the Pune venture), though both have small intakes. Alekar runs theatre, music and dance programmes for around fifty students and has negotiated a degree of autonomy unusual in the Indian University context: public performance work features strongly in the examined components. There is also a small unit in the School of Performing Arts at the University of Pondicherry.

State-funded training in 'traditional' forms exists, somewhat precariously, at the famous Kerala Kalamandalam for *Kathakali*, and some similar training in *Yakshagana* has been available at the research institute in Udupi. Elsewhere, it exists only alongside the courses or programmes mentioned in this section.

Other schools, academies and centres

There are however a number of academies and theatre companies which offer excellent training, combined in many cases with the chance to put it into practice in professional (even if poorly-paid) work. They owe their existence to the vision and commitment of dedicated individuals, but have in all cases moved beyond being exclusively linked to one charismatic figure or one performance mode. Examples are Panikkar's *Sopanam* (Trivandrum), (established in 1964); Mallika and Mrinalini Sarabhai's *Darpana* in Ahmedabad (established 1948); *Rangayana*, started by B.V. Karanth in Mysore in 1991 and now supported by state funding; K.V. Subbana's *Ninasam* at Heggodu in Karnataka (started as an amateur group in 1949, running as a theatre school from 1980, likewise state-government-funded). The work and influence of these institutions will be discussed further below: they indicate, individually and collectively, the diverse kinds of activity to be found in the contemporary scene and reflect in every case a particular vision of how traditional performance forms can be used in the current situation. They have been able to employ a permanent company (for one year at a time at Heggodu, for five years at Rangayana, fairly constantly at Darpana), tour productions, develop new work, hone performance skills, invite visiting directors and workshop tutors.

NINASAM THEATRE INSTITUTE

The institute is part of a cultural ensemble founded by K.V. Subbana and operating in Heggodu, a hamlet in rural Karnataka, since 1949. Originally an amateur drama society, it added a film appreciation and education unit. The theatre training institute was founded in 1980 and a touring theatre company (*Tirugata*) followed in 1985.

The institute offers a ten-month residential course (six days a week, fourteen hours a day) based on the NSD syllabus, which incorporates theory, history and practice in equal measure. The syllabus covers both Indian and western theatre and includes a similar range of performance training to that found in western drama schools. Intake is around fifteen per year, drawn if possible from all parts of Karnataka – but exclusively from Karnataka; Kannada and some English are the languages used. The institute receives state government funding and students receive a monthly stipend; they contract to work for one year following graduation in the repertory company, Tirugata, if invited. The Gandhian simplicity which characterises Heggodu as a place to live and work plays a strong role in the development and commitment of its students.

The institute explicitly records its aims as imparting relevant theatre training within Karnataka in order to use theatre practice as a form of mass discourse. Significant features both of the training institute and of the repertory company include focus on action at rural level and involvement with the community, including developments in response to expressed local needs. One purpose of selecting students from different parts of the state has been to 'seed' awareness and appreciation of theatre, and to pave the way for Tirugata touring performances. In contrast to NSD graduates, many Ninasam students have continued their involvement in theatre (around fifty per cent as full-time workers). Largely as a result of this, Ashoka comments that 'one can find trained theatre workers in any part of Karnataka now', a rare state of affairs in India (Ashoka 1995, 144).

Tirugata performs in all nineteen districts of the state, touring for around six months each year. Detailed records include financial breakdown and audience numbers (average 756 per show in the second season, many performances playing to over 1,000). Since this is touring theatre, it plays in many variable venues, often lacking facilities; company members fulfil all necessary performance-related tasks and the company (which includes women), operates a co-operative structure. Tirugata at first funded itself mainly from 'gate' receipts; of recent years a significant proportion of its funding derives from (local) sponsorship, suggesting that the recruitment policy has paid off in terms of developing not merely good will but also financial commitment of a relatively stable nature in different parts of the state. Members have also set up outreach activities, both in Karnataka and elsewhere (e.g. children's workshops in Maharashtra); and have initiated performances by Siddhi community members leading to significant shifts in attitude within the community and to recognition from without.

Funding has been derived from the state government, Sangeet Natak Akademi, the Ford Foundation, and careful touring economics. The institute has built a simple theatre with a large proscenium-arch stage and an auditorium for 600 – somewhat amazing in a hamlet of mainly thatched huts – plus studio/rehearsal space; the school has a good library and audio-visual facilities; tours have equipped rural centres with basic technical facilities. Like Rangayana (see below, also in Karnataka), it welcomes visits/ workshops by major Indian and overseas theatre workers (among them B.V. Karanth). Bharucha discusses the possibly sinister colonialist/political implications of Ford funding, but concludes that Heggodu has always been upfront about the money and clear about how to use it for structural and long-term support. Subbana has also been on the Executive Committee of another Karnataka operation at Udupi funded largely by Ford from the early 1980s to engage in research, extensive documentation, and the organisation of festivals and colloquia on *Yakshagana* under the direction of Prof. Haridasa Bhat. This too is characterised by good reporting, proper accounts and regular publications; Ford Foundation money and other spin-off international links have been directed to contributing to the maintenance and perhaps extension of folk forms both theatrical and musical (including puppets).

The plays chosen and directed by Ninasam personnel regularly include world classics and modern works as well as Kannada writers and Kannada versions of classical plays: in keeping with the educational mission, they do not merely pander to the entertainment ethos or to popular taste, though everything is made accessible in Kannada. Significant productions include a *Shakuntala* directed by Subbana; Brecht, Shakespeare and Molière have been successfully presented as well as works by e.g. Karnad. 'Constant experimentation, an uncompromising commitment to quality and an ambitious attempt at developing theatre as a means of cultural dialogue' inform this work (Ashoka, 145).

SOPANAM INSTITUTE OF PERFORMING ARTS

Kavalam Narayana Panikkar's institute, founded in Trivandrum in 1964, aims to contribute to the evolution of a new Indian theatre by using traditional (Malayalam) theatrical forms to address contemporary issues. Sopanam has staged many of Panikkar's own plays and he has directed new versions of classics by Bhasa and Kalidasa – in total twelve Malayalam works and five in Sanskrit, several of which have toured both in India and abroad. Sopanam provides performance training based on traditional practice (the martial art *kalari*, study of ritual forms like *Theyyam* and *Padayani*, training in local musical forms). The relatively small number of productions is explained by the fact that most of the performers have been part-time for much of the period; training might occur before the start of the day's work and rehearsal in the evening after it; only relatively recently has the institute acquired a permanent rehearsal and performance space. Panikkar's work however has achieved major recognition both in Kerala and throughout India: Singleton proposes that 'his intraculturalist approach to modern theatre is a defiant attempt to legitimize his performance heritage by resisting the dominant ideology through ritual practice' (Singleton, n.d. 12). His institution is small and remains within a fairly narrow, though significant, compass; but it has functioned consistently and established a strong reputation; his plays are published in Malayalam and several in English translation appear in Seagull Books list.

NATAKA KARNATAKA RANGAYANA

Founded by B.V. Karanth, this State Theatre is a fully professional repertory company located in a splendid building in Mysore, with two open air and one indoor performance spaces, which also host occasional visiting performances. The company numbers eighteen (all from Karnataka state), who receive a training which includes yoga, martial arts, acting, rhythm and music, design and stage-craft. It has mounted around thirty-five productions between its inception in 1991 and the end of 1997, including a variety of Indian forms, some as adaptations from fiction and poetry, and some half-dozen European plays. Visiting lecturers and workshop tutors feature strongly (most from India, some from abroad). The company has toured within and beyond the state, and on a couple of occasions abroad. Karanth, one-time Director of NSD, is a significant figure in modern theatre and his influence has been beneficial. The training and performance policy of the company seems reasonably open, but with solid roots in appropriate Indian forms. Currently things look healthy, but it is perhaps too early yet to judge whether state funding will lead to problems.

DARPANA ACADEMY OF PERFORMING ARTS

Indian performer Mallika Sarabhai, with her famous classical dancer mother Mrinalini, runs a Performing Arts Academy in Ahmedabad, Gujarat. The Academy, founded in 1948 by Mrinalini, encompasses relatively conventional dance instruction for children, a celebrated puppet troupe, a folk-dance company which has also revived a range of indigenous dances, an internationally renowned performance company and an extensive social and educational outreach programme (Darpana for Development, see below); recent revisions have initiated an expansion of the latter plus ventures in communication, more flexible multi-skilled training for the performance company and a shift from *ab initio* dance instruction to more advanced work. The Academy also includes a delightful amphitheatre overlooking the Sabarmati river which serves as a regular venue for home-grown and visiting performance of all kinds; it also frequently receives performance workers from many areas as collaborators for short or long periods; in both cases visitors come from other regions in India and also from abroad. The Academy has encouraged theatre from local groups in Gujarati, Hindi and English, as well as opening to a spectrum stretching across folk and classical Indian dance, north and south Indian classical music, puppetry and story-telling. The intention is to promote Indian performance forms of many kinds within an awareness of the national and international context, and to support innovation.

Both Mallika and Mrinalini Sarabhai perceive the creation of work of high quality rooted in indigenous tradition as profoundly empowering and celebratory, but also, when necessary, confrontational and unorthodox. Their work has targeted receivers at all social levels and in many different locations, particularly where it explicitly moves towards outreach, community involvement and performance as politics. Even where a largely 'bourgeois' audience is involved, Mallika's work (cited in Chapter 4) is never less than challenging to its artistic and sociopolitical preconceptions. As the only Indian performer in Peter Brook's *Mahabharata*, cast in the role of Draupadi, she forged a combative refocusing of herself as a woman and as an Indian which has permeated all her subsequent work.

Darpana currently is less of a basic training institution than a nexus for the instigation of creative activity. Over the years, Marxists have targeted its 'elitist' origins in classical dance and its apparent links with the mill-owning Sarabhai family, regardless of the fact that Mrinalini's philanthropic husband Vikram was a nuclear scientist, and that for many decades the Academy has been funded mainly from performance income, aided latterly by commercial sponsorship of the performance venue and occasional grants for specific projects; the development work, which is clearly not elitist or 'top down' in practice, is discussed below. Whereas the three other institutes discussed in this section see their brief as largely state-specific, Darpana's vision is essentially multiform, across a wide range of performance encompassing regional, national and international currents. Its philosophy construes that very multiformity as a conscious artistic and political choice, quite deliberately positioned against narrow vision of all kinds. There would seem to be a place for such a vision in the contemporary scene.

It is worth noting here that two of the four institutions discussed in this section are private and two public. Both the private operations receive some funding, usually on a project basis, from national or local sources (e.g. the ICCR – Indian Council for Cultural Relations). Otherwise they are reliant on sponsorship and/or performance payments. Clearly there can be problems both here and in the public domain, where political instability and sudden shifts of funding policy are likely to cause difficulties. Of course the story is not too dissimilar in many other parts of the world. India however has no public social security system, which means that life in the performance sphere is even more hazardous than elsewhere.

Side glances

Other performance work

This book has not dealt to any great extent with 'pure' dance forms or with puppets, though they are referred to in Chapter 3. It is however worth mentioning that these forms too are responsive in different measure to changing contemporary contexts: puppetry is particularly well-placed to respond imaginatively and is also amenable to educational and outreach activity. Notable examples are the Delhi-based puppeteer Dadi Padumjee, profiled in *STQ* 23, whose highly inventive and immaculately delivered work is on a par with the best in puppetry world-wide and spans the range from children's shows to politics, from exquisite miniatures to moving and powerful combinations of puppet and performer; and the late Meher Contractor's revival of many forms at Darpana Academy. Whereas some puppet forms (for example in Rajasthan) seem currently to have shrunk to a small and repetitive 'packaged' repertoire, others have adapted and flourish. There are delicate shadow-puppet forms similar to those from Indonesia, sturdy and comical rod and glove puppets, puppet versions of traditional theatre forms (*Kathakali, Yakshagana*).

Bharucha's study of Chandralekha, referred to above, focuses on perhaps the most outstanding example of innovation in dance. There is also a considerable amount of 'fusion'-oriented dance experimentation by established academies and individual performers. This is both intra-and inter-cultural: mixing *Bharatanatyam* and *Kathakali*; combining forms from Indian and western culture, sometimes by native Indian performers, sometimes by Indians living abroad or born abroad, sometimes by non-Indian performers with strong affinities to Indian culture. The success and quality can be variable, of course, as with any experimentation; the issue of trans-culturalism is evident again, but it is certainly not a simplistic one, and here as in other domains it is as much a question of Indian performers and forms doing the assimilation as of cultural domination or cultural piracy. Here as elsewhere in the current environment, Indian performance in practice displays a robustness, a self-assurance and an experimental openness. Even at the relatively conservative end of the spectrum, the most renowned *Bharatanatyam* training institute, Kalakshetra (Madras), engages in a degree of innovation, spurred on perhaps by Chandralekha's presence a few kilometers down the road.

Academic and professional discussion

This occurs via books (scripts by the above writers, articles in *Enact*, *Sangeet Natak Journal* (both of which have now ceased publication), *Literary Criterion*, *Seagull Theatre Quarterly* (from 1994) and other journals; the Sangeet Natak Akademi and Sahitya Akademi (academies of theatre/dance and literature) at state and national level also publish scripts, collections of texts and essays from Indian writing from the medieval period onwards. An important recent publication is *Rasa: The Indian Performing Arts in the Last Twenty-five Years* (Vol.II: Theatre and Cinema: theatre section edited by Ananda Lal) (Lal 1995), which contains thirty-four essays on theatre, both descriptive and evaluative, indicating the range of issues and forms of practice. Although discussion in some of these publications is highly abstract and removed from the practical theatre scene, much of it is also carried out by writers, directors and academics who have close and practical links with theatre in performance. Outstanding examples are the work of K. Ayyappa Paniker – poet, playwright, historian, critic and translator, editor of major collections including translations of Shakespeare's complete works into Malayalam; and the excellent coverage of the recent theatre scene, together with its antecedents, in *Seagull Theatre Quarterly*, whose contributors are invariably active theatre workers with recent direct experience. Talwar does however indicate an area of oversight when she points out that 'contemporary Indian theatre has been ignored by cultural analysts' (Talwar 1997, 94); here too *STQ* has made considerable moves to plug the gap.

These brief notes indicate some of the range of issues and forms of practice to be found currently in India. To examine them all fully would take several books. The bibliography and references indicate where further material may be found. I want now to look at precisely the category of work which Talwar claims has been neglected, and which also displays the ingenuity, multiplicity and energy characteristic of much contemporary practice.

Alternative practitioners and 'Theatre of Development'

Overview

Neelima Talwar claims that 'theatre of development' is a distinctive trend in Indian drama from the 1970s (Talwar 1997, 94). Categories of activity in this area include theatre and/as 'liberation', political intervention, agit prop, 'cultural caravans' and festivals, street theatre and other modes of educational promotion: social and community issues, health, educational schemes, theatre for and by women's groups, children's theatre. Though funding here too can be haphazard, if dependent on fickle politically-tied local sources and suspect, if dependent on 'foreign money' via Non-Government Organisations (NGOs), there is now throughout India a great wealth of theatre and performance work of this kind; often on a small scale, sometimes intermittent, but determined and dedicated. Some of this activity draws on the work of social theorists and theatre practitioners like Boal, Freire and Fanon.

Talwar (1997) gives 5 categories of theatre work under this heading (she uses the term 'plays', but it is more accurate to talk of theatre or performance work):

1. Theatre as a means of promoting science, or more generally what Das refers to as 'scientific temper' (Das, 1992): roughly, increased intellectual resources together with a critical attitude.
2. Performance as health education.
3. Topical political critiques.
4. Feminist plays or plays highlighting questions relating to women.
5. Performance in support of literacy drives.

(1997, 95)

I would add to these, performance work foregrounding other social and communal issues; more importantly, Talwar's scheme focuses exclusively on the *content* or aim of such performance and says nothing about its *methods*. These include:

1. 'Agit-prop' theatre, frequently neo-Brechtian in character, aiming at 'conscientisation' and raising political awareness.
2. Street theatre, processional theatre, cultural caravans (*jathas*), drawing on local folk forms including music, dance, comedy etc.
3. 'Theatre of the oppressed' (Boal-related work) aiming at audience involvement and empowerment as participants, debaters, co-creators, 'spectactors' (Boal).

Talwar does however contend that neither A.J. Gunwardana's term 'intermediary drama' (i.e. neither 'modern' nor 'traditional', recalling Sircar's 'Third Theatre') nor Rustom Bharucha's 'revolutionary drama' adequately circumscribe the range of development theatre. Its form does indeed derive from the merger Gunwardana points to, but its tone, Talwar proposes, 'is that of patient persuasion, provocation that leads to informed choices' (97). This however implies an emphasis on 'reasoning' which is not necessarily uniquely helpful as a way of understanding how many forms of theatre work.

Such theatre is frequently close to what Schechner calls 'environmental theatre', which uses found spaces and involves the community, though its underlying drive is what he categorises as 'confrontation theatre' (Schechner 1983). He later uses the term 'believed-in theatre' (*STQ* 18, 3), which stresses the direct links to the life-situation and the issues presented for all participants, performers and spectators. Another pertinent note is struck by Prabir Guha's suggestion 'invisible theatre' (*STQ* 12, 60): neither advertised nor reported.

However, it is important to note that theatre with a development focus does also take place in more conventional ('westernised') settings, for example in urban theatres and at arts festivals. The work of many of the playwrights discussed above falls at least sometimes into this category, as do dance and multi-genre performances by performers such as Mallika Sarabhai.

'Cultural awakening is arguably a crucial stage in the development of a people ... [to] stimulate the minds of the people to take creative control of their own destinies' (Van Erven 1992, 1). In India, work which falls into Talwar's category certainly has its beginnings in this kind of awareness, but in the contemporary situation things are perhaps more complex than the initial drive to move from a colonial past and a neocolonial present.

Talwar indicates that the roots of development theatre 'go back to the genesis of the drama of political protest in 1857' (95). At various times since, it has surfaced, usually under the impetus of leftist or nationalist political groupings or affinities. The recent growth (post-1960) is traced back to Sircar, with particular reference to his 'theatre of rural-urban links'. Theatre of development 'has internalised all these problematic nationalist concerns and aesthetic modes that break the historical barriers between the audience and performers' (98).

In so far as it has done this, it represents an important extension to the performance spectrum, both in terms of form and of the relationship between theatre and society. Nevertheless, there are also problems associated with the genre of theatre for development itself. These issues will be picked up below, but it is worth noting here firstly that theatre of this kind is found, in slightly different manifestations, in Africa, South America and elsewhere in Asia; secondly that it gives rise to questions about appropriate forms; and thirdly that, in India as elsewhere, a major question is 'development for whom?' Form and outcome are intricately linked and upon them depends the extent of any freedom which may be acquired. Where the provider is a government agency or a politically-motivated NGO, or where the method tends more to agit-prop than to participation, such freedom may be severely compromised.

The discussion below includes both 'street' (usually more specifically politicised) and 'development' (usually covering a more general social and educational spectrum) models, though there is also often a degree of overlap. It concludes with a discussion of the relationship of the kinds of performance and intention involved to kinds and degrees of freedom.

IPTA and after

Between the two landmarks positioned above comes the history of IPTA (Indian People's Theatre Association). That story needs to be taken up from the beginnings of Bengali theatre, outlined in Samik Bandyopadhyay's article in *STQ* 12: 'Bengali Theatre: The End of the Colonial Tradition?' (Bandyopadhyay, 1996, 50–59).

In formal terms these are to be found in post-World War I upheavals against colonial theatre culture, which was generally awful, overacted and melodramatic, exhibiting many of the worst features of European actor-managers' theatre and Indian excesses. Some writers and directors (e.g. Tagore and Sisirkumar Bhaduri) sought different directions – more poetic or more realistic – but, says Bandyopadhyay, also acquiesced in the 'authoritarian power of the colonial theatre aesthetic' (50). Hopes that a theatre for the urban intelligentsia might arise (as opposed to the '*babus*' – upper middle-class colonialist fellow-travellers who were patrons of colonial theatre); or even that specific political (e.g. nationalist) aims might be achieved were not realised until the World War 2 bombings by the Japanese in Dec. 1942 and the famine of 1942–6 in Calcutta and Bengal, which provided the necessary shock and material for new departures (August 1942 also witnessed a Rebellion).

IPTA was located together with other Communist Party 'front' artistic organisations at 46 Dharmatala St. in central Calcutta. The CP was legalised on 23 July 1942; after a long debate it decided to join the International Communist Movement in support of Allied resistance to Fascist threat, putting independence demands second. IPTA 'rediscovered' (56) folk forms and traditions, revived indigenous values and began to develop more realistic and critical stances.

Bandyopadhyay's desire to foreground certain trends causes him to be unnecessarily dismissive of Tagore's major place in Bengali theatre; that however is not his focus here. He notes that 'given the sheer range in geographical spread and numbers alike, the IPTA does not have a close parallel in Communist or Communist-led cultural movements anywhere else in the world.' (56) The same phenomenon applies to much contemporary development theatre which draws on considerable collective energy: e.g. a 1981 report by KSSP (see below) claims that the total audience for its science-based performance work was over 1 million; and a single play entitled 'The Girl is Born' was performed by the NGO Stree Mukti Sanghatana (Women's Liberation Movement) to 2,000,000 people in Maharashtra in the early 1990s (Furman 1999, 3).

Bijan Bhattacharya's *Agun* ('Fire') was a landmark production (1943); episodic in form, focused on the issue of famine/rationing, spreading a message of solidarity. Other works followed using a similar form and incorporating features such as songs, leading to the requirement of new acting styles, both naturalistic and poetic. (Major performers from this era included Sombhu Mitra and his wife Tripti, a cousin of Bijan Bhattacharya.)

IPTA thereafter becomes a constant point of reference for theatre workers, so that its influence is even more extensive than its actual historical/geographical span: it becomes the sign of a particular approach to theatre which is both characteristic of and central to the development of a specific (political) attitude to and concept of 'Indianness' in and through theatre. This approach draws on traditional forms with contemporary/satirical additions. (See also Eugène van Erven's discussion of Indian Theatre of Liberation in his *The Playful Revolution* [Van Erven 1992].)

IPTA remained active throughout the Indian sub-continent up to 1964, though Habib Tanvir says that its 'swan song happened ... in 1957', perhaps around the time that its 'anti-imperialist and anti-bourgeoise [sic]' thrust became less relevant (*STQ* 21, 152). This led on to the increasing presence of Indian playwrights writing in regional languages from the 1960s (see above), and the incorporation of folk/classical elements into experimental theatre from the 1970s, for example Utpal Dutt using *Jatra* in Marxist plays like *Surya Shikar*, 1972.

During this period Brecht was also popular (*The Life of Galileo* is the model for Dutt's above-mentioned play about conflict between establishment belief-structures and new forms of knowledge), but Van Erven slates the fashion for 'Brecht in saris' (Van Erven 1992, 115). He cites M.K. Raina, Sircar and Arun Mukherjee as the 'only three established Indian political theatre makers' who go beyond adopting Western or traditional forms to incorporate social criticism (though he doesn't produce an argument to say what's wrong with this, or indeed with Brecht). On the other hand, it's noticeable that Rustom Bharucha writes favourably of K.V. Subbana's use of Brecht, even when working with underprivileged and/or rural groups with little formal education: he praises Subbana's refusal to patronise them by not doing anything except popular or familiar models. The issue, not quite clearly posed by van Erven, is perhaps the extent to which Brecht's themes and strategies have been assimilated or 'Indianized' – as Talwar puts it (Talwar 1997, 101). As my argument elsewhere indicates, I think that, although certainly some practitioners have crudely lifted theatrical models indigenous or foreign, there are a great many more writers and directors than van Erven is aware of who have created a whole spectrum of ways in which such models have been profitably blended with presentation and analysis of contemporary issues.

Sircar, with his group Satabdi, has worked like Mukherjee in Calcutta. Mukherjee's position was that political theatre needs audiences and the disenfranchised don't come because they have no money; after 1974 Sircar insisted that all performances should be free, but this meant that he had to use amateur part-time actors and was not able to spend much time in local communities or travelling.

All these groups, directors and writers trace their origins in large part to the experiences and principles of IPTA. It is also worth picking up here a strand which increasingly feeds into the changing theatre scene, and which begins from some aspects of women's involvement in IPTA.

The story of Gul Bardhan (told in *STQ* 7, 36–48) is not untypical of (i) theatre workers in the IPTA/politicised situation, both pre- and post- the end of the colonialist period; (ii) women working in such groups; (iii) the history of theatre as part of arts/entertainment spectrum from 1930–1980.

A celebrated performer who later ran her own company, the main features of Bardhan's experience include: reliance on and/or need to break free from the 'star' system which continued the (male) actor-manager tradition; the extremely difficult and vulnerable economic situation of performers; swings of political fortune – her company was sometimes reviled, sometimes adopted by leading figures; the lure of Bollywood once a member is 'recognised' as 'folk' performer; the sense of camaraderie and resilience developed in working with a touring company; and the flexibility of performers manifested in their willingness to learn new skills.

Gul Bardhan worked with IPTA from 1945–52, and ran her own Little Ballet troupe from 1952 onwards. The 'central squad' of IPTA, based in Bombay, became a kind of drain, funnelling regional artists towards commercial film impresarios. To some extent it also became the model for 'national' ventures like the foundation of NSD, the Akademis etc., which subsequently proved to have considerable drawbacks. These and other pressures outlined above, difficult as they are to cope with, are not untypical of working with small (touring) companies anywhere. The significant thing is that Bardhan, as a woman, was able to operate in an otherwise largely male field. Her experience with her company shows many of the features associated with work anywhere in the world at the 'improvisatory' or developmental end of the theatre product spectrum. This is also true of the ventures described next.

The theatre group Theatre Union was founded from a women's collective formed in 1981 whose members included Anuradha Kapur, Maya Rao (both of whom have taught at NSD) and Rati Bartholomew. The group arose as a response to a dowry-death incident. In *Manushi*, Kapur and Rao created a play structured around the Punjabi folk form, which had 300 performances, mainly in the Delhi area, at first in colleges, later on request in community locations including on the street. They went on to do other plays on such issues as sutee, rapes at work and by the police, and one about partition which Sudhanva Deshpande, who characterises their work as vivacious and creative, describes as 'among the most haunting I have ever seen created on the street' (S. Deshpande 1997, 16). Betty Bernhard, an American researcher, has a book currently in press on performance as a method of countering the oppression of women in India.

Other manifestations of development theatre similarly draw inspiration from these roots or are directly associated with them. Chief among them are the activities in Delhi centring around Safdar Hashmi (both before and after his murder) and the work of the KSSP in Kerala.

Delhi: Safdar Hashmi

Hashmi was active from 1973–1989 with his street theatre group Janam. Janam means 'New Birth' and is short for Jana Natya Manch: People's Theatre Front. Hashmi, originally a journalist, sought to use political theatre to 'liberate ourselves from the stranglehold of colonial and imperialist culture' (van Erven 1992, 141); in his view, the problem with traditional forms is that endemic social and political structures (feudal, obscurantist etc.) are embedded in them. This suspicion emerges as a conspiracy theory towards what were seen as art promotion exercises (funded by middle-class and foreign capital) aimed at maintaining an obscurantist or exoticist version of 'Indianness'. Even today, Sahmat (the current name for the organisation) refuses to accept financial assistance from outside India, as does another Delhi-based activist theatre group, Nishant, run by Shamsul Islam. Hashmi, although cautious, did however make limited use of 'folk' elements and explicitly recognised that 'contemporary Indian street theatre has been drawing in equal measure from our folk and classical drama as well as from western drama' (Hashmi 1989, 11).

Janam gave around 4,000 performances of some twenty plays, mostly by Safdar Hashmi, of which eleven were translated into many Indian languages. The group espoused an alternative political agenda and cultural history, and proclaimed itself to be anti-dynasty; founded originally out of the breakup of IPTA and the split of the

Indian Communist movement into the CPI and the CPI(M), it gave festival performances and tours, sometimes to massive audiences, for example in Uttar Pradesh at election time. Most productions occurred either around major political events: for example under the state of Emergency declared by Indira Gandhi; or in the context of local political issues: *Machine,* a thirteen-minute play about workers' conditions at a chemical factory, is now 'legendary in working-class circles' (Van Erven 1992, 150): it had its première at a Trades' Union conference on 15 October 1978 and played the next day to 160,000 workers; it was then taken up by groups all round the country. Actors create the 'machine' of capital, as workers, bosses, security personnel; the play is 'stylized, lyrical, near-poetic', its 'abstraction and brevity lend it a certain simplicity' (Sudhanva Deshpande, 1997, 10).

In 1979 Janam produced *Aurat,* their most popular play (over 2,000 performances in eighteen years, translated and performed in almost every Indian language). This and other plays use basic elements in different combinations and formats: some in rhyme, some in naturalistic dialogue; some with songs as narrative elements, others where they function as commentary; different kinds of humour and degrees of documentary topicality. Further plays in 1980 about price rises and rationing were 'hugely popular', according to Deshpande (1997, 12), who describes this period as 'the salad days'. Other plays took up other agit-prop agendas and social/ political issues: the treatment of women, agricultural economics; *Apharan Bhaichare Ka* dealt with separatism, Sikh/Punjabi extremism, and conspiracy theories about Congress Party and US involvement in Indira Gandhi's murder.

After fifteen years Janam needed to establish itself on a professional footing in order to continue, and was planning to raise finance from film-writing and production and to build an institute and theatre; but Safdar Hashmi was killed by political opponents on January 1st 1989. National protests followed and the SAHMAT trust fund was established; many street-theatre groups were formed or revived throughout India following Hashmi's murder, including several using the same name as Hashmi's group, though in some cases their existence was short-lived; both January 1 and April 12 (Hashmi's birthday) have been regularly celebrated ever since as festivals of street theatre; one of the most popular plays by the Calcutta group Notun Chehara, with 800 performances since 1989, is *Safdar Marena (Safdar Doesn't Die).*

Sahmat (Safdar Hashmi Memorial Trust) organises events, exhibitions, street theatre; publishes books (including Hashmi's books for children), documentation, audio tapes and videos: it is dedicated to democratic, secular and pluralist values. It has established wide contacts with leading artists and organisations, and publishes an articulate and well-produced bulletin. Under the direction of Safdar's widow Mala, both the spirit and the substance of Hashmi's work continue to inform the organisation, which is important both in its own right and as a landmark for and key player in theatre of development activity.

The existence of this organisation and that of Samudaya and KSSP (see below) are major indicators of the profile of this work in India, which is however as yet largely unrecognised elsewhere. Talwar notes also that even in India, 'most serious inventories of contemporary Indian theatre do not include them' (1997, 103), perhaps because the work they do is not immediately recognised as 'theatre'. This work is often participatory (sometimes involving very large numbers), improvisatory, occurring in non-fixed locations and using an eclectic amalgam of forms. Yet of course many of these features are common not only to traditional and folk theatre forms in India, but also to an emerging world consensus about what might properly be called 'theatre'. Theatre historians are perhaps slow to catch up, but the kinds of shifts in understanding which the previous chapter has outlined have been occurring for several decades (see e.g. Roose-Evans, 1989 and Yarrow, 1992, re. shifts in European theatre). Jacques Lecoq defines the foregrounding of the improvisatory as a pointer to creative renewal; Schechner's work on performance as event and on environmental theatre signals other important dimensions. Theory has to accommodate to practice: whilst practice in the 'west' is changing shape by incorporating much from the east, Indian theatre, which has itself assimilated and transformed western models, is also changing in many ways, as this book attempts to indicate. The presence and influence of development theatre is one major aspect of that change.

Kerala

The Kerala Sastra Sahitya Parishad (KSSP), a state-wide education network with headquarters in Trivandrum, was founded in 1962. It has consistently organised 'cultural caravans' (*jathas*) throughout the state and sometimes further afield. It claims 2,000 affiliated branches and 60,000 members (1995 figures) organised according to a four-tier structure from state committee to local units covering ten to twenty sq.km. Its original brief was to spread science education and challenge religious domination; this has gradually extended to other issues, for example relating to environment and ecology, the question of dowry, the Bhopal disaster. KSSP describes its involvement in terms of three areas: agitative, educative and constructive. It has NGO status and raises funds by book publication and sales; it also receives donations and central/local government funding for specific R&D projects. There were links with Calicut University School of Drama (Trichur) for *jathas* and tours: plays dealing with political and social issues would be followed by discussion afterwards. In 1987 KSSP organised a nationwide cultural caravan (beginning with rehearsal first in Trivandrum, then leaving from five different points), culminating in a *jatha* in Bhopal and performances all over the country, including to 15,000 spectators in Calcutta. *Kala jathas* (cultural processions) move from village to village, stopping to perform and initiate discussion, leading on to follow-up debate and, where appropriate, action. They use plays, songs in the folk medium, and other cultural media. KSSP is affiliated to the All India People's Science Foundation Network and to national literacy and women's education campaigns.

Graduates from Trichur also started Root Theatre Co. in 1983, workshopping and performing various forms including western and contemporary, realistic and Sanskrit in villages to combat the influence of commercial touring comedy groups (of which there are about 500 in Kerala, mostly using untrained actors and predictable formats and material, but generating large amounts of revenue, especially for the manager); Root put on Sircar's *Bhoma* among other works.

Abhinaya (Trivandrum), founded in 1992, continues this work. The group holds annual festivals and plans to develop as an artistic centre/network; its focus is cultural, social and aesthetic. Several members worked with Footsbarn Theatre in France and have contributed their experience of European mime/physical theatre styles to produce an effective blend with Malayalam traditional material.

Karnataka

R.P. Prasanna founded Samudaya (Community) Theatre Co. in 1975 in Bangalore, and worked with groups in Mysore and Mangalore at the time of Indira Gandhi's Martial Law. Prasanna co-ordinated theatre of liberation groups for a one-month mobile festival to combat Mrs Gandhi's re-election attempt in Chikmagalur district (October-November 1979). Following on the success of this venture, thirty-two more Samudaya units were formed, working both with rural communities and with proscenium theatre in Bangalore. In 1981 there was a second *jatha* (festival) but activity declined after this and Prasanna left in the mid-80s to join NSD; he later moved to Heggodu. Samudaya continues however both to perform and to organise *jathas* periodically. Other social action groups also developed using some theatre, especially workshop methods, for example MESCA, with twenty groups in Karnataka and others in Tamil Nadu, Andhra Pradesh and Kerala, which organised street theatre and cultural caravans. A very successful play about child-labour achieved political and legal results. MESCA's co-ordinator Shashidara Adapa intended to build a new form of popular theatre from the grass roots, incorporating different forms, like puppets and painting (see van Erven 1992, 121–5).

Samudaya developed eight plays during its first year; its work included *Belchi*, based on the burning of Harijan labourers in Bihar in 1977 (2,500 performances to 1997) and *Struggle*, about a strike in a Bangalore factory, dramatised by the workers themselves. Other plays dealt with similar themes of murder, oppression, police brutality. Like *Machine*, the work arose from real-life incidents: Samudaya's aims were to 'experience and evaluate the scene at first hand, and to use theatre as an instrument of education, as an attack on feudal and semi-feudal values' (Bartholomew 1983, 19). The group initially drew inspiration from Sircar, who ran a two-week workshop for them; although the work of both Samudaya and Janam has many points of contact with Boal's Theatre of the Oppressed, his book (published in English in 1979) was not available in India at this time.

See also above under 'Academies' for details of K.V. Subbana's work at Heggodu with his organisation Ninasam.

Tamil Nadu

The ARP (Association of the Rural Poor) works with Harijans and often includes theatre as part of its educational programme which focuses on social and communal issues. ARP also operates in Andhra Pradesh, where it has worked in 500 communities. Some members were sent to the Philippines to learn the Boal-based methodology of the Philippine Educational Theatre Association. ARP operates five teams, each with fifteen members who work on two-year projects, meeting other teams monthly to discuss progress. It has also organised cultural caravans in Tamil Nadu, starting with workshops in Madras, again focusing on local, communal, caste and gender issues. Chennai Kalai Kuzhu has also operated from Madras since 1984, performing issue-based plays evolved from collective improvisation; its director, Pralayan, drew on experience with Samudaya and KSSP (see *STQ* 16, 72–88); in Andhra, APNM (Andhra Praja Natya Mandali) has units throughout the state, producing much original work and drawing on rural roots. Also in Madras (Chennai), Na Muthuswamy's Koothu-P-Pattarai has operated as a professional group for over two decades, addressing a variety of social issues by adapting folk forms (particularly *Therukoothu*) to contemporary situations.

Chandralekha started 'Skills' in Madras in 1980 to develop community relationships through enhancing skills in communication and the visual arts (e.g. to assist production of education aids): this 'cultural' focus was rare in development work at this period. Chandra was also involved in a street theatre project with Skills, an eight-minute piece on the death of democracy at the hands of political opportunism and corruption: she and Sadanand Menon were subsequently charged with sedition in 1982.

Calcutta and West Bengal

IPTA's beginnings in Calcutta are noted on pp. 178–80; activist and alternative models of performance continued to flourish under Sircar and Mukherjee; Nemai Ghosh's photographic history of Calcutta theatre since the 1950s draws on more than one hundred experimental groups active at any given point during that period (Ghosh 2000); Devi's plays derive from her social and political intervention in the lives of the disadvantaged and oppressed in West Bengal. In view of these strong traditions, plus the reputation of Calcutta as an intellectual centre and the presence of the influential Seagull Foundation for the Arts, it is not surprising that development activity flourishes.

Its principal proponent since 1985 has been the Boal-inspired collective, or 'cultural movement', Jana Sanskriti, directed by Sanjoy Ganguly, who scripts most of the plays in their final form; they deal with issues which include local politics, rape, communal harmony, alcohol and environmental concerns. Jana Sanskriti has thirty theatre teams, ten of them composed of all women, working in southern West Bengal. Ganguly has given workshops throughout India and has good links with Boal's Centre for the Theatre for the Oppressed in Rio de Janeiro and with other Boal workers; his group make use of Boal's Image and Forum Theatre strategies to create pieces drawn from the experience of the communities they live and work in. Jana Sanskriti declares that it 'seeks to stop the oppressed people from thinking that they are inferior, weak and incapable of analytical thought' in order to become able 'to plan constructive action' (Jana Sanskriti 1999; see also *STQ* 2 on Boal work and Jana Sanskriti).

Jana Sanghati Kendra, which originally worked with Jana Sanskriti, now operates with three all-woman teams and attempts to extend Boalian Forum Theatre techniques into a continuous cycle of performance and social action. Whereas Jana Sanskriti is independent, though associated with an NGO which takes forward the issues raised in performances into social action, Jana Sanghati is itself an NGO and works in collaboration with two 'trade union' organisations. Like many other similar ventures, it has devoted considerable thought to both the politics and the aesthetics of theatre work in this field. It uses the term 'Spontaneous Theatre' to summarise its focus, which combines an emphasis on improvisation and performer-input (along with the use of traditional performance-forms) with the desire to achieve a 'continuous cycle between social action and theatre' (Jana Sanghati 1999). This aims to ensure that theatre activity is continuously present as a way of engaging with local social and political concerns, and 'may lead to a blurring in the differences of roles between social activists, villagers and theatre activists'.

Seagull Theatre Quarterly has involved itself in two programmes of active intervention through performance: the first, a documentation of a project with sex-workers in the Kalighat district of Calcutta in 1994–6 (*STQ* 9); the second, co-ordinating an initiative called 'Theatre for Change', funded by the UK Network Foundation and organised by two small Calcutta NGOs. This 1997–8 initiative consisted of two parts, one working with disadvantaged children, the other with women victims of violence: Jana Sanskriti were engaged to conduct the latter. *STQ* 20/21 carries full documentation of the initiative, including interviews with many of the participants.

Other prominent Calcutta activist groups are Prabir Guha's Alternative Living Theatre and Pranab Chatterjee's Ritwick. The latter remains associated with the CPI (M), but Guha moved away from direct political involvement, worked for a time with Grotowski and operates a more Artaudian version of theatrical confrontation. He has also worked with Theatre Living Laboratory, a project in rural Bengal and Bihar aimed at social mobilisation of distressed women (see *STQ* 20/21, 92–8); in an article in *STQ* 12 he states that 'many such groups ... are spread all over India. They are committed to a kind of invisible theatre that seeks to propagate social change' (63), and names eleven theatre groups in just two blocks or zones of one district in West Bengal. Their members are drawn from marginalised communities and include tribals and Muslim women.

There is thus clear evidence of wide-ranging and persistent activity with a strong socio-political focus. The central debate about politics and aesthetics will be picked up below.

Gujarat

There is significant development theatre activity in Gujarat, including the experimental and street theatre work of Hasmukh Baradi's Garage Theatre (Ahmedabad). Baradi also publishes a journal.

Among other projects, including one using puppets and another mentioned in Chapter 3 (p. 82), Darpana Academy's development wing (Darpana for Development) has run a three-year project for social development entitled *Parivartan* ('Change') with Bhil tribes-people in northern Gujarat, funded by the Macarthur Trust and carried out in conjunction with a local NGO. Regular assessment of this project against its aims resulted in its extension for a further three years, both in the same group of thirty villages – where some 12,000 people saw the eleven productions developed – and in others. All members of the performance team were drawn from the target community; issues to be presented were decided in consultation with them. Similar schemes have been operated and are planned by Anita Desai in southern and eastern Gujarat (*Breaking the Culture of Silence*). This work included a six-day *padyatra* – walking to and performing in thirty-one villages.

Issues (bride price, witches, revenge feuds, women's health, inoculation, alcoholism) relate to tribal practice and belief-structure. Formats have included song, dance and folk theatre; discussion and intervention is promoted either by Boal structures (Image and Forum Theatre) or by post-performance sessions. Follow-up through NGOs and other regional forums or agencies (health provision, village council structures) has been initiated. Both schemes seek to move towards empowerment, particularly of women, in local political structures, paralleling aspects of Boal's 'Legislative Theatre'.

Performers already possessed some skills (singing etc.) but these were usually not regarded as 'performance'-oriented, rather as contributions to ritual events; they therefore received specific further training at several points, initially in the form of an extended workshop. Both quality of performance and effective interaction with and stimulation of the spectators are sought.

An interesting and salutary footnote to this activity is that it has in large measure evolved as a partnership between Darpana Academy (a private institution with no narrow political affiliation) and prominent ex-Bombay-IPTA member Kailash Pandya. Initially responsible, along with co-IPTA-veteran Jaswant Thaker, for reviving the Gujarati folk-form *Bhavai* (also with Darpana support), Pandya now co-ordinates major outreach programmes using folk forms for development work with tribals. Thaker's daughter, Anita Desai, also works in this field. The late Vikram Sarabhai, leading atomic scientist, humanitarian and benefactor of the arts, together with his renowned dancer wife Mrinalini, provided crucial support. The situation makes a nonsense of oppositional political posturing which tends merely to create alternative versions of the 'other' as villain rather than as victim, and thus to compound the situation by reinforcing the language and structure of embattlement.

Surveys and evaluations

Seagull Theatre Quarterly attempted to develop a nationwide profile of street-theatre groups through a questionnaire in August 1996; of thirty approached, only two responded, one from Kanpur and one from Calcutta, founded in 1984 and 1987 respectively; both of them, significantly, stress the need for effective networking (*STQ* 16, 89–90). Nonetheless, a national open-air theatre festival took place over five days in Calcutta in November-December 1996: fourteen groups participated, including *Jana Natya Manch, Satabdi, Jana Sanskriti, Chennai Kalai Kuzhu* and groups from Bhopal and Imphal (Manipur); directors included Sircar, Bansi Kaul, Sanjoy Ganguly, Sudhanva Deshpande; the chief guest was Moloyashree (Mala) Hashmi, Safdar's widow, still very active in *Jana Natya Manch*.

Sudhanva Deshpande stresses that, in terms of the situation in 1997, it 'is in south India ... that street theatre has become a truly people's movement' (S. Deshpande 1997, 17). As in the case of the *STQ* survey, 'street' here includes all forms of action-oriented theatre. Northern states show less consistency, with a few activist- and development-oriented groups in Uttar Pradesh, Madhya Pradesh, Orissa, Rajasthan and Maharashtra, several in Bihar, one or two in Gujarat, others in Delhi and Mumbai (Bombay) and one in Haryana; the important West Bengal spectrum is hinted at above; Punjab, in spite of severe political turmoil and terrorist activity, has a consistent record of new work, particularly that inspired and produced by Gurucharan Singh (see above). Information however is sometimes difficult to obtain (Deshpande specifies that little is available from 'disputed' states in the north-east); and groups of this kind are often unable to provide it, because they lack resources or time to do so, though there are, as often, problems arising from factionalism and impermanence. Material in *STQ* over the last few years has however begun to make up for this deficiency. The by no means exhaustive information offered above suggests that there is indeed a very considerable amount of this kind of theatre activity, which utilizes methods from the whole performance spectrum: Pralayan claims that it 'is now a necessity to understand that street theatre is part of the overall theatre movement' (*STQ* 16, 79). This is all the more remarkable in view of the very considerable problems it faces.

Many of these problems are similar to those found in other parts of Asia: lopsided finance often due to multinational interests, oppressive political and social structures, the marginalisation of large groups, poverty, undernourishment, censorship, lack of educational and public health services, state control of the media; plus difficulties of communication, multiplicity of languages, religious differences, restrictive attitudes and practices with reference to caste and class, gender and role: all of these are part of what street theatre and theatre for development seeks to combat, but they make consistent work and mutual support difficult. Other problems include a tendency to fragmentation and mistrust of the politics of other groups, so for example Marxists won't work with Catholics and/or those supported by foreign development agencies (see van Erven 1992, 137–139).

These structural difficulties are serious enough; they are compounded by the ideological complexities which underpin message- or aim-oriented performance practice and by the specifics of the socio-political context in which it operates. So do the methods of activist theatre induce resuscitation or death? Sudhanva Deshpande specifically excepts work aiming to empower women from a scathing dismissal of message-oriented street- and/or development-theatre, which is seen as part of the market system and devoid of artistic merit (Deshpande 1997, 3–4). Other evaluations concur in pointing to the ineffectiveness of performance where it is primarily 'talking down' (Deshpande, 4), 'one-way communication' (Desai 1997/8, 8) and 'top-down' (*Parivartan* Assessment 1998, 2).

Juan Diaz Bordenave, commenting on the propagandist use in Brazil of the folk verse form called *Folhetos*, says: 'I see in this discovery a lot of good, a lot of evil. The good is that the folk media are legitimate possessions of the people, part of their culture, and so, they have a right to be respected, supported and used. However (...) I am afraid that as soon as people realize that their folk songs, poems and art are being used for subliminal propaganda, they will let them die (...) to use those channels for an instrumental function of persuasion, in my view, is *cultural genocide*' (Bordenave, cit. in Das 1992, 94–5). Bordenave sees the outcome in the short-term as ineffectual and in the long-term as destructive.

On the other hand, Zakes Mda, discussing theatre for development in southern Africa, reproduces three categories of popular theatre with an educative aim drawn from an article by Pru Lambert: agitprop, participatory and conscientisation (Mda 1993, 50). Though the latter two are distinguished on some grounds, particularly with reference to establishment of goals, they both display many features found in successful enterprises discussed above; in particular, the higher the degree of conscious participation by the community, the greater the likely effect. Elsewhere in the same work, Mda also underlines the importance of using indigenous cultural forms and respecting the contexts in which they operate.

Baz Kershaw points out that much theatre concerned to improve conditions 'has assumed that the pictures of the world painted by Marxist and socialist political theorists are fundamentally accurate, reveal truths about "reality". Hence this tradition of theatre has tended to identify with the teleological "master-narratives" of historical or dialectical materialism' (Kershaw 1996, 138). Not only is this politically, philosophically and aesthetically naive, but it also fails to challenge the dominant *structures* of discourse; it merely inverts the *figures* whilst retaining the 'we're right, you're wrong' pattern. A more genuinely radical alternative, Kershaw implies, lies in Dorrian Lambley's identification of the '"poetic" in theatre, defined as a "visible gap between signified and signifier", as the source of its potential as a "credible language of opposition"'(Kershaw, 138–9).

In this understanding, *only* a change in form initiates real change in effect. Mala Hashmi says: 'drama has to be created and crafted even on the streets' (*STQ* 16, 1997, 71); Jana Sanghati is explicitly concerned 'to see that spontaneous theatre is effective both because of the power and relevance of its message and because of its attention to aesthetics' (Jana Sanghati 1999). In other words, crafting is essential because the form delivers the experience which contextualises the content; if that content is to be grasped as radically different from known (authorised) formulations, the grammar or syntax of performance has to be such as to initiate a new kind of conceptualisation, to enable a new positioning of subject and object, of self, world and otherness. The practices of ritual and street theatre are not so very different here; perhaps Forum Theatre and other participatory models do offer room for real change by keeping the 'gap' open.

In *STQ* 21, Anjum Katyal writes: 'Theatre as *process* is an empowering activity. It encourages self-expression, develops self-confidence and communication skills, and promotes teamwork, cooperation, sharing' (2). Tim Prentki's list of criteria for Theatre for Development include:

- Learner-centred participation;
- Articulation; finding a voice;
- Creating a fictional 'safe space';
- Exploring transgressive possibilities;
- Making use of theatre dynamics (relating);
- Highlighting and interrogating the communicative process;
- Offering transformative potential.

(Derived from Prentki 1998, 419)

Many of the practitioners discussed above would claim benefits of this kind in addition to significant social and political outcomes for their work. If this is so, it seems less likely that either the forms or the culture they are embedded in are under threat, because what is occurring is a revitalisation of the cultural soil (i.e. the participating individuals and communities) rather than the reverse. The danger may lie less in the adoption of theatre practices to the socio- (or psycho-) political sphere than in the sheer extent of such activity. Furman (1999) states that at any one time, 20–30,000 NGOs in India use performance to support their work. And Pralayan speculates that the logic behind more generous Government attitudes to NGOs is that 'the Government wants to gradually shift its social and cultural responsibilities on to the NGOs' (83). It is all the more difficult to maintain vigilance because this kind of activity does increasingly offer some forms of remuneration to those who otherwise have little chance of access to it.

STQ 16 (1997) is largely devoted to a review and discussion of street theatre in India; Brecht and Boal (and through him, Fanon) form part of a fan of reference which includes Sircar, IPTA and the kinds of work outlined above. Principal areas of discussion include what might be termed a politicised version of Schechner's 'braid', balancing artistic complexity and effectiveness of outcome. Van Erven quotes Bulhan's comment on Fanon's work, which suggests that 'true liberation requires the *simultaneous* transformation of the oppressed individual *within* an oppressed group and of the social conditions that caused the individual's distress in the first place' (van Erven 1992, 11). He also points to Freire's claim that 'true knowledge [comes] through invention and reinvention, through ... restless, impatient, continuing, hopeful, inquiry' (van Erven, 13). In other words, both 'liberation' and the 'knowledge' which furthers it are active and interactive: the relationship between the personal and the political, between the individual as constituted by social, economic, hierarchical and cultural-historical factors and society as open to change initiated and carried out by individuals is precisely the territory of theatre practice within a developmental perspective.

Performance can change its receivers' beliefs and attitudes, and hence – though more gradually in most cases – their behavioural patterns. But, as almost all 'committed' theatre artists have found, although such change may appear to be a matter of the reception and acceptance of 'external' material by a 'target' group, it rarely takes place in a radical and lasting way unless the receivers are actively engaged in the process. Top-down methods are largely ineffective in the long-term. So change is in fact dependent on the preparation of what receives the change: the inner economy and polity of the individual. Performance forms can prepare that ground by aesthetic and intellectual means; they can aim to affect the deepest levels open to them of emotional or rational activity, they can work through kinds of experience which are solitary and those which are enhanced or expedited by being shared. On some level they need to take into account a dynamics of performance and reception, of communication and participation, of openness and activation.

Since aesthetic experience frequently activates parts other techniques don't reach, form is never immaterial, in both senses of the term. Both the range of effects and the processes which enable them have been and continue to be vital across the whole spectrum of Indian theatre, as the *Natya Sastra* implies. The stages by which more extensive freedom and self-determination are acquired include the ability to distance and evaluate intellectually, the sensibility to enter imaginatively into 'other' kinds of experience, and the increasing facility to manipulate and play across this range of understanding and possibility. They move towards a more generous perception and activation of human action. Theatre which works in this way properly belongs within the field of consideration of contemporary practice, and it is playing a significant part in altering the shape of performance practice in India and elsewhere.

SUMMARY

Theatre activates and ritualises or marks, events. It makes them stand out as important, it energises them in order to propel them into the consciousness of its receivers – which it also seeks to activate by specific and conscious, though not merely superficially intellectual, means; and it thus offers them to these receivers as events taking part, coming alive, in their own sphere of consciousness and hence their own range of understanding and responsibility: it empowers.

Those Indian performers, teachers, writers and directors discussed above who seek to use traditional forms to ask new questions are at work in this area of interrogating, and of offering theatre back to communities from which it sprung and who have in the course of time been disenfranchised – by economic or political disinheritance, by loss of access, by exposure instead to processes of more passive consumption (e.g. tv). If I'm (and Schechner is too) right about the significance of performance in everyday life, these ought to be things which affect the structure of public and private life. Theatre as performance – whether for players or co-participating receivers – activates learning, understanding, knowing as an activity of the whole organism, body, brain, emotions: it causes changes in physiological functioning, it makes available kinds of behaviour (mental and physical) and a scope of feeling and perceiving which may previously have been suppressed or dormant.

The implications of the changing role of women in the contemporary performance scene, which picks up from the earlier analysis in Chapter 3 of their marginalisation throughout the history of most traditional forms (pp. 86–94), are considerable. Throughout the twentieth century they have been increasingly visible as performers and in other roles. In recent years, Anjum Katyal's challenging, astute and eloquent editorial writing and direction of *Seagull Theatre Quarterly* is a significant marker. One of the academies discussed above is run by two women, Mrinalini and Mallika Sarabhai. Kamaladevi Chattopadhyay and Kapila Vatsyayan have occupied leading roles in national institutions based in Delhi. Vijaya Mehta has run the National Centre for Performing Arts in Mumbai. Mala Hashmi's role is referred to above. Many women's performance groups now exist. The situation of women as performers – a role often perceived as conflicting with those traditionally ascribed to and considered suitable for women – though still in many cases difficult, is more tolerable than in many periods in the past, as evidenced in several interviews in *STQ*. Concomitantly, the role of women as portrayed in performance has shifted markedly, seen in characters created by both male and female writers (Karnad, Tendulkar, Devi, Dina Mehta, Kambar, to name but a few): they are angry, articulate, prominent, competent, resourceful. Both Mallika Sarabhai and B. Jayashree, among others, have presented 'alternative' stage versions of the 'traditional Indian woman' in the figure of Draupadi. They are part of a changing scene, or perhaps they are part of a process which is rediscovering its 'roots', not in some idealised history, but in the flexibility of available configurations of self and its modes of action which derive from participation in the full reach of creative activity.

Performance forms which reproduce stereotypes (the naturalistic in the west, the symbolic in the east; specifically in India the – melodramatic – Bollywood movie model; anywhere the excessively simplistic and message-oriented deployment of stock types, caricatures and easy targets) are reproductions of reproductions. Unless seasoned with a sharp dose of irony, they permit avoidance of, rather than access to, real events with an emotional, intellectual, personal and political dynamic. They mask off feeling as the sign of feeling, action as the typology of action.

Popular (entertainment-oriented) performance modes in east and west still largely reflect this. Where the west has learned from alternative modes or explored beneath the naturalistic surface (from Beckett to Barker, from Grotowski to Brook), challenging work results. Indian moves towards this mix of modes and models have been indicated above: Tanvir's and Karnad's writing for example, but also Satyajit Ray's films, irony at pan-Indian structures and rhetoric in the novels of Rushdie, Tharoor and Seth, the exploration of taboos and articulation of the unvoiced in development theatre, and much writing by women, dalits, etc.

If the business of art is to expose and challenge acquiescence in avoidance of the real, the particular task of theatrical performance is to locate, explore and enliven the full physical and emotional range of experience. Performance uses bodies and feelings. It makes them available. It aims to refine and to expand their range of modes and attributes, as well as to understand and celebrate them. Avoidance blocks access to them and negates their function. It is therefore important that performance modes operate in the difficult territory of the unfamiliar, the contestatory, the hybrid, whatever the perceived dangers.

This is particularly the case in India. It seems to me that there is an enormous need for individual and community empowerment, to contest apathy, centrism, communalism (facile and dangerous 'othering'), corruption and resignation in the face of it. Empowerment needs to work for the disadvantaged, to give them a voice and a stake. It also needs to work for the apparently advantaged who have access to education: the dominant methodology throughout the education system, which spreads its influence to many other spheres of public life, is that of 'passive learning' (a contradiction in terms which means in fact no learning at all, or the mere regurgitation of empty precepts or 'facts'), which produces conformism and cynicism. Active and participatory models of democratic and educational practice are urgently needed throughout the social fabric. That is the kind of model which much of the theatre work described in this chapter employs in one way or another. Such work needs to be supported and extended. The deconstruction or contestation of accepted forms and the elaboration of others is a question of ethics and politics as well as, and as a result of, aesthetics. The ability to experience and to think in new or alternative ways, which underpins behaviour, is essential to individual and social well-being.

CHAPTER SIX

Indian Theatre in the contemporary world: East-West traffic

INTRODUCTION: WHAT THE WEST HAS WON

One impetus for this book was the desire to account for western interest, in the period from 1940 to the present, in Indian theatre. In the chapters on text, performance and theory, I have explored ways in which Indian theatre works both as a model of processes of origination and as an opening into wider dimensions of being and understanding, whether that is perceived in aesthetic, political or psychological terms.

How that heritage is being handled in India is the subject of the previous chapter. What I want to do here, quite briefly, is firstly to sum up how the goals of western interest I outlined can be understood within other frameworks (approaches to knowledge) which I have encountered; and secondly, to ask whether the contemporary debate about interculturalism and cultural piracy adequately deals with the kinds of interaction which have taken place and are still doing so (including, for instance, the increasing presence of Indian or expatriate Indian companies and performers on the European and American performance scene).

Two riders might be inserted here. Firstly, what the west has got from the east is of course a lengthy and knotty piece of string of which the phase I draw on is only one end. G.N. Devy suggests for instance that the work of the eminent oriental scholar Sir William Jones led not only to one manifestation of Said's 'Orientalism', but also to the basis of both comparative literary studies and of linguistics (Devy 1997, 30–32). Moreover, Drew has indicated some of the extent of the debt of Plotinus and the whole western tradition of neo-Platonic thought to India (1987, 102; see also Malekin &

Yarrow 1997); and it has been suggested that, in common with Buddhism, much of Chinese and Japanese aesthetics draws on forms and practices generated within the Indian sub-continent. Here the traffic has been initially East-East, but it has continued into western orientalism at the end of the eighteenth and nineteenth centuries. Secondly, current debates about postcolonialism are themselves in no small measure carried on by or focused on 'exported' Indian artists or academics (Harish Trivedi cites Salman Rushdie and Gayatri Spivak as the Indian high-culture equivalent of the simultaneous 1994/5 acquisition of the Miss World and Miss Universe titles! Trivedi, 1997, 38.) Both these dimensions are beyond the scope of my discussion, but they indicate that the roots are deep and the traffic continues.

More specifically with reference to theatre, there have been major gains in terms of western programmes of actor-training and views of the performer/audience interaction (Artaud, Brook, Grotowski, Lecoq), in addition to the uses of anthropology in performance theory which have already been alluded to. More generally, the understanding of the concept of theatre itself has shifted, starting again from Artaud's fascination with eastern performance modes in contrast to the more verbally oriented theatre of the 1930s. The emergence of 'physical theatre', however vague and unsatisfactory that may be as a term, owes much to an awareness of different modes of using the body in space and different imaginative conceptions of the nature and role of theatre as perceived in eastern performance by western observers.

The preceding chapters will, I hope, have made it clear why it is appropriate to suggest that Indian theatre raises questions such as the nature of reality, the status and function of narrative and performance, and what the business of acting, and of attending acutely to what is enacted, discloses about the nature of the self and its modes of operation. Much significant theatre, and debate about theatre, raises such issues: the parallels between *Natya Sastra* and Plato's aesthetic theory have been alluded to; Shakespeare, Strindberg and Beckett are quite consciously exploring this kind of territory. The foregrounding of Indian material, performers, concepts and so on is a part of a process of engagement with issues which concern theatre anywhere at any time. Provided that is clearly understood it seems legitimate; where however the borrower claims or convinces him/herself that s/he is not simply using available analogies to answer questions specific to his/her own cultural context, but is in some way validating the relevance of the material to its own context, things become a great deal more woolly. Brook's *Mahabharata* may have worked well as an exciting performance metaphor, but it is doubtful whether it contributed much to the status or understanding of the epic in India.

Chapter I suggested that western impetus was fuelled at least in major part by a sense of lack. I would also argue that much in Symbolist and Modernist aesthetics goes back to the same sense of lack, or perhaps to *anamnesis*, the intuition that the lack conceals or points to what it is a lack of; and that, in spite of or behind the emphasis on materialist criticism, creative practice and theoretical challenge has continued to pursue that same quest. Let's go/we can't go; all we have, now, is our two hours traffic on the stage. In one respect, Indian theatre is a vast canvas; in another, it fuses and focuses the only sensible practice of life, which is to be as much as possible in each moment.

As the book has suggested, Indian theatre generates questions and invites new strategies in the following areas, all of which have been part of the realignment of western thought and practice in the last half-century:

(a) consciousness and self
(b) quantum models
(c) actor training strategies
(d) theatre and audiences
(e) theatre and anthropology.

The first two of these have mainly to do with ways of understanding the world; the last three with ways of transforming it. So although of course they in no way represent the totality of twentieth-century western preoccupations, what they do is to span the field in which these operate. To the first group could be added approaches to history, politics and psychoanalysis; to the second, methods from education, statecraft and psychotherapy.

Underneath each conceptual framework lie assumptions about what questions can be asked. The arts in the twentieth century have not been slow to grasp this opportunity, and the challenging of assumptions from radical perspectives has ranged from the visual (Cubism) to the narrative (plural narrators, intercutting time-frames and narrative modes from Joyce to Pynchon). Whereas in everyday terms it takes much longer for these shifts to penetrate (many people and institutions still operate as though Newtonian science had all the answers), the persistence and variety of these forays suggests a relatively continuous dynamic. In the course of this realignment, evident from the late nineteenth through most of the twentieth century, interplay between scientific method, speculative thought and imaginative act, drawing on new insights from physics to psychology, new technologies from photography to particle acceleration, impelled new forms to articulate experience. Perhaps the most significant – if even now far from fully acknowledged – outcome is to reveal nineteenth-century scientific materialism, post-Enlightenment thought and the models of self, world and reality which they embody as relative and historically circumscribed, only one possible model amongst many others.

These questions are summed up succinctly by de Nicolás:

> If the boundaries of atomic entities and events, and those things and events, as expressed by our commonsense language, such as I, you, space, time, birth, death, subject, object, etc., did not really invariently exist, what would then be the relation of what exists, and how would it then be apprehended?
>
> (1976, 32)

De Nicolás himself describes his initial arrival in India as a kind of turning inside out, and my own experience was similar. The encounter with otherness is of course, properly understood, an encounter with other reaches of the self. In so far as 'India' impels such an encounter, the results can either be a retreat into the known (which then erects external categories of the oriental or other) or a profound rethinking and reforming of it. To do the latter is to engage in an active process of self-renewal: theatre workers are already engaged by definition in active processes which involve at least the putting on the line of what passes for self, so they may be half-way there.

Twentieth-century western theatre theory and practice from many directions suggests a similar range of preoccupations, centring around questions like:

Is performance a way of becoming more

– coherent
– integrated
– whole/healthy
– present/available
– wise

- extensive
- free
- expressive
- significant
- productive
- unconditioned
- powerful?

And/or as Russell Hoban puts it in *Kleinzeit*: 'I, I? How can there be any *one* I?' What we have, perhaps desperately, tended to cling on to – the sense of the self as consistent or whole, as what Buddhist writer Alan Watts calls the 'skin-encapsulated ego', is simply not tenable any more: and the experience of theatre not only has to match that, it cannot help so doing by its very nature, and theories about it have to articulate what Shakespeare already displays: the duplicity of any belief in a single or inviolable self, and the multiplicity of being which performance can stimulate. (Think what happens to Lear, who wants to cling on to what he thinks he owns; and in contrast, what flexible but specifically human qualities derive from Prospero's awareness that the world of appearances is not all.)

As we have seen, Indian theory and practice constructs performance as a set of active processes which stimulate altered modes of perception of self and world. They thus rest, at least implicitly, on an active model of 'mind' which includes the possibility of such transformations. Neo-Platonic thought envisages a state in which individual intelligence has access to what Böhme calls 'der Ungrund', that without ground. Participation in the process of liberation from boundaries and operating at the originating point of form (as discussed in previous chapters) allows this possibility to be realised, for performers and receivers.

An actor performing ceases to be merely his/her everyday self. For Proust, 'involuntary memory' gives access to a state in which the self ceases to be 'contingent, mortal': Stanislavsky's 'emotion memory', though in part voluntary and focused on particular events and locations, is moving into similar terrain in so far as it enables the performer to link past and present versions of the self. Audiences cease behaving exclusively as individuals; individual audience members may sympathetically 'become' several characters. For Borges, the essence of the aesthetic is that it conjures up 'the imminence of a revelation which has not occurred': i.e. it enables the mind to sense the coming-into-being of form.

The east-west exchange which has long framed such issues continues in Symbolist and post-Symbolist aesthetics and surfaces again in the more recent 'turn to the East'. The difference as signalled here is that the medium (theatre and performance) is much less abstract, more public and communal, and hence in many senses more directly accessible. Artaud thought of theatre as the 'last group means of profoundly affecting the organism'. I'm not quite sure what he meant by last, but the rest of it seems to hit the mark. Carl Lavery views Genet's practice of ritual in theatre as 'a modern rite of passage, aiming to effect permanent change in the consciousness of its participants via a radical de-centering of subjectivity'; a process achieved by arriving 'at the point where differentiated subjectivity is confronted with sacred indifference' (Lavery 2000, ms). He argues that Genet is concerned to initiate experience of the 'existential sacred' as the ground on which to revise the 'social sacred' or totemic Order. In so far as Grotowski, Brook *et al* would, it seems, concur with this aim, it is possible to view this practice of theatre, as I have intimated in Chapter I, as one move to relocate, through aesthetic experience, dimensions of being which are by no means exclusively 'eastern' or 'western', but which may stand out as more readily identifiable in an 'alien' or 'exotic' culture (thus marking the repulsion and the fascination which close the spectrum). However, what is important is the extent to which that alien or exotic other is recognised as own.

On one hand then theatre may more recognisably offer possibilities for the suspension or extension of the known self, for the reconfiguration of self and world. This is located in the functioning of imagination central to Indian forms and clarified in the theory of *Natya Sastra*. On the other hand, theatre may also be able to accommodate the pluralistic model of being which may result, and which also seems to be reflected in the 'richness' of Indian performance modes as well as in their variety. Theatre presents this as dialogue, as interaction, as the physicalisation of two or more points of view, as negotiation between languages, assumptions, genders, roles. It is in a privileged position to deal with the demand for a multiplicity of forms and perspectives. I want to explore a little further some of the changes in theatrical practice which have resulted in the west from appreciation of these factors. They can be divided into three areas: performance training; understandings about performance forms; material for performance (textual or other).

PERFORMANCE TRAINING

Styles of performance training in western schools and academies have shifted gradually over the last decades; the shift has accelerated during the period. There is not necessarily a one-to-one correspondence between aspects of eastern (e.g. Indian, Japanese, Chinese) performance, the goals of particular western seekers (Artaud, Brecht, Barba, Brook) and integration into the performance training of companies and/or institutions. In some cases there has been: Barba specifically studied Kathakali in order to report back to Grotowski, who incorporated, adapted and then abandoned some of the techniques; Barba has also regularly invited Sanjukhta Panigrahi to work with his company in their search for performative presence, 'bios' or the 'extra-daily body' in performance. Mnouchkine, Brook and others have used eastern performers (actors, dancers, musicians) in their productions on an *ad hoc* basis, but in most cases they have not been asked to contribute to the long-term training of the company. But both in such companies and in theatre training institutions in general there has been an increasing awareness of forms other than those directly relevant to the western repertoire. Use of mask-work, both in training and in performance, has become more extensive and thorough. Training in specific techniques has been a feature of workshops (e.g. Zarilli on Kalarippayat, Pan Project on mask-work, CPR voice workshops) attended by performers and teachers. Schechner has also incorporated specific training in his productions and production style.

Other changes are less precisely attributable to direct contact with eastern thought and practice, but nevertheless reflect a quest for parallel forms of experience and production. The use of the neutral mask pioneered by Jacques Copeau from the 1930s and taken on by Jacques Lecoq has been central to a major strand in performance work of the last three decades, feeding into mask, mime and physically-inventive performance by companies like Théâtre de Complicité, Trestle, Mummerandada, Footsbarn, Mummenschanz, Cheek By Jowl, Moving Picture Mime Show, Bread and Puppet Theatre. The mask is used to instil familiarity with a 'resting' or transitional phase of consciousness, a 'stillness before movement'; it enables the performer to switch off, to disengage from the previous version of the persona, be that the everyday variety or a 'character-mask'. Its aim is ultimately what in Indian thought is known as *moksha:* liberation from attachment to the transient persona; as a training method it enhances mobility and functions in tandem with improvisatory methods to free up the performer's resources for play.

The idea of sacrifice, as analysed by de Nicolás, is not at all removed from the requirements of western performance trainers including Stanislavsky, Grotowski, Lecoq, Brook and others. Sometimes they have, not surprisingly, inherited from their own socio-historical situation or from acquaintance with others' glosses some overtones of the term which inflect their work in a particular direction (e.g. Grotowski's acceptance of and resistance to Polish Catholicism, Brook's adoption of Gurdjieff's sometimes contorted interpretation of the quest for the self). But the pursuit of abandonment of the egoic self (Grotowski), discovery of what precedes the already known (Lecoq, from Copeau, via the use of the neutral mask) or the emptiness of the space of performance in which the performer can operate (Brook, in a perhaps unconscious echo of both *Rg Veda*'s and classic Mahayana Buddhism's exposition of the *Asat*, or that which is not (yet) as the source of all material form) is fundamentally oriented in the same direction. How can I stop being what I have been taught/accepted to think I am in order to discover myself as a capacity to be more, to be other, to be that which thought cannot admit, which I didn't think I could be or didn't think others would allow me to be? And in spite of encrustations imposed on him by the Method and generations of apparently faithful 'realist' acting, Stanislavsky's most profound insight was that it is in those 'buried' but nonetheless accessible layers of the self that the motivation for present behaviour may be located, and located physically as sensation memory (which is therefore necessarily of the present moment, the moment of recall and the senses which are doing the recalling). In other words Stanislavsky's supreme offering to actors is the chance to learn how to live the genesis of action, which predicates form and intention; and in order to arrive at that you have to give up (temporarily, but with possible long-term consequences) what you might like to think you are at the moment.

If there is any really significant change which has occurred in performance style in the west in the last thirty years, it has less to do with particular directors or designers and more to do with the increasing presence of performers (and directors) trained in this kind of methodology. Performance can only change if performers change. Increasing exposure to workshops and performances by practitioners from other cultures has resulted in a more eclectic training programme for western performers, which has at least in part produced more flexible performers.

Of course this is not always the case; the superficial acquisition of a few 'bolt-on' techniques does not in itself produce a radical shift, and it certainly flirts with charges of piracy or consumerist packaging. But there are many companies and performers – among them those mentioned above – whose meeting with different styles has been more thorough and prolonged, and who have taken some care to familiarise themselves with the bases of those styles. Indeed in several instances trainers and directors of Indian origin, resident in western countries or regular visitors as workshop-leaders/directors, are the providers. Jatinder Verma directs Tara Arts, which works with British performers of Asian descent; there are many other similar dance and theatre ventures in the UK, like Tamasha Theatre and Shobana Jeyasingh's dance work, which provide a slightly different slant on the notion of cultural transfer. Kalamandalam Vijayakumar directs the Kala Chethana *Kathakali* troupe, which provides regular workshops for schools and colleges throughout the UK as well as promoting both 'traditional' *Kathakali* performances and *Kathakali* treatments of European material. John Martin, who directs Pan Project and works extensively in many countries with performers – actors, dancers and musicians – from different ethnic traditions, interprets 'multi-culturalism' via practice not as a kind of 'least offensive' or lowest common denominator *masala* (after the model of most 'Indian' restaurants in the UK, or the U.S.A. version of a multi-ethnic state, where 'difference' tends to get tacitly edited out under the assumption that everyone really wants to be 'American' ...), but as the joyous play and interplay between performers assured in their own traditions and able to experiment and seek affinities from that base. His success is testified by vibrant collaborations such as *Itan Kahani*, a dance and story-telling show bringing together Africa and India in the shape of Peter Badejo and Mallika Sarabhai, which charmed and excited audiences in four continents. Here again there are complex attitudes and processes at work which extend beyond acquisition on the part of the 'western' client. Performance-training (not all those receiving it in these contexts will go on to become performers at all, let alone performers of Indian forms) here plays a role as a general educational tool, and its very 'naturalness' or unassuming position is itself significant. What may emerge from it is a kind of 'de-orientalising' of forms which have hitherto been framed off as 'exotic'. Participants begin to recognise that such forms work

through the (relatively similar) body of any human bein.
they provide ways of developing expressive skills and attrib.
can be pleasurable, useful and ultimately integrative.

The opposite is sometimes true of attempts by wester.
'fuse' forms, for example classical western ballet and *Kathak*
Bharatanatyam. I have seen several disastrously gooey amalgams, which
not infrequently suffer from an excessive deference towards the
'foreign' culture (as great a handicap as excessive disrespect). They
tend to fall into the category of the bliss trip characteristic of the
adoption of Indian *gurus* by western seekers.

UNDERSTANDING OF PERFORMANCE FORMS

'Understanding' in this context includes exposure as an audience to
different forms, leading to increasing familiarity, and exploration of
the cultures, contexts and theoretical framing of such forms. The
former has, in parallel with the developments described above, not
merely increased quantitatively in line with greater international
exchange opportunities, but also changed qualitatively, though
perhaps to a lesser extent than for participants and performers, as
such forms become more familiar and less exotically 'other'. Here
again the picture is not simple, and there are grounds for arguing that
Brook and Mnouchkine, for example, have merely reinvented
orientalism under a contemporary liberal mask. However, the
increasing presence of Hindi movies, as well as the consistent if
marginal presence of high-quality Indian 'art-cinema' in e.g. the UK
and USA, plus the frequency of Indian music and dance recitals in
many major cities, provides a background of increasing 'normality'
which assists the 'deintoxication' process. That said, Indian theatre
or theatre-related performance is still definitely not the norm, and
where it does occur it usually plays to an audience which is largely
self-selecting by virtue of ethnic origin or specialist interest.

In the second area, that of cultural analysis, there is of course an
extensive debate in progress. That debate, like most academic
debates, is located within a small number of select institutions and
carried out by individuals who have devised their own code for the
purpose. Since the code effectively excludes anyone else (including,
for the most part, the people it is actually supposed to be talking
about, i.e. those who produce the cultural activity), it is doubtful
whether the issues of the debate affect many who participate in or
receive performance, or the public at large. Some of the questions do

however get filtered out as issues in cultural politics. And here too the fact that this debate has, for whatever reason (guilt may be a significant factor) concerned itself with the morality of cultural exchange, does at least put in the limelight a consideration of 'alternative' performance modes. It is quite possible that the business of considering them may in itself be another disguised form of colonialist appropriation or marginalisation; but as I indicated previously, there are this time round a considerable number of prominent 'colonised' voices taking part.

John Russell Brown, a frequent visitor to India, raises some relevant questions in a recent essay (Russell Brown 1997), which refer to both the areas discussed so far. He is doubtful about (Brook's and Mnouchkine's) attempts to acquire the apparently detachable exotica of costume, techniques or texts ('raiders across a boundary, they bring back strange clothes as their loot and try to wear them as if to the manner born', 19), but suggests that what may be more legitimately garnered is a set of questions about one's own theatrical forms, 'an increased awareness of what theatre may be' (27). The questions he frames are not so far away from what Barba, Grotowski and others have been looking for.

Russell Brown asks whether it would be possible to find ways of developing the following:

- 'transparency of [*Kudiyattam*] performance', which evokes greater imaginative activity on the part of the audience;
- sharper sense of the improvisatory in performance;
- different conventions for audience behaviour;
- shifts in audience-stage relationship;
- greater flexibility in relationship between performers and musicians (e.g. less rigid scoring);
- more intensive/devotional actor-training;
- inner stillness of performers (and in puppetry, of operators).

(Russell Brown 1997, 27–30)

As I noted above, significant changes have been underway in the European theatre scene in terms of the gradual internalisation of the perceptions and methods of Copeau, Artaud, Lecoq, Dario Fo, Keith Johnstone and others. Much of this development is outlined in Frost & Yarrow, *Improvisation in Drama* (1990); its knock-on effects continue in the work of the companies mentioned above, in the teaching of Lecoq and former colleagues like Philippe Gaulier, in the work in the USA and Canada of Johnstone, Schechner *et al*, in the increasing flexibility of performance styles and operation (a kind of return in many cases to almost medieval modes of touring theatre using pack-up and go sets, out-front performance styles, mask and mime, puppetry and low-tech machinery, multi-skilled performers etc.). Not all of this by any means derives from acquaintance with eastern modes, but in some cases it does and in others it is cognate with such modes and follows similar principles.

The things Russell Brown hopes for have in fact been making their way into western theatre for several decades: the current recognition by both audiences and 'established' theatre managements of the work of e.g. Schechner, Tara's Jatinder Verma and Complicité's Simon McBurney is an indication that they are beginning to arrive. That, it has to be said, operates against the background of or in competition with the increasing reliance on high-tech gimmickry in commercial theatre; but it nevertheless represents a radical revaluation.

To Russell Brown's wish-list could be appended examples of companies or training methods found in the west which at least attempt, and often in some measure succeed, in fulfilling the criteria he seeks. He himself suggests that acting styles appropriate to the sparseness of say a Beckett text are conducive to imaginative participation; neutral mask work is one way of moving towards it for performers, and the precise attention to breathing and physical control which is increasingly required of performers – and to a considerable extent is based on eastern training schedules – is another measure.

Improvisation of many kinds lies at the basis of much work of contemporary performers and directors, from Mike Leigh and Caryl Churchill at one end of the spectrum through Dario Fo to Théâtre de Complicité. Shifts in stage-audience relationship were central to the work of Grotowski and Kantor and are found in much post-war writing and performance work, including for instance Weiss's *Marat/Sade*, Brook's *Mahabharata*, increased flexibility in stage /auditorium design from the prestigious fringe venue The Gate to the publicly-funded Barbican and the processional and carnivalesque style of Barba's Odin Teatret or Bread and Puppet Theatre. Mnouchkine, Pan Project and others have used musicians from different ethnic traditions together, creating relationships amongst themselves and with other performers which are much more reciprocal and less rigid. Stillness and 'presence' is sought after by many trainers, notably Barba, Grotowski, Copeau, Brook (see also Yarrow 1997b).

As I have suggested above, the search for these qualities and modes of performative behaviour is locatable throughout this century (to say the least). The 'turn to the east' is only one of the forms it takes; and there has, as Drew (1983) and others have pointed out, been more than one turn. The search is important because it is for vital areas of creative activity and imaginative response, for qualities fundamental to a sense of renewal and empowerment. If it so happens that India has often seemed a promising treasury to raid, I hope the preceding chapters have given some clues why, in terms of performative traditions and the understandings underpinning them, this should be so. But Russell Brown is right: the search is not, fundamentally, about piracy or decorative acquisitions; it is about qualities in the seeker which, for whatever reason, his own cultural context does not appear to stimulate. The reasons for this in the current century have to do with mind-sets fostered by materialist and historicist prejudice (see Malekin & Yarrow 1997a); artwork has frequently been concerned with circumventing or subverting orthodoxy, and hopefully it will continue to find one of its principal *raisons d'être* in such activity.

MULTICULTURAL CURRY

Aesthetically and in terms of ways to understand and articulate extended models of performance it is clear that the west has gained; it seems less obvious that India has 'lost' anything, since in any case it has been, as the previous chapter in particular shows, in process of debating and delivering all kinds of possible attitudes to and uses of its own multifarious traditions.

It is also appropriate to note here that the traffic hasn't been all one way: India has assimilated and continues to assimilate much from the west, and that process is as complex and as problematic as its opposite. The current spectrum of forms and languages available to performers in India is the richer – not necessarily enormously so, but nevertheless significantly – for those acquired from elsewhere, voluntarily or involuntarily, which have long been part of Indian experience and have in recent years been more consciously than ever foregrounded, debated, positioned as 'other' and as integral, and in all of this intense activity further woven into the fabric of theatre in contemporary India.

It is moreover the case that we currently live at a historical moment which in some ways looks, even in a global sense, both particularly open to the relocation of ethnic or indigenous traditions and faced by issues of multiculturalism. The break up of monolithic blocks and composite states, extensive relocation or reaffirmation of ethnic groupings, strong presence of increasingly large numbers of citizens of mixed racial origins; South Africa, Yugoslavia, the USSR, Germany: these are some of the places and forces which have brought questions of language, cultural tradition and identity to the forefront of global and national political agendas. The issues are about self-perception, borders between self and other, educational and socialisation practice, human rights, economic allocation. Within this scenario performance has begun to operate as a political, educational and psychosocial player: the work of Augusto Boal, ranging from his initial designation of 'Theatre of the Oppressed' to his current concern with 'Legislative Theatre', spans much of this spectrum. With specific reference to India, I looked in some detail at aspects of 'Development Theatre' in the previous chapter, for the issues are both intra and inter-cultural.

The importance of such work, both in India and elsewhere (it is widely used in Africa and South America as well) is on the one hand that it locates performance within political and educational practice – in other words, it leads beyond a view of theatre and performance as entertainment objects reinforcing cultural or political stereotypes, and foregrounds their potential as means of individual and social empowerment; and on the other hand that it helps to celebrate diversity and indigenous tradition by drawing on such forms in order to focus on contemporary issues. Performance, which in the previous section was discussed as a means of cutting loose from fixed versions of identity, is here utilised as a way to locate cultural identity. The contrast may appear strange, but previous chapters have argued for such a degree of flexibility. Identity in play is identity both posited and suspended, like the balls of a juggler.

As the book has argued, this metaphysical virtuosity has practical implications. This is especially relevant in situations where the 'identity' one is locating or confronting is itself multiple. Children of mixed parentage; second or succeeding generation immigrants; those living in regions with strong cultural and linguistic traditions but required to speak a language and live by systems imposed by a larger political entity (state, political model). In these cases the need to 'perform oneself' is itself a form of juggling; but, although the opposite claim is one of the principal and most absurd blind spots of fundamentalists of many kinds, we all, wherever we were born or live, are in profound ways genetically, culturally and linguistically plural. Performance, because it is active and participative, because it creates communities, because it is enjoyable, and because it works directly and organically to tap into affect and expressivity, bypassing many of the blocks associated with perceived linguistic 'competence' or hierarchical status, is one of the most effective means of exploring that plurality: so in this sense the evocation of multiculturalism may have a crucial role to play in the psychology and politics of community.

Pan Project's recent London venture, *Interface 98*, consciously exploited these resources in order to promote celebration, understanding and respect within and between communities of different racial origins. The venture comprised: (i) ongoing workshops with young people, led by artists rooted in 'ethnic' traditions but working within an international context; some of this activity issued as large-scale performance events; (ii) a series of events including theatre, dance and music, by innovative international companies; (iii) a linked series of debates, organised by the International Theatre Institute and with the participation of artists, teachers, academics, and arts workers (including for example Richard Schechner and Tony Feegan, Educational Director for LIFT). The work profiled was distinctive for emerging from regional cultural contexts but being energised by meeting with other cultures and forms, reflecting both how multiracial communities use art as an articulative practice and how such work thrives on cross-border experimentation.

Some of the main issues which arose were:

— renegotiating stereotypes
— assimilating different forms organically
— language, identity, cross-fertilisation
— promoting the 'unloved' in oneself
— acknowledging otherness within and without
— reconciling the 'local' and the 'global'
— 'hybridisation': plus-value or submission?
— is 'multiculturalism' a technique or a way of being?
— avoiding hijack by 'isms'.

Of course many nationalities and ethnic traditions were represented at these events. The issues, however, are part of a scenario which includes current problematics of western negotiations with the 'Indian', attempts by performers of Indian origin living and working in the 'west' to come to terms with themselves and their activity, and encounters by practitioners within India with aspects of their own traditions and of other kinds of practice. Such practitioners, some of whom are discussed in Chapter 5, would recognise many of the issues listed above as relevant to the contemporary Indian scene; and that scene is itself increasingly part of a global dialogue.

Each term or issue within that dialogue itself represents a spectrum, a range of attitudes and options across which practice must continuously negotiate. There is no single 'solution': each artist or group, each work or venture, charts its own response and in so doing helps to redraw the map. The whole picture interfaces or overlaps with the 'postcolonial', itself capable of several different readings as Homi Bhabha, Harish Trivedi and Rustom Bharucha, among others, have pointed out. Strategies of resistance and strategies of renewal likewise overlap. Although 'theory' is often both suspiciously regarded as a neocolonising practice and appears to retreat behind thorn-hedges of jargon, its presence on the scene at least signals that the debate is widespread. And many of the concerns it tackles are close to those outlined above.

In terms of this book then, the narrative line, which has run from questions about western aesthetic and psychospiritual lacunae through investigation of the theory and practice of Indian forms in traditional and contemporary manifestations, now places its itinerary against an international canvas. But the focus here too, as throughout, is on the practice and participation in theatre as engaging originating zones or degrees of human action and as extending the freedom to play across the whole range of human possibility. The topics above highlight the need for a practice which takes performers — and an ideally co-participatory audience — into and through internal and external insecurity, which can articulate a confidence and a form of identity which is flexible and free-ranging, which can draw on multiple resonances and 'languages': what Bharucha, speaking of Chandralekha, describes as a '"rootedness" in self which enables them to be "at home" in a widely disparate range of circumstances' (Bharucha 1995b, 17).

This implies a sense of 'self' which lies somewhere beyond language, nationality or personality as narrowly defined; somewhere closer to the 'not not I' and the 'ontological acrobatics' Schechner and Emigh find in performance situations which take participants through liminality as a kind of ritual operation. The meeting place functions as the root of all systems of exchange: the most promising guarantee of free trade.

As I have tried to argue throughout, the disclosure of that capacity in and through performance is both an aesthetics and an ethics which situate 'theatre', as understood and practised in India in many ages and forms, as a radical engagement with the enduring and the contemporary.

Bibliography

Arambam, Lokendra (1997). 'Experimental Theatre in Manipur: at a Critical Juncture'. *Seagull Theatre Quarterly* 14/15, pp. 16–21

Ashoka, T.P. 'Kannada Theatre', in Lal, Ananda (Ed.), *Rasa: The Indian Performing Arts in the Last Twenty-five Years. Vol. II: Theatre and Cinema*, pp. 141–148. Calcutta: Anamika Kala Sangam

Bandyopadhyay, Samik (1996). 'Bengali Theatre: The End of the Colonial Tradition?'. *Seagull Theatre Quarterly* 12, pp. 50–59.

—— (1997). 'The New Karnas of Manipur'. *Seagull Theatre Quarterly* 14/15, pp. 73–90

Barba, Eugenio and Savarese, Nicola (1991). *The Secret Art of the Performer*. London: Routledge

Bartholomew, Rati (1983). 'Samudaya's Jatha, Karnataka'. *How*, vol. 6, nos. 1–2, Jan.–Feb.

Beckett, Samuel (1977: orig. 1938). *Murphy*. London: Calder

Bedi, Indira (1999). *Reading Emotion: Functional Linguistics and the Theory of Rasa*. Norwich: PhD Thesis, University of East Anglia.

Bernal, Martin (1987). *Black Athena: The Afroasiatic Roots of Classical Civilization*. London: Vintage

Bharucha, Rustom (1991). 'A View from India', in Williams, David (Ed.), *Peter Brook and The Mahabharata*. London: Routledge, pp. 228–252

—— (1993). *Theatre and the World*. London: Routledge

—— (1995a). 'Government Policy: Anatomy of Official Cultural Discourse', in Lal, Ananda (Ed.), *Rasa: The Indian Performing Arts in the Last Twenty-five Years. Vol. II: Theatre and Cinema*, pp. 39–52. Calcutta: Anamika Kala Sangam

—— (1995b). *Chandralekha: Woman, Dance, Resistance*. New Delhi: Harper Collins India.

—— (1998) *The Theatre of Kanhailal*. Calcutta: Seagull

Bohm, David (1980). *Wholeness and the Implicate Order*. London: Routledge and Kegan Paul

Borges, Jorge Luis (1962). *Labyrinths*. Trans. James E. Irby. London: Penguin

Brook, Peter (1990). *The Empty Space*. London: Penguin

Byrski, M. Christopher (1974). *Concept of Ancient Indian Theatre*. New Delhi: Munshiram Manoharlal Publishers Pvt. Ltd.

Campbell, Patrick (1996) (Ed.). *Analysing Performance*. Manchester: Manchester University Press

Capra, Fritjof (1976). *The Tao of Physics*. London: Fontana

Chaitanya, Krishna (1986). 'The Aesthetics of *Kathakali*'. *Sangeet Natak* 80, April–June, pp. 20–25

Chandrika, B. (1993). 'Drama as Ritual', in Narasimhaiah, C.D. and C.N. Srinath (Eds.), *Drama as a Form of Art and Theatre*. Mysore: Dhvanyaloka, pp. 108–115

Coomaraswamy, Ananda K. (1956). *The Transformation of Nature in Art*. New York: Dover Publications

Das, Varsha (1992). *Traditional Performing Arts: Potentials for Scientific Temper*. New Delhi: Wiley Eastern

Desai, Aditi (1997/8). 'Breaking the Culture of Silence: Theatre for Women, Health and Development'. Project notes and reports. Ahmedabad: Drishti

Desai, S.D. (1990). *Happenings: Theatre in Gujarat in the Eighties*. Gandhinagar: Gujarat Sahitya Akademi

Deshpande, G.P. (1995). 'Birth of a Play: the Documentation of a Process' (interview). *Seagull Theatre Quarterly* 7, pp. 3–16

Deshpande, Sudhanva (1997). 'The "Inexhaustible Work of Criticism in Action": Street Theatre of the Left'. *Seagull Theatre Quarterly* 16, pp. 3–22

Devi, Mahasweta (1987). *Truth Tales*. London: The Women's Press

—— (1997). *Five Plays*. Calcutta: Seagull

Devy, G.N. (1992). *After Amnesia: Tradition and Change in Indian Literary Criticism*. New Delhi: Orient Longman

—— (1997). 'Comparatism in India and the West', in *Critical Theory, Western and Indian*, Ed. Prafulla C. Kar. New Delhi: Pencraft International, pp. 12–35

Dharker, Rani (1997). 'The Appropriation of Indian Folk Theatre: Ramlila's New Avatar', in *Critical Theory, Western and Indian*, Ed. Prafulla C. Kar. New Delhi: Pencraft International, pp. 112–121

Drew, John (1987). *India and the Romantic Imagination*. Oxford and New Delhi: OUP

Elam, Keir (1991). *Semiotics of Theatre and Drama*. London: Routledge.

Emigh, John (1996). *Masked Performance: The Play of Self and Other in Ritual and Theatre*. Philadelphia: University of Pennsylvania Press

Frost, Anthony & Yarrow, Ralph (1990). *Improvisation in Drama*. London: Macmillan

Furman, Lou (1999). 'Beyond the Stage: Reflections on Street Theatre of India'. Website at Http://www.wsu.edu:8080/~furmanl

Ghosh, M. (1951–61). *The Natyasastra Ascribed to Bharata Muni*. Calcutta: Asiatic Society of Bengal

Ghosh, Nemai (2000). *Dramatic Moments: Theatre in Calcutta Since the 60s*. Calcutta: Seagull

Gopal, Ram and Dadachanji, Suresh (1951). *Indian Dancing*. Bombay: Asia Publishing House.

Gopalakrishna, Sudhana (1993). 'Metatheatricality: A View from Kathakali', in Narasimhaiah, C.D. and C.N. Srinath (Eds.), *Drama as a Form of Art and Theatre*. Mysore: Dhvanyaloka, pp. 53–56

Grotowski, Jerzy (1969). *Towards a Poor Theatre*. Tr. Eugenio Barba. London: Eyre Methuen

Gupt, Bharat. *Dramatic Concepts: Greek and Indian* (1994). New Delhi: D.K. Printworld (P) Ltd.

Hashmi, Safdar (1989). *The Right to Perform: The Selected Writings of Safdar Hashmi*. New Delhi: Sahmat

216

Hofmannsthal, Hugo von (1952). 'The Letter of Lord Chandos', in *Selected Prose*, trans. Mary Hottinger and Tania and James Stern. New York: Bollinger

Indian Express, 12/2/98 (New Delhi): 'Travails of Theatre' – interview with Madeeha Gauhar by Shamshul Islam

Iser, Wolfgang (1978). *The Act of Reading: A Theory of Aesthetic Response*. Baltimore: Johns Hopkins U.P.

Iyengar, Sameera (1998). 'A Space for Theatre: the Prithvi Theatre Festival'. *Seagull Theatre Quarterly* 18, pp. 70–79

Iyer, K. Bharatha. *Kathakali* (1983). New Delhi: Oriental Books Reprint Corporation

Jain, Kirti (1995). 'Theatre training: Some Issues', in Lal, Ananda (Ed.), *Rasa: The Indian Performing Arts in the Last Twenty-five Years. Vol. II: Theatre and Cinema*, pp. 63–70. Calcutta: Anamika Kala Sangam

Jana Sanghati Kendra (1999). 'The Ideas on which our Work is Based'. Newsletter.

Jana Sanskriti (1999). Newsletter.

Jauss, Hans J. (1982). *Towards an Aesthetics of Reception*. Brighton: Harvester

Kale, Pramod (1974). *The Theatric Universe*. Bombay: Popular Prakashan

Kanellakos, Demetri P. (1972). 'Four Levels of Speech or Utterance'. *Creative Intelligence* 2, pp. 15–21

Kar, Prafulla C. (Ed.) (1997). *Critical Theory, Western and Indian*. New Delhi: Pencraft International

Karanth, K.S. (1973, new edition 1997). *Yaksagana*. New Delhi: Indira Gandhi Centre for the Arts/Abhinav

Karnad, Girish (1972). *Hayavadana*. Bombay: OUP

—— (1989) *Tughlaq*. In *Three Modern Indian Plays*. New Delhi: OUP

—— (1990) *Naga–Mandala*. New Delhi: OUP

—— (1998) *The Fire and the Rain*. New Delhi: OUP

Katyal, Anjum (1994–9). Editorials to *Seagull Theatre Quarterly*, in particular nos. 9, 14/15, 17, 20/21

Kershaw, Baz (1996). 'The politics of performance in a postmodern age', In Patrick Campbell (Ed.), *Analysing Performance*, pp. 133–152. Manchester: Manchester University Press

Kulke, Hermann & Rothermund, Dietmar (1990). *A History of India*. London: Routledge

Kushwaha, M. (1994). 'The Validity and Scope of Rasa as a Critical Concept', in Narasimhaiah, C.D. (Ed.). *East West Poetics at Work*. New Delhi: Sahitya Academy, pp. 77–87

Lal, Ananda (Ed.) (1995). *Rasa: The Indian Performing Arts in the Last Twenty-five Years. Vol. II: Theatre and Cinema*. Calcutta: Anamika Kala Sangam

Lalitha, K. and Susie Tharu (Eds.) (1995). *Women Writing in India* (2 vols.). New Delhi: Oxford

Langer, Susanne (1953). *Feeling and Form*. New York: Scribner's

Lavery, Carl (2000). *Sacred Revolution: The Politics of Abjection and Narcissism in the Theatre of Jean Genet*. PhD thesis, University of East Anglia

Lokendrajit, Soyam (1997). 'An Artist's Response to Contemporary Reality: a Case of Two Directors. *Seagull Theatre Quarterly* 14/15, pp. 26–29

Mahesh Yogi, Maharishi (1966). *The Bhagavad Gita: A New Translation and Commentary (Chapters 1–6)*. London: Penguin

Malekin, Peter & Yarrow, Ralph (1997a). *Consciousness, Literature and Theatre: Theory and Beyond*. London: Macmillan

Martin, John (1997). 'Pre-Expressivity: Some Thoughts from the Rehearsal Floor', in *Presence and Pre-Expressivity 2*, *Contemporary Theatre Review*, Vol. 7, Part I, pp. 49–57

Mathur, J.C. (1964). *Drama in Rural India*. London: ICCR, Asia Publishing House

Mda, Zakes (1993). *When People Play People: Development Communication through Theatre*. London: Zed Books

Mehta, Dina (1993). *Brides are not for Burning*. Calcutta: Rupa

Merrell-Wolff, Franklin (1973). *The Philosophy of Consciousness Without an Object*. New York:

Meyer-Dinkgräfe, Daniel (1994). *Consciousness and the Actor*. Frankfurt am Main: Peter Lang

Moirangthem, Nandakumar (1997). 'Writing for Sumang Leela'. *Seagull Theatre Quarterly* 14/15, p. 160

Mukerji, Sumitra (1994). 'Encounters with Cultures: Contemporary Indian Theatre and Interculturalism'. *Seagull Theatre Quarterly* 4, pp. 3–12

Nandikesvara (1981). *Abhinayadarpanam*. Ed. and trans. M. Ghosh. Calcutta: Manisha Granthalaya Pvt. Ltd.

Nair, D. Apakuttan and Paniker, K. Ayappa (1993). *Kathakali. The Art of the Non-worldly*. Bombay: Marg Publications

Narayan, R.K. (1994). *Gods, Demons and Others*. London: Minerva

Narasimhaiah, C.D. (Ed.) (1994). *East West Poetics at Work*. New Delhi: Sahitya Academy

Narasimhaiah, C.D. and C.N. Srinath (Eds.) (1993). *Drama as a Form of Art and Theatre*. Mysore: Dhvanyaloka

Natyasastra. See Ghosh, M.

de Nicolás, Antonio (1976). *Meditations through the Rg Veda*. Boulder, Colorado and London: Shambhala

Paniker, K. Ayyappa (1986). 'The Mask-Dance of the God of Death in Patayani', in G. Sankara Pillai (Ed.), *The Theatre of the Earth is Never Dead*, pp. 1–7

—— (1993) See Nair, D. Appakuttan

Panikkar, Kavalam Narayan (1992). *Karimkutty* and *The Lone Tusker*. Calcutta: Seagull

—— (1995) 'Federation in Culture', in Lal, Ananda (Ed.), *Rasa: The Indian Performing Arts in the Last Twenty-five Years. Vol. II: Theatre and Cinema*, pp. 109–114. Calcutta: Anamika Kala Sangam

Parivartan Project: 'The Next Step': An Assessment 1995–1998. Ahmedabad: Darpana for Development

Pillai, G. Sankara (Ed.) (1986). *The Theatre of the Earth is Never Dead*. Trichur: School of Drama, University of Calicut

Pradier, Jean-Marie (1997). *La Scène et la Fabrique du Corps*. Bordeaux: Presses Universitaires de Bordeaux

Prentki, Tim (1998). 'Must the show go on? The case for Theatre of Development'. *Development in Practice*, Vol. 8, No. 4, pp. 419–429

Raha, Kironmoy (1995). 'Bengali Theatre', in Lal, Ananda (Ed.), *Rasa: The Indian Performing Arts in the Last Twenty-five Years. Vol. II: Theatre and Cinema*, pp. 119–124. Calcutta: Anamika Kala Sangam

Rajagopalachari, L. (1951). *Ramayana*. Bombay: Bharatiya Vidya Bhavan

Ramachandran, C.N. (1993). 'Folk Theatre and Social Structures – Tentative Comments.' In Narasimhaiah, C.D. and C.N. Srinath (Eds.), *Drama as a Form of Art and Theatre*. Mysore: Dhvanyaloka, pp. 17–23.

Ramayana. See Rajagopalachari, L.

Richmond, Farley P., Swann, Darius L. and Zarilli, Philip B. (1990). *Indian Theatre: Traditions of Performance.* Honolulu: University of Hawaii Press

Rothermund, Dietmar. See Kulke, Hermann

Rough Guide India 1994

Roy, Arundhati (1998). *The God of Small Things.* New York: Harper Collins

Roose-Evans, James (1989). *Experimental Theatre.* London: Routledge

Rushdie, Salman (1982). *Midnight's Children.* London: Picador

Russell Brown, John (1997). 'Theatrical Tourism'. *Journal of Literature & Aesthetics,* Vol. 5 No. 1 (Jan.–June), pp. 19–30

Ryder, Arthur W. (n.d.) *Kalidasa. Translations of Shakuntala and Other Works.* London: Dent

Sarabhai, Mrinalini and Mitchell, John D. (1992). *Staging a Sanskrit Classic:* Bhasa's *Vision of Vasavadatta.* New York: IASTA

Seagull Theatre Quarterly (1994–99). Nos. 1–23: especially Nos. 2 (Jana Sanskriti), 14/15 (Theatre in Manipur), 16 (Street Theatre), 20/21 (Theatre for Change); other articles are referred to under author's name.

Shah, K.J. 'Bharata's *Natyasastra:* I, VI & VII Adhyaya (with Translation, Notes, Comments and Glossary)'. Unpublished paper located in Dhvanyaloka Literary Criterion Centre, Mysore.

Schechner, Richard (1983). *Performative Circumstances: From the Avant Garde to Ramlila.* Calcutta: Seagull Press

—— (1985). *Between Theater and Anthropology.* Philadelphia: University of Pennsylvania Press

—— (1988). *Performance Theory.* London: Routledge

Singleton, Brian. (n.d.) 'K.N. Panikkar's *Teyyateyyam:* Resisting Interculturalism Through Ritual Practice'. Unpublished ms.

Sircar, Badal (1989). *Evam Indrajit.* Trans. Girish Karnad. In *Three Modern Indian Plays.* New Delhi: OUP

—— (1978). *The Third Theatre.* Calcutta: Sircar

Somorendra, Arambam (1997). '*Sumang Leela* (The Courtyard Play): an Introduction'. *Seagull Theatre Quarterly* 14/15, pp. 152–154

Stok, Zbigniew & Hänssler, Erika (1981). Production note to *Van Gogh, suicide through society,* by A. Artaud. Zürich: Stok Kammertheater

Talwar, Neelima (1997). 'Theatre of Development in Independent India', in *Critical Theory, Western and Indian,* Ed. Prafulla C. Kar. New Delhi: Pencraft International, pp. 94–111

Tanvir, Habib (1996). *Charandas Chor.* Trans. Anjum Katyal. Calcutta: Seagull

Tapas, Vijay (1995). 'Marathi Theatre' in Lal, Ananda (Ed.), *Rasa: The Indian Performing Arts in the Last Twenty-five Years. Vol. II: Theatre and Cinema,* pp. 171–178. Calcutta: Anamika Kala Sangam

Tendulkar, Vijay (1989). *Silence, the Court is in Session.* In *Three Modern Indian Plays.* New Delhi: OUP

Thakkar, B.K. (1984). *On the Structuring of Sanskrit Drama.* Ahmedabad: Saraswati Pustak Bhandar

Tharoor, Shashi (1994). *The Great Indian Novel.* London: Picador

Tharu, Susie. See Lalitha, K.

Theweleit, Klaus (1987, 1989). *Male Fantasies* (2 vols.) Cambridge: Polity Press

Thiyam, Ratan (1997). 'The Audience is Inside Me'. *Seagull Theatre Quarterly* 14/15, pp. 62–72

Valéry, Paul (1957). *Oeuvres*. Paris: Gallimard

Van Erven, Eugène (1992). *The Playful Revolution. Theatre and Liberation in Asia*. Bloomington: Indiana U.P.

Varadpande, M.L. (1992). *History of Indian Theatre. Loka Ranga. Panorama of Indian Folk Theatre*. New Delhi: Abhinav Publications

—— (1990). *Mahabharata in Performance*. New Delhi: Clarion

Vatsyayan, Kapila (1980). *Traditional Indian Theatre: Multiple Streams*. New Delhi: National Book Trust

Williams, David (Ed.) (1991). *Peter Brook and The Mahabharata*. London: Routledge

Williams, Raymond (1968). *Drama in Performance*. Harmondsworth: Penguin

Wright, Elizabeth (1996). 'Psychoanalysis and the theatrical: analysing performance'. In Patrick Campbell (Ed.), *Analysing Performance*, pp. 175–190. Manchester: Manchester University Press

Yarrow, Ralph (1986a). '"Neutral" Consciousness in the Experience of Theater'. *Mosaic* 33/3, pp. 1–14

—— (1986b). 'The Potential of Consciousness: Towards a New Approach to States of Consciousness in Literature.' *Journal of European Studies* 14, pp. 1–20

—— (1990). See Frost, Anthony

—— (1992) (Ed.) *European Theatre 1960–1990*. London: Routledge

—— (1997a). See Malekin, Peter

—— (1997b) (Ed.). 'Presence and Pre-expressivity'. *Contemporary Theatre Review* Vols. 7/2 and 8/1

Index

Bold type for words indicates the title of a play or other work; figures in **bold** indicate a particularly important or summary reference.

Aajir 156
Adapa, Shashidara 186
aesthetics 4, 11, 20–2, 38, 41, 62–3, 65–7, 73, 87, **95–100**, 104–116, 121, 123, 125–7, 144, 150, 178–9, 185, 194, 199–200, 202–3, 210, 213–4
abhinaya 70, 79
Abhinaya Theatre Group 185
absurd theatre 7, 8, 111, 146
actor-trainers/training 4, 6, 11, 14, 19, 29, 100–1, 121, 145, 154–5, 159, 164, 166–175, 181, 190, 200, 203, **204–7**, 208–9
Agashe, Mohan 163
Agni 37, 51–3, 123, 140
Agra Bazaar 154
Agun 179
aharya 78
Ahmedabad 82–3, 146–7, 169, 172, 189
Ajoka 157
Akademis 147–8, 159, 164, 170, 175, 181
Akharas 84
alaukika 79
Alekar, Satish 152, 155, 162–3, 168
Alkazi, Ebrahim 162, 167
Alternative Living Theatre 188–9
Amnesty International 158
anand(a) 66, 70, 116, 122, 137–8, 140
angika 78
Andhra Pradesh 69, 83, 186–7

Ankia-natta 83
Antarnatya 163
Apharan Bhaichare Ka 183
ARP (Association of the Rural Poor) 145, 186–7
Arambam, Lokendra 159–61
Aristotle 101, 104, 107, 109, 131
Artaud, Antonin 5, 8, 11, 15, 28, 34, 60, 96, 122, 128, 189, 199, 203–4, 208
Aryan 39, 45, 87
Ashoka 39
Ashoka, T.P. 165–6, 170–1
Assam 69, 83, 142, 158
Atharva Veda 66, 78
Atman 10
audience 6–7, 12, 21–2, 29, 36, 50–1, 59–61, 63, 69, 70, 72, 80, 82, 88, 99–100, 102–3, 107–8, 112–3, 117–8, 121–2, 136, 140, 144, 154, 161, 163–4, 177–8, 180, 190, 200, 202, 207–9, 213
  see also reception
Aurat 183
avatars 9
Ayurvedic 78

Badejo, Peter 206
Balinese theatre 86, 103
Bandyopadhyay, Samik 155–6, 160–1, 178–9
Bangalore 185–6
Baradi, Hasmukh 189

Barba, Eugenio 3, 6, 8, 12, 14, 28, 65–6, 100, 103, 110, 113, 127, 129, 143, 204, 208–9
Bardhan, Gul 135, 181
Bartholomew, Rati 181, 186
Bayen 156
Beckett, Samuel 7, 10, 12, 21, 25–6, 40, 53, 96, 112–3, 121, 196, 209
Bedi, Indira 105, 123
Begum Barv(w)e 152, 155, 163
Belchi 186
Bengal 34, 83–4, 179, 187, 189, 191
    Bengali language, culture 57, 154–5, 161
    Bengali theatre 150–2, 162–3, 178–9
Bhabha, Homi 213
Bhaduri, Sisirkumar 178
Bhagavad Gita 49
Bhagav(w)ata 36, 67, 70, 76, 85, 88
Bhagav(w)ata Mela 68, 77
Bhaona 83
Bharata Muni 11, 16–18
Bharatanatyam 65, 78, 87, 121, 149, 174–5, 207
Bhartendu Natya Akademi 167
Bharucha, Rustom 3, 21, 26, 29, 80, 115, 127, 130, 138–9, 141, 144, 148, 161, 170, 174177, 180, 213
Bhasa 55–6, 85, 106, 111, 126, 148, 153, 171
Bhat, Haridasa 171
Bhatt, Uzra 157
Bhattacharya, Bijan 179
bhava 55
Bhavabhuti 55
Bhavai 13, 67, **82–3**, 153, 166, 190
Bhima 82, 120
Bhoma 152, 154, 185
Bhopa 69
Bhopal 64, 69, 162, 164, 185, 190
Bhuta 54, 70
Bihar 82, 86, 142, 186, 189, 191
'bios' 103, 204
Black Athena 2
Boal, Augusto 72, 101–2, 128, 176–7, 186–90, 194, 211
Bohm, David 117, 124
Bombay (Mumbai) 84, 138, 146–7, 153, 159, 161–4, 181, 190–1, 196

Bordenave, Juan Diaz 192
Borges, Jorge Luis 115, 135–6, 202
Brahma 9, 37, 42, 56
Brahman 9, 10, 26, 52
Brahmin/ic 10, 45, 66, 70, 87, 92, 149
Brecht, Bertolt 12, 15–16, 28, 47, 60, 79, 100–2, 107, 128, 154, 171, 177, 180, 194, 204
Brides are not for Burning 155
Brook, Peter 3, 8, 12, 14–15, 28–9, 34, 100–1, 113, 121, 144, 173, 196, 199–200, 203–5, 207–9
Buddhism 8, 199, 202, 205
Burra Katha 67, 69
Byrski, M.Christopher 17, 105–12, 124

Calcutta 137–8, 145–7, 154, 159, 161–4, 168, 179–80, 183, 185, 187–8, 190
Calicut, (Kozhikode) University School of Drama 145, 168, 185
Capra, Fritjof 5, 9, 10, 117
Carnatic music 76
carnival/esque 16, 51, 73, 84
Carrière, Jean-Claude 34
caste 13, 38, 47, 71, 83, 86, 132, 142, 145, 153, 187, 191
catharsis 104, 121
Centre for Performance Research (CPR) 28, 204
Chaitanya, Krishna 79
Chakravyuha 161
Chakyars 69
Chakyar Kuttu (Koothu) 51
Chandrika, B. 111
Chandralekha 127, 139, 149, 174–5, 187, 213
Charandas Chor 152–3
Chatterjee, Pranas 188–9
Chattopadhyay, Kamaladevi 196
Chekhov, Michael 6
Chattisgarh 153
Chhau
    Mayurbhanj 82
    Purulia 13, 82
    Serakaila 82
Chennai Kalai Kuzhu 187, 190
China 142

Chitra Katha 36
Cholas 39
Chorus Repertory Theatre 148
Chranas 84
Churchill, Caryl 90, 209
chutti 77
Cixous, Hélène 140
Coleridge, Samuel Taylor 24
Contractor, Meher 174
commedia 14, 21
communalism 157, 197
Communism 179, 182, 189
communitas 83
consciousness I, II, 14–16, 18, 41–2,
    48, 52, 54, 65, 97, **113–26**, 132,
    137, 142–6, 195, 200, 204
Copeau, Jacques 6, 14, 100, 117, 153,
    159, 204, 208
Csikszentmihalyi, Mihaly 24
'cultural piracy' 4, 58, 102–3, 144,
    175, 198, 206, 210

Darika 70
Darpana Academy 82–3, 169, **172–3**,
    174, 189–90
Das, Varsha 68, 176, 192
Dave, Janak 82
death 47, 49, 74–5, 92, 94, 107, III,
    II9, 136, 140, 155, 201
Derrida, Jacques 10, 35, 125
Desai, Anita 189–90, 192
Deshpande, G. P. 59, 150, 162
Deshpande, Sudhanva 182–3, 190–2
desire 107–II3, 125, 139–41
Despande, P.L. 84, 163
devadasis 93, 149
Devi, Mahasweta 45, 59, 88, 143, 151,
    155–6, 163, 187, 196
Devi, Rukmini 87
Devy, G.N. 102, 198
Dhaka 157
Dhaker, Rani 154
dharma 39, 42, 73
Dhritirashtra 49
Dionysos 85, II6
director(s) 55–6, 58, 67, 100, 138,
    145, 154, 159–60, 162–3, 165–7,
    175, 180–1, 195, 205–6, 209
Dodatta 77

Doordarshan 148, 167
Drama in Performance 96
Drama Review, The 71
Draupadi 82, 87, 89, 91–2, 139, 173,
    196
Dravidian 39, 45, 70, 87
Drew, John 2, 106, II9, 210
Dubey, Satyadev 164
Durga 37
Durodhyana 82, 120
Dushyanta 106–7
Dutt, Utpal, 130, 144, 152–3, 163,
    180

Ebotombi, Harokcham 'Sanakhya' 159
economics see funding
Elam, Keir 96–99, II4
Eliot, T.S. 52
Elkunchwar, Mahesh 59, 151, 163
Emigh, John 24, 34, 80, 91, 138, 213
Enact 151–2, 175
English (language) 13, 22, 34, 56,
    59–60, II3, 147, 151–2, 155, 157,
    169, 172–3
'efficacy-entertainment' 51, 65, 67, 70,
    102, 127, 194
entertainment 40, 47, 76, 83, 87–8,
    II8, 146, 159–60, 181, 196, 211
entheos II6
epic(s) 19, 32, 35–6, 38, 41, 43–7,
    49–51, 56, 66, 70, 89, 106, 143,
    152
epos 39
Evam Indrajit 151–5, 154, 159
'extra-daily' 6–7, 12, 15, 17, 24, 41, 65,
    102, II2, II7–8, 120–2, 127, 138,
    204

'fan' 16, 60, 64–5, 75, 78, 130, 194
Fanon, Fritz 2, 176, 194
Faust 101, 109
Flood, The 59
Fo, Dario 12, 100, 208–0
Folhetos 192
Ford Foundation 73, 147, 170–1
Forster, E.M. II9–20
freedom I, **20–27**, 66, 91, 94–5, 122,
    127, 136–9, 141, 178, 180, 192,
    186, 194–5, 202, 204, 213

Freire, Paulo 176, 194
Freud, Sigmund 18, 80, 141
Frost, Anthony 208
Funding/economics 27, 29, 67, 82, 87,
    100, 132, 143–5, 147–8, 159–60,
    162, 164, 167–74, 176, 178,
    181–2, 189, 191, 195

Gandhi, Indira 183, 186
Ganesh (Ganapati) 38, 42, 85
Ganguli, Usha 164
Ganguly, Sanjoy 164, 187–8
Garage Theatre 189
garbha 105
Gargi, Balwant 157
Gauhar, Madeeha 157–8
Gaulier, Philippe 208
Goethe, Johann Wolfgang 63, 101, 104
Genet, Jean 7, 12, 15
Ghashiram Kotwal 163
Ghosh, Manmohan 113
Gilani, Benjamin 146
Gita-Govinda 57, 84
Godot, Waiting for 112, 146
gods 17–18, 37–8, 47, 51, 71–2, 74,
    85, 88–9, 92, 109, 115–6
Gondhal 69
Gopal, Ram 78
Gopalakrishnan, Sudhana 118
Great Indian Novel, The 49
Greek theatre 37, 69, 110–1
Grotowski, Jerzy 3, 6, 8, 12, 14–15, 19,
    28, 100, 110, 113, 138, 154, 189,
    196, 199, 203–5, 208–9
Guha, Prabir 177, 188–9
Gujarat 82, 87, 172–3, 189–90, 191
Gunwardana, A.J. 177
gunas 9–10, 78
guru 19, 67, 101, 207

Hanuman 57, 79, 83, 91
Harijan 186
Haryana 191
Harsa 55
Hashmi, Mala 184, 190, 193, 196
Hashmi, Safdar 22, 27, 145, 153, 164,
    182–4
Hayavadana 152, 154, 165
Heisenberg, Werner 10

Heggodu 159, 165, 169–71, 186
Hesse, Hermann 66
hijaras 86, 93
Hindu/ism 36, 41, 80, 93, 102, 142,
    152–3
Hindi language, theatre 57, 150, 155,
    161–2, 164, 165, 167, 173 (see also
    Indian languages)
Hindi cinema see Indian cinema
Hindustani music 76
Hoban, Russell 53, 202
Hyderabad University School of
    Performing Arts 168

identity 4, 6, 20, 22ff, 121, 130–1,
    136, 142–5, 152, 155, 166–7,
    211–2
Imphal 146, 190
improvisation 6, 23, 68, 80, 84, 88,
    100, 119, 153, 181, 184, 187, 205,
    208–9
India(n)
    aesthetics see aesthetics
    culture 45, 58, 63, 66, 87, 93, 127ff,
        134, 139, 140, 142ff, 182, 184,
        187, 205, 208–9
    cinema 44, 47, 65, 70, 84, 148, 156,
        162, 164, 167, 181, 196, 207
    dance 51, 57–9, 70–1, 76, 152,
        172–5, 177, 207
    history 57, 66, 87, 152, 196
    Independence 4, 33–4, 46, 49, 58,
        142, 144, 146, 149, 154, 167
    languages 2, 34, 50, 55, 57–8, 63,
        65, 83–4, 132, 147–8, 151–3,
        155ff, 162–3, 165, 167, 180,
        182–3, 191, 210
    music 58–9, 63, 70, 80, 82–5
    politics 66, 127ff, 142ff (see also
        politics)
    religion 50, 66, 86–7, 191
Indian Council for Cultural Relations
    (ICCR) 174
Indian Express, The 157, 163
Indian People's Theatre Association
    (IPTA) 4, 130, 145, 148, 153, 167,
    178–82, 187, 190, 194
Indian Theatre: Multiple Streams 13,
    28 (see also Vatsyayan)

Ionesco, Eugène 7, 10, 113
Iser, Wolfgang 80, 98
Islam 93, 114
Islam, Shamsul 182
itihasas 39
Iyengar, Sameera 164
Iyer, K.Bharata 78, 88, 114

Jain, Kirti 168
Jaloos 157
Janam (Jana Natya Manch) 27, 145,
    153, 164, **182–4**, 186, 190
Jana Sanskriti 164, **187–8**, 190
Jana Sanghati Kendra 188, 193
jathas 177, 184–6
Jauss, J.R. 98
Jeyasingh, Shobana 28, 206
jo-ha-kyu 111
Johnstone, Keith 6, 8, 208
Jones, Sir William 33, 198
Jokumaraswami 152, 165

Kabuki 54, 88, 103
Kaikeyi 49
Kala Chethana *Kathakali* Troupe 49, 206
Kalakshetra Academy 175
kalam 70
Kalarippayat 171, 204
Kale, Pramod 78, 113–6
Kali 9, 37, 70, 86–7, 89, 139
Kalidasa 33–4, 55, 63, 89, 104, 126,
    153, 171
Kaliyogam 77
Kambar, Chandrasekhar 139, 152, 162,
    165, 196
Kanara 73
Kanellakos, Dmitri 39
Kanhailal, Heisnam 159, 161
Kannada 57, 76, 150–1, **164–6**, 169,
    171
Kanpur 190
Kantor, Tadeusz 12, 96, 209
Kapoor, Jennifer }
Kapoor, Prithviraj } 163
Kapoor, Sanjna }
Kapur, Anuradha 181
Karanth, B.V. 145, 164–5, 167,
    169–70, 172
Karanth, K.S. 28, 77

Karimkutty 12, 152–3
Karnabharam 161
Karnad, Girish 58, 60, 128, 139,
    145–6, 151–2, 154, 162, 165, 171,
    196
Karnataka 69, 73, 77, 83, 145, 148,
    162, 164, 169, 172, 185–6
Kashmir 142
kathak 70, 207
kathaka 69
kathakara 83
Kathakali 13–14, 36, 54–5, 63, 65, 68,
    70, 73, **76–82**, 86, 88, 118, 120,
    147, 149, 153, 168, 174, 204, 206
Kathmandu 157
Katiyakkaran 36, 67, 82, 85
Katyal, Anjum 86, 137–8, 158–9, 193,
    196
Kaul, Bansi 153
Kauravas 39, 42, 44, 49, 91
Kerala 69, 71, 73, 77, 83, 128, 138,
    145, 148, 171, 185–6
Kerala Kalamandalam 77, 168
Kerala Sastra Sahitya Parishad (KSSP)
    145, 179, 182, **184–5**, 187
Kershaw, Baz 192
Kochi (Cochin) 77
kolakarran 71
Koothu-P-Pattarai 187
kris 86
Krisna (Krsna, Krishna) 37, 41, 51, 70,
    91, 141
Krishna-attam 71, 80, 141
Kristeva, Julia 107, 125, 140
Kurukshetra 39
Kurus 39
kuttambalam 77
Kuttiyatam (Koodiyattam, Kudiyattam) 13,
    36, 44, 63, 68–9, 77, 79, 87, 118,
    149, 153, 208
Kuttu 36, 69

Lacan, Jacques 7, 14, 23, 107, 125,
    135, 141
Lahore 157
Lal, Ananda 27, 29, 34, 133, 148,
    150–1, 157, 159, 161, 164, 168,
    175
Lalitha, K. 155

Langer, Susanne 6, 24
language, linguistics 19–20, 33, 35, 38, 40, 46, 53–4, 65, 97, 99, 105, 107, 109–10, 118, 123–4, 135, 144, 207–8
lasya 86
laukika 79
Lavery, Carl 203
Lear 49, 108, 113, 136, 147, 202
Lecoq, Jacques 6, 8, 14, 100, 117, 184, 199, 204–5, 208
Lewis, Alun 119
Life of Galileo, The 180
lila 9, 48, 83, 85, 122
liminality 12–13, 20, 26, 40–1, 47, 72, 141, 154, 213
Little People's Theatre 163
logos 39
Lokendrajit, Soyam 158–9
loss 25–6, 49, 53, 106–113, 119–20, 136, 139–40
Lucknow 167
Lyotard, Jean-François 10, 44

Macarthur Trust 189
Macbeth 44, 108, 112–3, 120, 147, 159, 161
Machine 183, 186
Madhya Pradesh 56, 69, 191
Madras (Chennai) 187
Madurai (MK University) 168
Mahabharata 34-37, 38–40, 42–43, 45–49, 50, 56–8, 63, 73, 76, 82, 85, 87, 89, 91, 109, 113, 128, 148, 153, 161, 173, 200, 209
Mahanirvan 155, 163
Maharashtra 34, 36, 69, 84, 147, 170, 179, 191
Mahesh Yogi, Maharishi 121, 126
Majumdar, Debasis 163
Malani, Nalini 138
Malayalam 57, 150, 152–3, 171–2, 175, 185
Malekin, Peter 1, 48, 122, 198, 210
Mangalore 185
Manimekhalai 56, 82, 113
Manipravala 57
Manipur/i 70, 88, 132, 142–3, 148, 154–5, **158–61**, 163, 165, 167, 190

Manipur State Kala Akademi 159
manis 86
Manthara 49
Marat/Sade, The 209
Marathi 57, 150–1, 161–2
Margi Academy 77, 149
Markandeya 74
Martin, John 136, 206
Marxist 84, 95, 127, 130ff, 144, 173, 180–191–2
mask(s) 15, 23, 26, 82–3, 85, 88, 204, 209
Mathura 70
Mauryas 39
maya 9, 10, 23, 106, 114, 126
McBurney, Simon 209
Mda, Zakes 192
Medea 113, 138–9
mediaeval European theatre/art 37, 65, 67, 83
Mehta, Dina 155, 196
Mehta, Vijaya 84
Menon, Sadanand 187
Menon, Vallatol Narayana 77
MESCA 186
metatheatre 75, 85, 118
Meyer-Dinkgräfe, Daniel 74, 113, 115, 121–2, 126
Meyerhold, Vsevolod 8, 11, 100
Midnight's Children 142
Mitra, Manoj 163
Mitra, Sombu 163
Mitra, Tripti 163
Mnouchkine, Ariane 3, 12, 14, 28, 100, 204, 207–9
Modernism 5, 10, 21, 34, 200
Mohiniattam 87
Moirangthem, Nandakumar 160
moksha 25, 82, 204
Mother of 1084 156
Mrcchakatika 55, 84, 153
Mudiyettu 70, ·86
mudras 11, 77, 79
Müller, Max 37
mukha 105
Mukherjee, Arun 180, 187
Mukerji, Sumitra 145–6, 149, 151, 153–4
Munshiji 84–5

Murphy 40
music see India(n)
Muslim 93, 142
Muthuswamy, Na 187
Mysore 145, 169, 172
myth 39–41, 50, 58, 63, 66–7, 89, 165
mythos 39

NGOs 178, 185, 188–9, 193–4
Nadeem, Shahid 157–8
Naga-Mandala 128, 152, 154, 165
Nair, D. Appakuttu 77, 79–80, 118
namaghara 83
Nambiars 69
Narayan, R.K. 46
narrative 32–3, 35–6, 39, 42–3, 46–9,
    50, 55–6, 58, 66–70, 76, 85, 183,
    199–200
Nata 66
National School of Drama (NSD) 159,
    162, 164, 166–8, 170, 172, 181,
    186
natya 105
Natya Sastra 4, 11, 16, 17, 18, 19, 21,
    22, 32, 37, 38, 55, 62–3, 66–7, 77,
    79, 95, 99–101, 104–5, 107–8,
    113–27, 149, 195, 199, 203
Nautanki 68, 84, 87, 153
Naxalite 142, 156, 163
Naya Theatre 154
Nayaka 82
Neutrality 114, 120, 126, 137
neutral mask 6, 15, 121, 204–5, 209
New Delhi 51, 145–7, 159, 161–2,
    164–5, 167, 182, 191
Nicolàs, Antonio de 117, 119–20, 201,
    205
Nietzsche, Friedrich 18
Ninasam **169–171** (see also Heggodu)
nirvahana 105
Nishant 182
niyatapti 106
Noh 11, 14, 43, 54, 111
Not I 53
Notun Chehara 183
Nuñez, Nicolàs 15

Odin Teatret 103
Oja-Pali 69

Omcheri (N. N. Pillai) 59, 151–3
onnegata 88
orientalism 2, 21, 28–9, 34, 63, 144,
    182, 198–9, 201, 206
origin 1, 11, **16–20**, 42–3, 51, 53, 62,
    64, 66, 84, 86, 110–1, 122, 139,
    149–50, 202, 213
Orissa 69, 82–3, 86, 191
    Orissi dance 28, 103

Pabuji Ki Phad/Pada 36, 67, 69
pacha 77
Padumjee, Dadi 174
padyatra 189
Pallavas 39
pakarnattom 79, 118
Pakistan 142, 157
Pan Project 28, 204, 206, 209, 212
Pandavas 39, 42, 44, 49, 89, 91
Pandavini 69
Pande, Mrinal 155
Pandya, Kailash 82, 190
Pandyas 39
Panigrahi, Sanjukhta 28, 204
Paniker, K. Ayyappa 74–5, 77, 79, 80,
    82, 94, 112, 117–8, 130, 175
Panikkar, Chitra 77
Panikkar, Kavalam Narayan 36, 56, 58,
    60, 72–3, 80, 105, 111, 127, 130,
    138, 145, 147–8, 150–3, 169, 171–2
Panini 125, 139
para 125
Parivartan 189, 192
Parvati 42, 89
Passage to India, A 119
pasyanti 125, 129
Patayani 74, 117, 171
Pebet 161
Perform/ance/er 7, 11–12, 17–20, 29,
    32–3, 36, 38, 41–43, 45–48, 51–2,
    57, **61–94**, 114ff, 134, 137, 143,
    150, 181, 191, 194–5, 197, 201–2,
    205, 209, 212, 214
    event 5–8, 12–13, 21, 22, 33, 51, 62,
    64–5, 73, 88, 97, 102–3, 111–2,
    127, 130, 133, 146, 184, 195, 212
    forms, models 4, 13, 34, 61–4, 130,
    139, 1433, 156, 164, 184, 199,
    203, 208

status 5, 61–2
styles 58, 85, 153, 204–5, 209
techniques 6, 14, 34, 66, 69
text 4, 34, 43, 53, 62, 80, 100,
   104
theory 28, 95–6, 100ff, 104, 107,
   113, 125, 184, 199
Philippines Educational Theatre
   Association 187
physical theatre, physicality 6, 8,
   13–15, 20, 153, 159, 199
physics 5, 10, 40, 108, 117, 201
picture showmen 36, 69
Pillai, G. Sankara 71, 73–4
Plato 10, 104, 119–20, 126, 196
'play' 6–11, 16, 23, 40, 48, 52, 64, 66,
   80, 82–3, 85, 93, 122, 124, 140–1,
   195, 205–6, 211, 213
Playful Revolution, The 180
Plotinus 198
poesis 41, 116
politics 4, 10, 11, 16, 21, 24, 26, 27,
   46, 55, 66, 82, 84, 86–7, 89,
   91–96, 103, 119, 125, 129–30,
   135, 138, 142–167, 176–194,
   197, 200, 208, 211–2
Pondicherry University School of
   Performing Arts 168
postcolonialism 27–8, 31, 58, 60, 127,
   143–4, 146, 149, 177, 180, 199,
   208, 213
Powada 69
Pradier, Jean-Marie 1, 2, 134
Prakrit 33, 46, 57
Pralayan 187, 191, 193
Prasanna, R.P. 145, 165, 185–6
pratimukha 105
Prentki, Tim 193
Prithvi Theatre 162–4
Prospero 49, 112, 126, 202
puja 123
Pune 84, 146, 161–2
   University School of Performing
   Arts 168
Punjab 142, 183, 191
Punjabi language, theatre 86, 153,
   157–8, 182
puppets 36, 50, 69, 83, 156, 171–4,
   186, 189, 208–9

Puranas, The 63, 83, 87
Pushkar 64

Radha 89, 141
Radha, Kironmoy 162–3
Raina, M.K. 56, 180
Rajas 78
rajsic 77
Rajasthan 36, 69, 82, 174, 191
Rajagopalachari, L. 56
Rakesh, Mohan 152
rakshasic 77
Rama 9, 37, 39, 41, 44, 48, 79, 86, 89,
   91
Ramachandran, C.N. 82
Ramayana 35–40, 42, 46, 48–50,
   56–7, 62, 83, 87, 109, 153
Ram Lila 9, 67, 82–3, 102–3, 154
Ramnagar 83
Rangayana 159, 165, 169–70, 172
rang(a)lo 82, 85
Rao, Maya 181
Rasa: The Indian Performing Arts in
   the Last Twenty-five Years (Vol.II:
   Theatre and Cinema) see Lal,
   Ananda
rasa 11, 41, 55, 66, 74, 89, 95, 104,
   110, 114–6, 122–3, 125–8
rasika 11, 125
rasas 78
Raslila 51, 66–7, 70, 84
Ravana 39, 44, 49, 58–9, 79, 83, 91
Ray, Satyajit 196
Reception/reception theory 4, 8, 18,
   22, 35, 41, 42, 43, 44, 52, 54, 63,
   65–6, 79–81, 93, 95–101, 113–6,
   121–4, 129, 133, 137, 143, 194–5,
   202 see also audience
Rg Veda (Rig Veda) 37, 38, 51–3, 66,
   78, 116–7, 123, 125, 205
rhema 39
rhythm 19, 35, 50, 54, 59, 71, 77–8,
   112, 114, 117, 121–2, 124, 171
Richmond, Farley P. 29, 61, 66–7, 145
Rilke, Rainer Maria 12
rites, ritual 12, 22, 24, 32, 38, 52, 54,
   58, 64, 66–7, 70–1, 73–6, 79, 85–7,
   93, 102, 111–2, 115–7, 123, 145,
   152, 165, 171–2, 190, 193, 213

Roman theatre 37
Root Theatre Co. 185
Rushdie, Salman 142–3, 196, 199
Russell-Brown, John 208–10
Ryder, Arthur 33

sacrifice 19, 26, 52, 66, 75, 105, 111, 116–7, 123
Safdar Marena 183
Sahmat (Safdar Hashmi Memorial Trust) 182, 184
Samarth, Alaknanda 113, 138–9
Sama Veda 66, 78
samhita 11
Samudaya 145, 165, 184–7
sandhis 105
Sankaradeva 83
Sanskrit 19, 37, 40, 46, 57, 63, 83, 104, 115–6, 126, 171
Sanskrit drama 4, 22, 33, 34, 38, 50, 55–7, 62–7, 71, 76, 79, 80, 85, 87, 95, 104–113, 147, 153, 157, 164, 185
Sarabhai, Mallika 135–6, 138–9, 169, 172–3, 177, 196, 206
Sarabhai, Mrinalini 169, 172–3, 190, 196
Sarabhai, Vikram 173, 190
sardar 84
Sartre, Jean-Paul 120
Satabdi 145, 154, 164, 180, 190
sat-chit-ananda 137
Sati-Savitri-Sita 44
sattva 78
sattvik 77
Saussure, Ferdinand de 97
Savary, Jerôme 12
Savarese, Nicola 14, 103
Schechner, Richard 4, 6, 12, 14, 16–17, 23, 25–6, 28, 37, 62, 64–6, 70–1, 78, 102, 111–3, 127–8, 130, 143–4, 146, 154, 177, 184, 194–5, 204, 208–9, 212–3
Schiller, Friedrich 80, 109
script/ing 33, 48, 55, 58–9, 101, 153, 179, 181–3, 186–8
scroll painting see picture showmen
Seattle, University Theatre 157
Seagull Theatre Quarterly 86, 88, 133, 137–8, 144, 153–5, 158, 160,

163, 174–5, 177, 180–1, 187–8, 190–1, 193–4, 196
Secret Art of the Performer, The 103
self 4–8, 11–16, 21–26, 75, 80, 86, 93–4, 103, 109–10, 117–20, 122, 128, 135–141, 143, 152, 155, 161, 196, 199, 201–3, 205, 211–2
semiotics 34, 58, 95–101, 114, 123, 134
Seth, Vikram 196
Shakespeare, William 7, 17, 21, 35, 72, 101, 104, 108, 146–7, 171, 175, 199, 202
Shakti 9
Shakti, The Power of Women 135, 139
Shakuntala 89, 91–2, 106
Shakuntala 33, 106, 171
Shah, Naseeruddin 146
shaman/ic/ism 14, 22, 36, 64, 72, 116
Shilappadikaran 56–7, 82, 113
Shiva 9–10, 37, 42, 46, 51, 75, 78, 82, 85, 89, 110, 122
sidhis 38
Sikh 142, 183
Silence, the Court is in Session 151–2
Singh, Gurucharan 157, 191
Singleton, Brian 130–1, 150, 171
Sircar, Badal 22, 145–6, 151–5, 157, 159, 162–3, 178, 180, 185–7
'Third Theatre' 177, 194
Sita 44, 48–9, 58, 79, 86, 89, 91–2, 139
Sita's Daughters 139
soma 114ff
Somorendra, Arambam 160
sound 53–4
Sopanam 56, 145, 148, 169, 171–2,
Spartacus 154, 159
Spivak, Gayatri 199
Sri Lanka 39
Stanislavsky, Konstantin 6, 8, 11, 24, 54–5, 99–101, 107, 110, 138–9, 202, 205
Strindberg, August 199
Struggle 186
Subbana, K.V. 145, 165, 169, 171, 180, 186
Sudrak 162–3

Sudraka 55
Sumang Leela 159–60
Sundaram 162–3
Surya Shikar 180
Suta 69
Sutradhara 36, 70, 76, 82–3, 85, 118, 165
Swann, Darius L. 67, 145
Swapna Vasavadattam 56
'Symbolic Order' 7, 10, 15, 16, 21, 23, 92, 94, 112–3, 131, 134–6, 141, 161
symbolism 8, 10, 200, 203

Tagore, Rabindranath 178–9
Talé-Danda 152
Tal-maddale 69
Talwar, Neelima 175–7, 180, 184
tamas 78
tamsik 77
Tamas(h)a 67, 84
Tamasha Theatre 206
Tamil Nadu 77, 82–3, 145, 186–7
Tamil language/culture/drama 56–7, 82, 150
Tandava 86
Tanvir, Habib 22, 56, 58, 84, 145, 151–3, 162, 164, 180, 196
Taoism 8
Tapas, Vijay 163
tapas 50
Tara Arts 28, 206, 209
Tempest, The 104, 108, 112, 126, 128
Tendulkar, Vijay 59, 151, 162–3, 196
text(s) 4, 6, 19–20, 32–5, 45, 47–8, 50, 54, 55–60, 80–1, 83, 96, 99, 107, 122, 153 (see also 'performance-text')
Thaker, Jaswant 190
thanathu 138
Tharoor, Shashi 49, 196
Tharu, Susie 155
theatre
  anthropology 28, 33, 40, 95, 102, 127, 129ff, 199–200
  'classical' 32, 36, 62, 64, 67, 70, 82, 87, 149, 159, 180
  criticism 32, 60, 96ff, 151, 175, 200

'of development' 153, 166, 170, 172–3, **176–8**, 181–2, 184, 187, **189–94**, 211
'environmental' 64, 103, 128, 154, 177, 184
'folk' 32, 33, 36, 58, 66–7, 70, 73, 82–3, 105–6, 128, 145, 152–9, 165–6, 171, 177, 179–82, 184–5, 187, 189, 192
history 1, 17, 28, 29, 30, 54, 64, 97, 131–2, 172–3, 181, 184, 200
'of the Oppressed' 186, 188, 211
political 16, 59, 94, **142–67**, 176ff
  see also politics
practitioners 2, 27, 28, 101, 114, 127, 145, 176, 180, 193, 205, 213
proscenium arch 16, 52, 65, 146, 159, 163, 170, 186
professional 67, 84, 101, 146, 150, 160–1, 168, 183, 187
'physical' see physical
'rich' 34, 54, 58, 97
street 65, 68, 145, 154, 156–7, 165, 176–8, 182–4, 186, 189–94
theory 1, 17, 28, 30, 32, **95–141**, 213
tradition/al 3, 4, 8, 21, 22, 28–9, 33, 58, 127, 145, 147, 149, 153, 158, 162–3, 165, 171, 173–4, 182, 184, 188, 210, 213
Theatre Academy (Pune) 162–3
Théâtre de Complicité 21, 204, 209
Theatre Living Laboratory 189
Theatre Union 181
Therukoothu 13, 36, 67–8, 73, 82, 153, 187
Theweleit, Klaus 136
Theyyam 13, 54, 58–9, 70–73, 88, 120, 171
Theyya Theyyam 58
Thiyam, Ratan 43, 58, 145, 147–8, 159, 161–2, 167
Thottam 70–1
Tirugata 165, 169–70
Tongbra, G.C. 160
Top Girls 90
tragedy 75, 104–113, 122
transcendence 11, 15–20, 73–5, 114, 122

transformation 52, 65, 67, 79, 94, 102,
110, 115, 124, 128, 130, 133, 138,
143, 145, 165, 194, 202
transportation 65, 128
tribhanghi 121
Trichur (Thrissur) 73, 77, 145, 147–8,
168, 185
trimurti 78
Trivandrum (Thiruvananthapuram) 77,
145, 149, 169, 171, 185
Trivedi, Harish 199, 213
Tughlaq 151–2, 154
Turner, Victor 12, 26, 83, 102, 111,
127, 143, 154
Tulsidas 83
turiya 120

Udayana 106–7
Udipi 147–8, 168, 171
Ujjain 56, 63–4
Upanishads, The 26, 116
Urvashi and Johnny 156
Uttar Pradesh 84, 87, 183, 191

vac 35
vachika 78
V for 136
Valmiki 42
Van Erven, Eugène 29, 177, 180,
182–3, 186, 191, 194
Van Gennep, Arnold 12
Varadpande, M.L. 29, 43, 61, 66–7,
72, 84, 130
Varanasi 9, 83, 102–3, 154
Vasavadatta 56, 106
Vatsyayan, Kapila 13, 15, 28–9, 56–7,
61, 63, 66, 68–9, 74, 76–7, 82–5,
89, 127, 133, 148, 196
Vedas 8, 11, 17, 35–37, 38, 113, 115,
124, 143
    Vedic chanting 35
    Vedic (Sanskrit)aesthetics/
    linguistics/phonetics 51, 95, 104,
    110, 116, 125–6
Verma, Jatinder 28, 206, 209
veshas 82
Vijayakumar, Kalamandalam 206

vimarsa 105
Vishnu 9–10, 37, 78
Vidus(h)aka 36, 46, 67, 69, 82, 84–5
Viswaamitra 56
Vrindavan 51, 70
Vyasa 42

Water 156
Watts, Alan 26, 202
'web' 60, 64–5, 75, 130
Weiss, Peter 209
Williams, David 3, 29
Williams, Raymond 96
Wilkins, W.J. 37
Winnicot, D.L. 26, 80
Winter's Tale, A 107–8
women
    as performers 8, 61, 82, 84, 86, 93,
    133–141, 160, 170, 173, 176,
    181, 188–9, 196
    as directors/artistic directors 86,
    172–3, 176, 181, 196
    as writers 133, 155, 196–7
    representation of 44, 50, 77, 86, 89,
    93, 113, 134, 155, 157, 176,
    183, 196
    marginalisation of 46, 93, 132, 135,
    138, 152, 156, 188–9, 195
Wright, Elizabeth 7
writers 55, 58–9, 96, 124–5, 145–6,
150–166, 172, 175–6, 178, 180,
182, 184, 195

Yajur Veda 66, 78
Yakshagana 28, 36, 48, 63, 67–8, 70,
76–7, 82, 84, 86, 88, 120, 166,
168, 171, 174
Yama 38
Yami 38
Yarrow, Ralph 48, 122, 184, 199,
208–10
Yatra (Jatra) 68, 83–4, 166, 180
Yudhisthira 49

Zarilli, Philip B. 14, 28, 67, 145, 204
Zeami 11
Zia-ul-Haq, General 157